GET READY TO MAKE THE CAKE

Set Your Budget—Even if you have $2 per person, you can have a custom-made cake. If you have more, the sky's the limit!

Numbers Count!—A small wedding will require a small cake. A large party gives you more flexibility; all of the cake can be on display, or, if you're on a budget, showcase a small decorated cake and keep an extra undecorated cake in the kitchen to slice and serve.

Note the Date—A midsummer wedding suggests a different cake from what would be desirable at a winter holiday reception. A winter-white color scheme, anyone?

Pick Your Flavor—Your wedding cake should feature flavors that you love. If you love puckery lemon, then include it. Are both of you chocoholics? Don't leave out chocolate!

Determine Your Style—Is your wedding formal or on-the-beach casual? Your cake should fit your level of formality.

Logistics Lowdown—Assess your ability and situation. Do you have the time to make the cake? Will you need to borrow or buy any equipment? Do you have refrigerator space?

Make Lists—Lists are helpful for organizing ingredient and equipment needs as well as your week-to-week and day-to-day approach.

Practice!—From piping buttercream decorations to get them even to making a sample miniature version of your cake, familiarize yourself with techniques and try out the flavors you've chosen before making the final commitment.

WEDDING CAKES
YOU CAN MAKE

Designing, Baking, and Decorating
the Perfect Wedding Cake

DEDE WILSON

WILEY

Wiley Publishing, Inc.

This book is printed on acid-free paper. ∞

Published by Wiley Publishing, Inc., Hoboken, New Jersey
Published simultaneously in Canada

For general information about our other products and services, please contact our Customer Care Department within the United States at (800) 762-2974, outside the United States at (317) 572-3993 or fax (317) 572-4002.

Wiley also publishes its books in a variety of electronic formats. Some content that appears in print may not be available in electronic books. For more information about Wiley products, visit our web site at www.wiley.com.

Library of Congress Cataloging-in-Publication Data:
Wilson, Dede.
  Wedding cakes you can make : designing, baking, and decorating the perfect wedding cake / Dede Wilson.—1st ed.
    p. cm.
  Includes index.
  ISBN 0-7645-5719-X (alk. paper)
  1. Wedding cakes. 2. Cake decorating. I. Title.
  TX771.W475 2005
  641.8'653—dc22   2004025816

Printed in the United States of America
10 9 8 7 6 5 4 3 2 1

To Moses Acosta, my Dad

It is because of his love of food and me that I have a career that feeds my soul

CONTENTS

Acknowledgments vi

Preface vii

EVERYTHING YOU NEED TO KNOW ABOUT MAKING A WEDDING CAKE 1

Dreaming and Planning Your Cake 2

Baking, Frosting, Assembling, and Decorating Your Cake 20

Get It There on Time and Intact: Storing and Transporting Your Cake—Safely! 51

Add a Little Pizzazz! Presenting Your Cake 54

THE ESSENTIAL RECIPES 59

Essential Cakes 60

Essential Moistening Syrup 68

Essential Buttercream 69

The Wedding Cakes 73

Essential Vanilla Wedding Cake 75

Lemon Blackberry Cake 79

Swirled Marble Cake with Sour Cream Fudge Frosting 85

Raspberries and Cream Cake 89

Lemon Coconut Cupcake Tower 95

Strawberry Shortcake and Meringue Cake 101

Marzipan and Orange Essensia Cake 107

Nutella Cake 111

Orange Mocha Cake 115

Hazelnut Praline and Apricot Cake 119

Chocolate-Covered Caramel Cake 125

Valentine's Day Cake 131

Italian Rum Cream and Fruit Cake 135

Brown Sugar, Pecan, and Peaches Cake 143

Gilded Mocha Cake 149

Chocolate-Covered Cherry Cake 155

Sources 162

Index 166

Acknowledgments

Without my first book on wedding cakes, this one would never have been born. The first book was the brainchild of my agent and dear friend, Maureen Lasher. She has championed me throughout and always has great ideas—as does her husband Eric, who advocates for me at every turn.

Big thanks to my editor Linda Ingroia, who believed that this second wedding cake book should be realized and breathed life into the project. This is our fourth book project together, but the first of such magnitude and beauty. Linda, I hope you are as proud of our baby as I am.

Adam Kowit, the assistant editor, has studied every word of this manuscript (literally!) and has not only kept my concept and ideas from running amok, but his sharp mind has made this book better than it ever would have been without his guidance. And although it was not in his job description, he also kept me positive and calm throughout. Every conversation with him left me feeling like the book was going to be even better than I had thought possible. I hope I get to work with him again.

I thoroughly enjoyed meeting and conversing with Paul DiNovo, who designed the cover of this book. It was immediately apparent to me that we spoke the same language. The beauty of the photographs and the intent of my words are enhanced by his involvement.

When I found out who would be photographing my cakes, I was tickled pink! We had an all-female photo shoot team and I think the feminine touches are apparent, welcomed, and give the book the lovely essence that it has.

My sincere thanks to the following: Zeva Olebaum, the photographer with a fabulous aesthetic eye. She is a joy to work with and the book is as much hers as mine. My words are one thing, but nobody would buy a book on wedding cakes without gorgeous pictures. Her assistants Stephanie Johnson and Brica Wilcox helped us get through the long days as efficiently as possible. Karen Tack, food stylist extraordinaire. I had been a fan of her work prior to our meeting and feel blessed to have partnered with her on the cake assembly for the photographs. Cathy Cook, the prop stylist, brought us such a brilliant array of fabrics, backgrounds, and props that every morning Zeva and I felt like little girls playing dress-up for the cakes. They "wear" her suggestions beautifully.

A huge thank you to our amazing culinary school students and food stylist volunteers: Vivian Lois, who made several trips for us to gather equipment and props; Misako Urayama, who, among other necessary tasks, made the gorgeous leaf tablecloth on page 118; and Rachel Baumgartner, who earned the title of Miss Buttercream for the numerous batches we had her whip up! I hope all three of you know how important your presence was in bringing this book to life.

Robert Schueller from Melissa's came through with care packages of perfect berries and kumquats to grace the cakes.

Beryl Loveland from Beryl's sent equipment and props (check out the gorgeous silver cake base on page 154). She has been a supporter of my work for years and I encourage all of you to give her your business. She will have (or can get) what you need when you are planning your special cake.

To my three children, Ravenna, Forrester, and Freeman; I love you.

And as always, thank you to Mary McNamara for being my baking buddy and Juanita Plimpton for keeping me sane and fit.

PREFACE

Welcome to the world of delectable, homemade, gorgeous wedding cakes! If you are reading this page then I assume you already have an interest in creating a spectacular wedding or other large celebration cake at home, either for yourself, a family member, or a friend. This book is for you. I will help you, the average (but ambitious) home baker, make the cake of your dreams—the perfect wedding cake!

How to Use this Book

When you think of a wedding cake, the image of a towering, elaborately frosted and decorated creation comes to mind and the image can be daunting. How come it doesn't fall over? How many does it serve? How does it taste? How do you prepare and bake such large layers? In short, if you want to bake one yourself, where do you start?

While any large celebration cake does take some time and planning, it doesn't have to be daunting. Just consider me your wedding cake fairy! All the instruction and handholding you need to turn the skills used in making a regular 9-inch cake into a multi-tiered wonder are in this book. I will look over your shoulder as you proceed.

To help you in this endeavor, I have divided the book into sections. The sections are presented in the logical order that you will follow when making a celebration cake. The initial section helps you to figure out what kind of cake you want to make, then guides you through all the steps that go into making, storing, transporting, presenting, and serving your cake. The middle section includes essential recipes. The final, long section presents cakes of every flavor and for every occasion, each with an accompanying photograph.

Section one, "Everything You Need to Know About Making a Wedding Cake" is comprised of four chapters. The first, "Dreaming and Planning Your Cake," will help you focus your ideas, constraints, and logistics into a plan for designing the cake of your dreams. To help you pick the flavors you want your cake to have, I've also included a handy chart showing what recipe components make up the cakes featured in the book, as well as a second chart suggesting additional combinations for designing a cake that is uniquely yours. The second, "Baking, Frosting, Assembling, and Decorating Your Cake," is a hands-on chapter that describes the steps and techniques that go into making a wedding cake. All of the complete cakes in the book make use of these steps, so I encourage you to review and consider them in advance—even to practice the techniques using a one-tier, 6-inch sample version of the cake you want to make. You will later refer back to this chapter as a guide when making the cake for the big day.

The third chapter, "Get It There on Time and Intact: Storing and Transporting Your Cake—Safely!," takes you through the storage and transportation phases. These might not be the most glamorous stages, but they are very important, as you will most likely have to move the cake at some point. Finally, "Add a Little Pizzazz! Presenting Your Cake" is a small chapter that offers tips on display table decoration to give your cake a little extra "wow" factor, a guide for cutting and serving the cake, and ideas for plate decoration and embellishing serving pieces.

The second section, "Essential Recipes," gives you the basic recipes for all of the cakes in this book. Here you will find the

Essential Yellow Cake, Essential White Cake, Essential Chocolate Cake, all three of which are broken down into tier sizes (6-inch, 8-inch, 9-inch, 10-inch, 12-inch, and 14-inch) so most of the math is done for you! Recipes for the Essential Moistening Syrup and Essential Buttercream also reside here. These two recipes are used in almost all of the following cakes and I further encourage you to use them as basic building blocks to make cakes of your own.

The final section, "The Wedding Cakes," is the colorful heart of the book, offering 16 luscious cakes—vanilla cakes, chocolate cakes, cakes with nuts, cakes with fruit, round cakes, oval cakes, and square cakes. There are cakes for showers or smaller parties and others for large receptions. Each is unique, designed to appeal to different taste preferences and represent a diverse visual aesthetic. In addition, I have designed each cake with a mood in mind ("lighthearted," "contemporary," or "sophisticated"). Thinking about a carefree garden wedding? How about the Lemon Blackberry Cake, which evokes that spirit? If a princess ball-gown dress and hundreds of pink roses is what you're after, take a look at the Raspberries and Cream Cake. Or, perhaps you are looking to present an elegant, urban feel—turn to page 149 for the Gilded Mocha Cake. I am sure that one of these cakes will appeal to you or spark your imagination.

As with all my books, I have included a comprehensive Sources section in the back so that you can find all the equipment and ingredients that you need to bake the perfect cake.

It is my sincere hope that this book brings you inspiration and guidance, motivation, and vision; that through my words you can create your own perfect wedding cake. Once you have made your first awe-inspiring attempt, I hope you will continue to use the book for any and all large celebration cakes that grace your life. I am always free to answer questions, troubleshoot problems, and hear about success stories. Email me at dede@dedewilson.com or visit me online at www.dedewilson.com. I am looking forward to hearing from you! Now, let's create and bake . . .

Everything You Need
to Know About
Making a Wedding Cake

DREAMING AND PLANNING YOUR CAKE

Y̶ou have a dream, a vision of the wedding cake you want to create. Here's where you start making it happen.

You may have already baked your share of buttery, moist layer cakes covered with delicious frosting. Maybe you've earned a reputation for baking birthday cakes or other special-occasion cakes, and perhaps you've also mastered fancy cake decorating. You may create elaborate cakes, or you may turn out a mean batch of cupcakes. Whatever stage you're at, even if your skills aren't that sophisticated, if you love to bake and are willing to plan properly and work patiently, you can make a spectacular wedding cake.

Planning and creating wedding cakes raises questions that don't have to be considered with smaller cakes. Many people design wedding cakes based on a theme, mood, or style that the couple wants to achieve for their wedding. What kind of mood do you want your cake to have? Is it formal or casual? Will the reception be at a fancy reception hall or on the beach?

Then there are the technical questions. What kind of flavors do you want to use, and what decorations? How do you decide in advance how the cake should look or how large the tiers should be? How many pounds of butter and sugar will you need and what size pans?

Before heading into the kitchen, you should consider these questions, which I will help you answer in this chapter. There are many things that may influence the cake. The taste and look may stem from the love of a specific flavor or the design detail of a fabric—maybe from the color or shape of a dress. The cakes I present in this book represent a broad array of flavors, styles, and level of formality. I have striven to show you the broad range from which you can choose. Most importantly, I hope you will use my cakes as ideas that will lead you to find the perfect cake for you or the bride-to-be.

Now it's time to take notes.

How to Brainstorm the Cake of Your Dreams

Brainstorming will help you determine a list of the important considerations for the cake, which you can then hone into a vision of the ideal cake for the wedding at hand.

Here's what to do. If you are the bride (or groom!), you can do this alone or with your beloved. If you are close to the wedding couple, find out if the bride and groom both want to make decisions about the cake or if just one of them will be taking on the responsibility.

Take a piece of paper and a pen (or sit at your computer), and think about the wedding cake. Write down ideas and preferences in terms of taste, looks, setting, and what have you. Do not censor anything that pops into your head, even if ideas overlap or contradict each other. If a pink pig comes to mind because you collect little piggy figurines, so be it (I'll explain later). Write it all down. The list can be single words, phrases, nouns, adjectives, descriptions of pictures in your mind, whatever. (If you are more of a visual person, you can also collect a pile of magazines, and start tearing out images of things that might help shape the vision for the cake such as flowers, colors, and patterns. Then write or type out the corresponding list.)

Your brainstorming session might go something like this:

List

White chocolate	Not too feminine
Round	White chocolate
Roses	Moist
Large	Ice cream
Outdoors	Purple
Chicken	Pink pigs
Gold	White chocolate

From this list, you can see something taking shape and you can begin to get a framework for a cake. Chocolate is obviously a priority, white chocolate in particular. Roses come in many colors, sizes, and shapes. Try to imagine which roses fill your heart and mind with joy and make a note of it. Are they pink, red, or lavender? Small and tightly furled or full-blown and open? They could be placed on or around the cake.

The word "round" would indicate round tiers (the circle of love and life, perhaps?). "Outdoors" would indicate that the wedding is a casual outdoor affair, so the cake should fit within that setting. Nothing too formal, which probably means stacked tiers are the way to go. Tall, leggy pillars usually lend an air of formality.

A lemony chicken dish will be served at the meal, so that is probably why "chicken" came to mind. With lemon in the main meal, you might want to forgo the flavor in the cake.

Gold may have come to mind because you were thinking about the yellow gold rings and the gold thread running through the embroidery on the dress. Is this something to echo in the cake's decorations? Perhaps some gold leaf could embellish the tiers?

Ice cream served with the wedding cake is a fun idea (ice cream with the cake is OK; an entire ice cream wedding cake is a bad idea—it would be too difficult to maintain unless you lived in the North Pole), so this list serves as a reminder to mention that to the caterers (and it means that there is an ice cream flavor to select).

Purple is the color of the lisianthus flowers in some of the arrangements . . . should that color be integrated as well? And what of those pink pigs? Well, you (the bride or groom) have always collected pink pig figurines and there just happens to be a darling girl and boy pig pair that you have had since you were a child. The size is right, they are evocative of a personal passion . . . maybe suggest that they stand in as a cake topper? I mean, why not? This cake should represent the couple celebrating the big day, and being untraditional or whimsical will make the cake that much more special.

The important thing to remember is that there is no wrong way to brainstorm. Just keep the thoughts flowing until you come up with a list of ideas, words, colors, flavors, and concepts and you will see the cake taking shape. You might be surprised how it all comes together—and you might learn something about what is important to you or the bride and groom. No two lists will be the same, but that's the point! REMEMBER: The design of your cake should be and will be uniquely yours.

Questionnaire for the Bridal Couple: Defining the Perfect Cake

Before you begin the actual baking process, you need to know what size tiers to bake, what equipment to gather, and how to organize the steps to get you from raw ingredients to final creation. To accomplish this goal, you need to start at the beginning, and that means asking some further questions.

This questionnaire, in conjunction with the brainstorming session above, will help you find the perfect cake. The purpose of this questionnaire is to get you thinking practically about the cake.

QUESTION #1: WHAT IS THE BUDGET?

Weddings are supposed to be about romance but by now I am sure you know they are also about the numbers in your checkbook. While your cake might not break the bank to the extent that the dress or liquor budget might, it is still a concern. If you have a large budget for a fancy shindig, then your cake should be similarly spectacular. On the other hand, if the hope is for a small group of barefoot friends on the beach with the dog as your best man, then a cake of similar attitude is appropriate. In this way, the whole wedding budget will affect your approach to the cake.

To give you a place to start, know that the average wedding cake in the United States costs about $5 a slice. (That may not seem like much unless you realize that $500 for a cake to feed 100 is a significant amount of money, especially if you only have $10,000 for the whole wedding.) Your cake does not have to cost anywhere near that much, even if you use high quality ingredients, as you will be when using these recipes. You might be able to save up to half of the cost of a purchased cake.

My point is not for you to come up with a specific dollar amount for your cake, as it will range. Some of you might need equipment, such as cake pans or a cake decorating turntable, others just ingredients. Also, take into consideration where you are serving your cake. If the reception is at a restaurant or banquet facility, the cost of a cake might be included in their food budget. Ask if you can bring a cake in from the outside and deduct an agreed upon amount from the reception bill. You don't want to pay for a cake twice! Actually, this can be a sticking point, as some facilities do not let outside food come on-site, so ask this question early on. This goes for whether you are making your own cake or a cake for a friend or family member. If you are making the cake, I suggest you make the call to be sure.

Question #2: When Is the Wedding?

You might wonder what this has to do with the cake. Well, if the wedding is in September, then autumnal colors might come into play in the cake decoration. Or, a winter white scheme might look great on a December cake. A cake for an outdoor midsummer wedding needs to be heat-proofed as much as possible. The day of the week counts, too. If you are delivering a cake on a Sunday, and realize that you forgot something, you might not be able to find a store open to supply you with last-minute needs. By knowing all of this ahead of time, you can plan. Similarly, Friday or Saturday night traffic could wreak havoc with a delivery, so be prepared! Don't forget to consider time of day the cake will be served. If the cake is coming after an extravagant evening sit-down meal, then the slices can afford to be a bit smaller and you can plan the size of your cake accordingly. If cake and champagne are the featured items at a short mid-afternoon reception, then the cake servings should be generous.

Question #3: How Many Guests Are Coming?

The number of guests is directly related to the size of the cake, so this is very important. (The bride and groom should be aware that their RSVP date should be early enough for the caterers and bakers to plan accordingly.) Don't forget to count musicians, photographers, clergy, etc. I have even worked with couples who forgot to count themselves! Everyone counts!

Except for children. Don't get me wrong, I love kids (I have three), but a child under 10 should be counted as half an adult. Seventeen-year-old boys should probably be counted as four adults, but I promise you that my serving sizes are generous enough to cover your final number if you get it as precise as possible. This means that even if a few more people show up, you will be fine.

Question #4: How Formal Is the Wedding?

As mentioned above, the formality level of the wedding in general will set the tone for the cake. Cakes with large separations, such as pillars, are considered more formal. A cake with pillars might look out of place at a simple country wedding, while a stacked cake of short stature with fresh pansies might not be dramatic enough for a black-tie wedding. Consider the formality of your dress, the room, the food, and the flow of the party in general, and take this into consideration when designing the cake.

Question #5: What Flavors Are Essential?

This is all-important. I do not believe in cakes that are made for beauty and ceremony only. I believe they should be eaten—and enjoyed! In fact, the majority of the time my cakes are used as the dessert, as opposed to a symbolic addition. The flavor of your cake should be one that you or the wedding couple adore. If strawberry shortcake is the groom's favorite dessert, then why not incorporate it into the wedding cake?

If a day without chocolate for the bride is like a day without sunshine, then make the wedding cake as chocolate-filled as you like. The days of white cake with white icing, or vanilla on vanilla as the only choice, are long gone. Unless, of course, vanilla is a favorite flavor, in which case you will want to integrate fresh vanilla beans to maximize the vanilla taste.

On the other hand, are there flavors that you (or the bride or groom) simply do not like, or cannot eat? If one member of the couple dislikes coffee flavor in dessert, then do not even consider it. And if the bride or groom is allergic to nuts, then do not include them anywhere in the menu, including the cake. Remember, this is a special day and the cake, especially the flavor, should reflect the bride and groom's tastes. If Uncle Lou is allergic to nuts but the groom loves them—well, this isn't Uncle Lou's wedding, is it? There is no way you can please 100 guests, so I suggest making the cake you or the wedding couple want.

Of course, a wedding cake can incorporate several flavors, as you'll see in the cake recipes appearing later in this book. For now, you're just brainstorming the flavors you absolutely love (or can't stand) to create a starting point for envisioning your cake.

QUESTION #6: WHAT IS THE STYLE OR MOOD OF THE WEDDING?

This question is to get you thinking about design preferences. A tailored streamlined look, perhaps? Or feminine ruffles and bows? How about color? A pure and simple white cake with a few roses? Or something untraditional? If a chocolate cake is preferred, have you considered dark chocolate frosting on the outside? This look would be considered somewhat outside the "norm," but is doable, beautiful, and delicious.

Colors in wedding dresses are certainly appealing and popular, and the same goes for wedding cakes. Fresh flowers are as appropriate as sculpted white chocolate roses. Dark chocolate curls can be tantalizing, and crystallized flowers look exquisite. If it speaks to the bride and groom and adds up to the ideal cake, then it should be considered.

Choosing the Cake-to-Be

Now that you've brainstormed and thought about the practical elements of wedding style, time, and flavors, you can make some real choices about the components of your cake. The next page shows a chart that breaks down the cakes in this book by flavors of cake, frosting, filling, and moistening syrup. The 16 cakes in this book represent my favorite flavor combinations and styles and those most frequently requested by bridal couples. But wedding cake flavor and design choices are infinite; I offer you just a slice of what is possible. You could elect to make one of my cakes, or let them open your eyes to possibilities. So, to help get you thinking, I've added a second chart giving you other ideas of wedding cakes that could be made from the recipes in this book. Maybe one of these will be your favorite.

The Wedding Cakes, by Flavor

Essential Vanilla Wedding Cake: Yellow Cake ✳ Vanilla Bean Moistening Syrup ✳ Vanilla Buttercream Filling ✳ Vanilla Buttercream Frosting

Lemon Blackberry Cake: Yellow Cake with Lemon Zest ✳ Lemon Moistening Syrup ✳ Lemon Curd Filling ✳ Fresh Blackberry Jam Filling ✳ Lemon Curd Buttercream Frosting

Swirled Marble Cake with Sour Cream Fudge Frosting: Marbled Yellow Cake ✳ Vanilla Bean Moistening Syrup ✳ Sour Cream Fudge Frosting

Raspberries and Cream Cake: White Chocolate Cake ✳ Raspberry Eau de Vie Moistening Syrup ✳ Raspberry Buttercream Filling ✳ Fresh Raspberries ✳ Vanilla Buttercream Frosting

Lemon Coconut Cupcake Tower: Coconut White Cake ✳ Lemon Moistening Syrup ✳ Lemon Curd Filling ✳ Vanilla Buttercream Frosting

Strawberry Shortcake and Meringue Cake: Yellow Cake ✳ Vanilla Meringue Discs ✳ Fresh Sliced Strawberries ✳ Vanilla Bean Moistening Syrup ✳ Vanilla Buttercream Frosting

Marzipan and Orange Essensia Cake: Marzipan Orange Cake ✳ Orange Essensia Moistening Syrup ✳ Orange Marmalade Buttercream Filling ✳ Vanilla Buttercream Frosting

Nutella Cake: Yellow Cake ✳ Frangelico Moistening Syrup ✳ Nutella Filling ✳ Light Chocolate Buttercream Frosting

Orange Mocha Cake: Yellow Cake with Orange Zest ✳ Orange Moistening Syrup ✳ Espresso Ganache Filling ✳ Orange Buttercream Frosting

Hazelnut Praline and Apricot Cake: Yellow Cake with Ground Hazelnuts ✳ Frangelico Moistening Syrup ✳ Hazelnut Praline Buttercream Filling ✳ Apricot Jam Filling ✳ Vanilla Buttercream Frosting

Chocolate-Covered Caramel Cake: Chocolate Cake ✳ Caramel Moistening Syrup ✳ Caramel Buttercream Filling ✳ Milk Chocolate Buttercream Frosting

Valentine's Day Cake: Chocolate Cake ✳ Crème de Cacao Moistening Syrup ✳ Crème de Cacao Buttercream Filling ✳ Chocolate Buttercream Frosting

Italian Rum Cream and Fruit Cake: White Cake ✳ Rum Moistening Syrup ✳ Vanilla Bean Pastry Cream Filling ✳ Vanilla Buttercream Frosting

Brown Sugar, Pecan, and Peaches Cake: Brown Sugar Pecan Cake ✳ Peach Liqueur Moistening Syrup ✳ Fresh Sliced Peaches ✳ Caramel Buttercream Frosting

Gilded Mocha Cake: Yellow Cake with Bittersweet Chocolate Shavings ✳ Kahlua Moistening Syrup ✳ Ganache Filling ✳ Espresso Buttercream Frosting

Chocolate-Covered Cherry Cake: White Cake with Bittersweet Chocolate Shavings and Kirsch-Soaked Dried Cherries ✳ Kirsch Moistening Syrup ✳ Chocolate-Covered Cherry Buttercream Filling ✳ Vanilla Buttercream Frosting

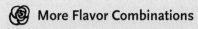

More Flavor Combinations

These alternative flavor combinations include variations on the recipes in this book. Refer to the Syrup, Filling, and Frosting Amounts chart on page 31 to determine how many batches of each recipe to make for the cake sizes you're using.

Marzipan Orange and Chocolate Cake: Make Marzipan Orange Cake ✳ Make Orange Moistening Syrup ✳ Fill with alternating layers of Chocolate Ganache and Orange Buttercream ✳ Frost with Orange Buttercream ✳ Decorate with Chocolate Plastic roses, leaves, and tendrils, using dark chocolate instead of white

Brown Sugar, Walnut, and Rum Caramel Cake: Make Brown Sugar Pecan Cake, substitute walnuts for pecans ✳ Make Rum Moistening Syrup ✳ Fill and frost with Caramel Buttercream ✳ Decorate with fresh ivory colored roses

White Chocolate Espresso Cake: Make White Chocolate Cake, substituting Yellow Cake for White Cake ✳ Make Kahlua Moistening Syrup ✳ For filling, make Espresso Buttercream starting out with White Chocolate Buttercream instead of Essential Buttercream (for White Chocolate Buttercream, follow Chocolate Buttercream recipe and substitute white chocolate) ✳ Frost with White Chocolate Buttercream ✳ Decorate with fresh deep burgundy colored roses

Amaretto Praline Cake: Make Yellow Cake with Ground Hazelnuts, substituting ground almonds for hazelnuts ✳ Make any liqueur moistening syrup, using amaretto for the liqueur ✳ Fill and Frost with Amaretto Buttercream—follow Crème de Cacao Buttercream recipe and substitute amaretto for the liqueur ✳ Decorate cake sides with crushed almond praline—follow Hazelnut Praline recipe and substitute almonds for hazelnuts ✳ Decorate tops and sides with Chocolate Plastic Leaves, using both white and milk chocolate plastic, in all sizes and shapes

Kirsch Cherry Cake: Make White Cake with Bittersweet Chocolate Shavings and Kirsch-Soaked Dried Cherries but omit the chocolate shavings ✳ Make Kirsch Moistening Syrup ✳ Fill and frost with Vanilla Buttercream ✳ Decorate with bunches of fresh Queen Ann cherries, deep red bing cherries, and lemon leaves

Lemon Drop Cake: Make White Chocolate Cake ✳ Make Lemon Moistening Syrup ✳ Fill with alternating layers of Lemon Curd and Lemon Curd Buttercream ✳ Frost with Lemon Curd Buttercream ✳ Decorate with piped buttercream vines and leaves, fresh yellow pansies, roses, and strips of candied lemon zest

Tropical Coconut Rum Cake: Make Coconut White Cake ✳ Make Rum Moistening Syrup ✳ Fill and Frost with White Chocolate Buttercream—follow Chocolate Buttercream recipe and substitute white chocolate ✳ Decorate with half toasted, half raw, long-shred sweetened coconut patted over the cake (see page 99) and fresh cattleya orchids in pinks, purples, and yellows

Chocolate Praline Cake: Make Chocolate Cake ✳ Make Frangelico Moistening Syrup ✳ Fill with Hazelnut Praline Buttercream ✳ Frost with Chocolate Buttercream ✳ Decorate sides with crushed Hazelnut Praline

Chocolate Raspberry Cake: Make Chocolate Cake ✳ Make Raspberry Eau de Vie Moistening Syrup ✳ Fill with Raspberry Buttercream ✳ Frost with Chocolate or Vanilla Buttercream ✳ Decorate with Dark Chocolate Curls and fresh raspberries

Black and White Cake: Make White Chocolate Cake, substituting Chocolate Cake for White Cake ✳ Make Vanilla Bean Moistening Syrup ✳ Fill and Frost with White Chocolate Buttercream—follow Chocolate Buttercream recipe and substitute white chocolate ✳ For decoration, pipe buttercream border and flood the tops of tiers with Chocolate Ganache (see page 153) ✳ Decorate further with White Chocolate Plastic roses, leaves, and tendrils

Get Organized

~~~~~~

Now that the cake and design concepts have been chosen, you need to get organized and get ready to bake. This section offers organizational lists and information all focused on helping you to be as prepared as possible for the task at hand.

The first thing is to make sure you have the equipment that you need and then gather together your ingredients. You might need to order equipment or ingredients through mail order, so planning ahead is crucial. I suggest that you have everything in your kitchen a full 2 weeks before you plan to start baking, so you will have time for last-minute adjustments. Here are some things to consider:

1. Do you need any equipment? Refer to the equipment list on page 000 and make a list of what you need, such as cake pans (size to be determined by cake design chosen), oven thermometer, icing spatulas, etc. Don't forget cardboards to support the tiers, pillars or wooden dowels, and a base for your cake. Beg, buy, or borrow a cake decorating turntable—it is a must!
2. Do you need specialty ingredients or decorations that need to be sought out or ordered ahead such as almond paste, crystallized flowers, fresh flowers, gold leaf, etc.?
3. Refer to the Baking and Organizing Schedule (see page 50) to help plan a timeline for making the cake. Make your own notes on what days you will be shopping, baking, frosting, decorating, and so on. Take into account anything you know ahead of time, such as that the florist closes at 2:00 pm on Saturday, or there is always traffic between you and the delivery site on Sunday.

CAKE SIZE CHARTS

The following two charts will help you determine what size pans to use to make sure you end up with the necessary number of servings. The first chart tells you how many servings each cake tier will provide.

First, it is important to understand the difference between a cake layer and a cake tier. For our purposes, a cake layer is a layer of cake as it is unmolded from the pan in which it was baked. Once cake layers are assembled with filling and frosted, the result is a complete cake tier. In this way, a cake tier is made up of cake layers. Most of the cakes in this book are made up of 2 cake layers which are split in half, so each tier is actually made up of 4 layers of cake, with 3 layers of filling. This chart also shows popular pan size combinations that yield the size cakes most often needed. Now, when you add up a 6-inch, 10-inch, and 14-inch tier, you get 78 to 110 servings. This might seem odd and chances are your party does not have exactly 78 guests or 110 or even a nice round number like 90. What to do? Always have a little extra. For every 10 guests, if you plan on 1 extra slice, that should be plenty.

You could scale back a bit if your budget is tight. If you have 130 guests coming but you like the shape of a 3-tiered, 6-inch, 10-inch, 14-inch cake, then you need cake for at least an additional 20 guests. How do you do this? You can make an additional small tier (such as a 9-inch) and have that in the back to be sliced and served. This extra tier does not have to be displayed, just made available for serving. This is not only easier than adding a tier to the cake on display, but it is economical as well because this extra cake, while it will have the same cake, filling, and frosting as the display cake, does not have to be elaborately decorated. No one will see it, except as slices on a plate.

The second chart details pan volumes. It is important to know volume because ultimately volume determines serving size. For instance, an 8×2-inch cake pan has almost double the volume of a 6×2-inch pan. A mere 2 inches greater in diameter and you have twice the amount of batter in there! When you are deciding on tier sizes for your cake, this kind of information is very important and can help guide your decision.

Used in conjunction, these charts will help you figure out what size tiers you need to combine for a wedding cake of your own design.

Cake Pan/Serving Size Chart

Often, wedding cake serving sizes are small. I believe this is because, unfortunately, many wedding cakes are looked upon as showpieces. They are not considered tasty enough to be dessert. I am sure you have heard someone say, "Oh that looks too pretty to eat." To me, these are awful words! My cakes are designed with taste being of prime importance. They are absolutely good enough to eat and good enough to be the grand finale of such a special occasion. Because your guests will love these cakes—to eat and to look at—I calculate generous serving sizes. This is why my serving size chart might not match those in other wedding cake books. Please use my chart when making the cakes presented here.

Also, I assume that you will be eating the top tier so the totals for combined cake tiers take this into consideration. The tradition of saving the top layer and freezing it for the first anniversary is widespread, but hardly appetizing. I am not a fan of defrosted cake. If you really want to approximate this tradition, I suggest making an identical small cake at the first anniversary and enjoying it freshly made.

If you are planning to use the cake as dessert instead of as part of an elaborate selection of desserts, which I encourage you to do, then use this chart literally. If the cake is part of a dessert buffet, or is coming after a particularly ample feast, then each tier can be cut into more pieces.

For an actual cake-cutting diagram chart, see page 58.

Round Tier	Number of Servings
6 inches	Serves 8–10
8 inches	Serves 12–16
9 inches	Serves 16–22
10 inches	Serves 23–34
12 inches	Serves 36–48
14 inches	Serves 47–66

Oval Tier	Number of Servings
$5^5/_8$ inches × $7^3/_4$ inches	Serves 11–13
$7^5/_8$ inches × $10^3/_4$ inches	Serves 24–32
$9^7/_8$ inches × 13 inches	Serves 32–40

Square Tier	Number of Servings
6 inches	Serves 10–12
10 inches	Serves 25–36
14 inches	Serves 50–70

Rectangular	Number of Servings
13 inches × 9 inches × 2 inches	32–40

Popular Round Tier Combinations	Number of Servings
6 inches, 9 inches, 12 inches	Serves 60–80
6 inches, 10 inches, 14 inches	Serves 78–110
8 inches, 12 inches	Serves 48–64
6 inches, 8 inches, 12 inches, 14 inches	Serves 103–140
6 inches, 10 inches, 12 inches, 14 inches	Serves 114–158

Cake Pan Volume Chart

The volumes below are for the pans most often used when making large celebration cakes. While the rectangular pan might not figure into any of your tiered presentation cakes, it is very useful for the extra servings often needed behind the scenes. It is a common "brownie" pan, so you probably have one in your kitchen.

Note that the volume amounts are for water filled to the brim. This, of course, is not how you fill your cake pans with batter, but it does give you a true volume amount for the pans themselves.

Pan Size	Volume
ROUND	
6 inches × 2 inches	3³⁄₄ cups
8 inches × 2 inches	7 cups
9 inches × 2 inches	8²⁄₃ cups
10 inches × 2 inches	10²⁄₃ cups
12 inches × 2 inches	15¹⁄₂ cups
14 inches × 2	21 cups
OVAL	
5⁵⁄₈ inches × 7³⁄₄ inches	4 cups
7⁵⁄₈ inches × 10³⁄₄ inches	8 cups
9⁷⁄₈ inches × 13 inches	12 cups
SQUARE	
6 inches × 6 inches × 2 inches	5 cups
10 inches × 10 inches × 2 inches	12 cups
14 inches × 14 inches × 2 inches	24 cups
RECTANGULAR	
13 inches × 9 inches × 2 inches	15 cups

Ingredients and Equipment

When it comes time to make a large celebration cake, you want to be sure to begin with the highest quality ingredients, and you will need some equipment that is specific to the task, such as a heavy-duty cake turntable. I have made thousands of cakes but I could not make a professional looking cake without a cake-decorating turntable and the proper icing spatulas. Read this section and acquaint yourself with these items, and refer to the Sources section in the back of the book to order them if you cannot find them near home.

INGREDIENTS

Flour—All the cakes in this book use cake flour. It has a lower protein content than all-purpose flour and produces cakes with a more tender crumb. Make sure to purchase regular cake flour, not cake flour that is labeled "self-rising," which contains leavening and salt. Cake flour is very finely milled and can easily attract moisture so proper storage is critical. I keep mine in an airtight plastic container at room temperature because I go through it so quickly. Store yours in the freezer if you plan to store it for a while.

These recipes were tested with flour that was stirred first to aerate. Then I use the dip-and-sweep method of measuring: scoop up the flour using the proper size dry measuring cup, then level off by scraping any excess back into the container. This is best accomplished with the flat blade of a knife. Do not shake or tap the flour down as the flour will compact and skew your measurement.

Granulated Sugar—This is simply referred to as "sugar" throughout the book. Measure in a dry measuring cup. The sugar in these recipes was measured using the dip-and-sweep method (see above).

Brown Sugar—All recipes will specify light brown or dark brown sugar. Brown sugar must be packed into dry measuring cups to yield an accurate amount.

Confectioners' Sugar—When you buy confectioners', or powdered, sugar it has a small percentage of cornstarch

The Incredible Shrinking—or Expanding—Cake

Determining Yield: All of the recipes in this book have a yield. But the yield is expressed in terms of a range, such as a 10-inch tier will serve 23 to 34. This is because if the cake is served as dessert, with no other desserts offered, then it will serve the small amount (23) since I assume you will cut larger pieces. If the cake is accompanied by a scoop of ice cream or sorbet, or some fresh fruit, the serving number might fall in the middle of the range. If the cake is just part of a large dessert buffet, then you can afford to cut smaller slices and the yield will be the largest amount (34). See page 58 for a diagram of how to cut cake tiers.

Actual Number of Servings: There is another matter to consider which is that a completed three-tier cake might serve 110 maximum, but you have 112 guests. In this case, I'd say, don't worry about it. The cake you have chosen will suffice. However, if you have 120 people coming, then you need an extra tier, either built into the cake or one behind the scenes. And, while we are talking numbers, I suggest that you always have a little extra, as opposed to cutting it close or trying to be exact to one specific number.

Here is a formula that I follow:

* For a party of 50 to 75, I figure on having 5 extra servings.
* For a party of 75 to 90, I figure on having 8 extra servings.
* For a party of 90 to 110, I figure on having 10 extra servings.
* For a party of 110 to 125, I figure on having 12 extra servings.
* For a party of 125 to 160, I figure on having 15 extra servings.

I have developed this formula from years of experience. It takes into consideration the fact that some folks will take seconds, and that last-minute guests attend the reception. Believe me when I tell you that not everyone RSVPs! It is a generous plan to insure that you will never run out of cake. If there is any extra left over, you can offer it to the hard-working caterers and banquet servers or even to a lucky few who might want to take some home.

---

added to prevent clumping. It is sometimes labeled as "10×," which refers to the fact that it is 10 times finer than granulated sugar.

Butter—I only use sweet, unsalted butter and prefer using a reputable national brand, such as Land O'Lakes. Refrigerate what you need and freeze the rest. It will keep frozen for months. Always keep it well wrapped, or it will pick up strong flavors and odors from other foods. Remember, when creaming butter for cake batter or using it to make buttercream, the butter should always be at room temperature.

Eggs—All of the eggs used in these recipes are graded size "large." It does make a difference. Two large eggs equals three medium eggs and obviously the difference between small and jumbo is even greater.

Many of the recipes call for separated eggs or only whites or yolks. Cold eggs separate more easily than room temperature eggs. The white is stiffer and more viscous and the yolk is less prone to breakage. However, in general, the eggs should be at room temperature when they are actually incorporated into your other ingredients or when the whites or yolks are whipped. Room-temperature eggs will give you maximum volume. Health regulations suggest not letting eggs stay at room temperature for more than 1 hour, so plan accordingly.

Milk—Use whole milk. You may experiment on your own with skim, 1%, or 2%, but the recipes were tested with whole milk.

Sour Cream—Use full-fat sour cream.

Baking Powder and Baking Soda—Leaveners, like other ingredients, must be measured accurately to maximize their usefulness. When the correct amounts are added, they help to lighten the batter, and create height. Because the cake recipes in this book are broken down into multiple sizes, some of the ingredient amounts are odd, such as "3/4 teaspoon" of baking soda. Just use 1/2 teaspoon plus 1/4 teaspoon and proceed. Unconventional, I know, but necessary for the varied sizes.

Baking powder is made up of acid, an acid-reacting salt, and bicarbonate of soda. The type used in these recipes is called double-acting baking powder and is the standard type sold in supermarkets. It is called double-acting because it works in two stages: first when exposed to moisture, and a second time when exposed to heat. When baking powder is in the presence of moisture (provided by the liquid in the batter such as eggs or milk) the acid-reacting salt reacts with the bicarbonate of soda, creating carbon dioxide gas. This gas helps to expand the air bubbles created by the creaming process, which gives greater volume to the cake. These expanded pockets of gas are set when the cake is baked.

In an emergency, you can make your own baking powder by combining 2 parts cream of tartar and 1 part baking soda; this is for immediate use only and will not store well. I tested the cakes with purchased baking powder.

Baking soda, or bicarbonate of soda, is used in batters that have an acid component, such as cocoa, chocolate, etc. Its addition helps to neutralize the acid as it releases carbon dioxide gas. Recipes that are leavened only with baking soda must be baked immediately as the reaction will begin as soon as the acid in the batter and the baking soda are combined.

Baking powder should be replaced every 6 months; baking soda should last a year or more. To test freshness, baking powder can be stirred together with water and there should be a vigorous bubbling action. For baking soda, you can stir some together with an acidic liquid such as lemon or orange juice. If fresh, this too should bubble. Of course, you should also check for expiration dates on containers.

Cream of Tartar—This acidic white powder is a by-product of the wine-making process. In this book it is used in small amounts to help stabilize whipped egg whites.

Chocolate

Unsweetened Chocolate—This is also called chocolate liquor, bitter chocolate, or baking chocolate. It is quite bitter

 Storing Chocolate

In general, unsweetened, bittersweet, and semisweet chocolates can be stored for up to a year. Milk and white chocolates have a shorter shelf life and should be used within 6 months of purchase.

Keep all chocolates well wrapped in plastic wrap or a ziplock) baggie and in an airtight container, free of moisture. Do not refrigerate or freeze.

Most chocolate is bought "in good temper," which means that the ingredients, which form an emulsion, are stable and the chocolate will look shiny and smooth. If it acquires grayish streaks during storage, it has developed "fat bloom," which simply means that the cocoa butter has become unstable and risen to the top. Don't worry; it looks unsightly, but the cocoa butter will mix back in upon melting. Do not, however, use this type of cosmetically impaired chocolate for shaving off curls or making other decorations.

To Temper Chocolate

Tempering is a precise melting procedure that stabilizes the fat crystals in the cocoa butter and prevents the chocolate from streaking after cooling.

1 Start with the desired amount of chocolate as stated in the recipe and chop it very finely.
2 Place about two-thirds of it in the top of a double boiler with gently simmering water in the lower half of the double boiler. The water should not touch the top pot's bottom.
3 Stir gently to encourage melting, but not vigorously, which will add air.
4 Do not allow chocolate to heat above 115° for semisweet and bittersweet and 110° for milk or white chocolate. As soon as the chocolate is melted, remove from heat and wipe the bottom of the pot to eliminate any chances of water droplets reaching the chocolate, which would cause it to seize.
5 Add about one-third of the remaining chopped chocolate and stir gently. The residual heat will melt it. You want to cool the chocolate down to 79°.
6 Add the remaining chocolate, in two more stages if necessary, to cool the chocolate further, continuing to stir gently until 79° is reached. Any unmelted chocolate can be removed and reserved for another use.
7 Place the pot back over hot, not simmering, water, and rewarm gently. Semisweet and bittersweet chocolates should be brought up to 88°; milk and white chocolates should be brought up to 85°. Do not allow any chocolate to rise above 90° or you will have to begin the entire process again (but you can use the same chocolate over again).
8 The chocolate is now ready to use.
9 To test the temper, spread a teaspoon amount thinly on a piece of aluminum foil and allow it to cool. The chocolate should look shiny and smooth. Any dull spots or streaks indicate that the chocolate is not in good temper.
10 Please note that it is easiest to temper at least 8 ounces of chocolate and it is really not that much more difficult to temper 3 or 4 times that amount. If you have any left over, it can be allowed to harden; then you can chop it up and fold it into your favorite ice cream.

and has no added sugar. Do not substitute unsweetened chocolate for semisweet or bittersweet chocolate.

Bittersweet and Semisweet (Dark) Chocolates—While it stands to reason that semisweet chocolate is sweeter than bittersweet, and this is usually the case, there is actually no federal standard differentiating the two. Use taste as your guide. They can be used interchangeably in most recipes.

Dark chocolates I like to work with include: Scharffen Berger Bittersweet, Mercken's Yucatan Vanilla, Callebaut Bittersweet and Semisweet, Valrhona Guanaja, Caraque, Manjari, and Caraibe.

When buying chocolate, make sure that cocoa butter is the fat listed in the ingredients, and not cottonseed or some other vegetable oil. True chocolates will have cocoa butter as a component. (See page 14 under Milk and White Chocolates for further explanation.)

A note on supermarket semisweet chocolate chips: the standard chocolate chips that you have probably bought for cookies are formulated to hold their shape when exposed to heat. They do not make good melting chocolate. For these recipes, it is best to search out bulk chocolate.

Milk and White Chocolates—Milk chocolate has the addition of milk solids and usually a higher sugar content than semisweet. There are, however, a new bunch of "extreme" milk chocolates that have recently appeared that are almost halfway between a traditional milk chocolate and a semisweet.

White chocolate is not actually chocolate at all, according to the FDA, as it does not contain any of the essential chocolate liquor (the mash resulting from raw cacao beans). High quality white chocolate will contain cocoa butter, however, and is the only type that I use. Lesser quality ones will contain other types of fats that are not indigenous to the cocoa bean, such as cottonseed oil or palm kernel oil. It is the cocoa butter in the higher quality brands that gives white chocolate a "chocolaty" aroma and taste.

Both milk and white chocolates can be temperamental during melting. In general, melt slowly and do not heat above 110°. Use an instant-read thermometer, or a chocolate thermometer, for best results. I prefer to melt these chocolates over hot water, not in the microwave, because it allows me more control over the temperature and I can keep a constant eye on the melting process.

Couverture Chocolate—These are chocolates with a high cocoa butter content—at least 32%. This makes the chocolate more fluid when melted and is the coating of choice by professional chocolatiers when making truffles and candies. It must be tempered before use in order to get a shiny, beautiful end product. Use it for making perfect curls, dipping nuts, and other decorative chocolate shapes. Couverture chocolate can be found at cake decorating supply stores and some specialty food stores.

Compound Chocolate or Confectionery Coating—This is not actually chocolate at all because it does not contain cocoa butter, which is legally required (in the USA) for the product to be labeled real chocolate. These coatings contain oils such as palm kernel, cottonseed, and soy. The taste, without the cocoa butter, is not as chocolate-like and the texture is not quite as smooth. Confectionery coatings come in dark, milk, and white flavors, as well as various colored and flavored ones that I steer away from. Due to its very stable nature, compound chocolate does not require tempering, which makes it very easy to work with.

Although I prefer to use real, tempered chocolates for such decorations as curls, you may use compound chocolate. Your job will be much easier, but the taste does suffer somewhat. The one exception I find to this rule is using white, milk, and dark chocolate coatings when making chocolate plastic (see page 000). I find the taste just fine and the plastic is a little easier to work with. (This can make the difference between being able to make a chocolate flower successfully and not being able to do it at all, so try it, by all means.)

Cocoa—For the recipes in this book, I used Dutch-processed cocoa as well as natural cocoa. Use whichever is called for in a particular recipe.

Extracts and Oils—I use only pure vanilla extract. Neilsen-Massey brand is a good one. Almond extract also comes in both imitation and pure versions; use the pure extract. I do not like lemon or orange extracts and will not use them, as I find their flavors artificial tasting. Instead, I prefer to use fresh rinds and juices or oils.

Lemon, orange, and lime oils are made by Boyajian and available from Williams-Sonoma. They are actual oils extracted from the rind of the fruits, with no bitter contamination from the pith. They are pure tasting and impart a wonderfully fresh taste to baked goods.

Coloring—I do not use food colors a lot, but when I do, there is a choice of type, depending on the use. If I want a bright or opaque color, I might use a paste or gel. For a delicate dusting of color on a white chocolate rose, I might use a powder. Do not rely on the liquid food colors from the supermarket. Their liquid nature can wreak havoc with certain recipes (such as melted chocolate) and the colors are basic.

Pastes, gels, and powders come in a kaleidoscope of colors and can be found at specialty food stores and through mail order. The colors can even be blended to create custom colors. There are also many metallic powders available in silver and gold tones. They mimic the real thing quite well. I never tint the buttercream for the exterior of the cake a deep solid color, as such high concentrations of color may stain teeth and tongue—not something you want guests to have to worry about.

Ingredient Substitutions—I have not included a substitution chart because these cakes were tested with specific ingredients to give you reliable results. When you are making a cake for your family and decide to substitute skim milk for whole milk, the worst that can happen is that your small, everyday cake does not work out exactly as planned. This book is filled with cakes meant for life's most important occasions. If you want to experiment in this way, make test cakes first to review results, and refer to a substitution chart in a reliable baking book for suggestions.

EQUIPMENT

To make these recipes, your kitchen must be outfitted with certain utensils and pieces of equipment. I have given specific suggestions within recipes—such as using a whisk to fold in ingredients—because you will get good results by doing so. Familiarize yourself with your kitchen and its contents; you will get the most out of what you have—and probably come up with new uses for old tools. There will probably be at least a few pieces of equipment (say, a wedding cake base) that you have to borrow or buy. Refer to the Sources section in the back of the book to order them if you cannot find them near home.

Ovens and Oven Thermometers

These recipes were tested on both home gas and electric ranges and the baking times have taken this into consideration. Internal oven temperatures can vary from the dial temperatures by as much as 25° to 50°. Because of this, I strongly suggest using an oven thermometer and adjusting your oven accordingly.

Also, one very important factor that is not often mentioned in baking books is the necessity of a level oven. Your floor may not be perfectly level, and if it is not, your oven is sitting on an angle and your cakes may bake up lopsided. Use a carpenter's level to assess the situation and rectify the situation if necessary (see page 28).

Heavy-Duty Mixer

In my wedding cake business, I depend on my mixers. I have a 20-quart Hobart (which is a commercial machine) and a 5-quart countertop KitchenAid. I tested all of these recipes with the 5-quart KitchenAid and suggest that you use the same machine. The KitchenAid mixer not only has a good size capacity, it also has the power to handle large loads. If there is one investment to be made before making these cakes, this is it! In fact, when I was hired to make my first wedding cake, I took the deposit and bought my first KitchenAid as I knew it would be well used in years to come—it is still going strong.

The KitchenAid comes with a stainless steel bowl, a wire balloon-shaped whip, a flat beater and a dough hook. The dough hook doesn't figure into any of the recipes in this book, but the other attachments are used in many recipes. The balloon whip incorporates air into whipped cream, buttercream, and eggs; the flat beater creams butter and most cake batters.

It is handy to have an extra stainless steel bowl, which can be purchased separately, especially when a recipe calls for creaming butter and then you need a clean, grease-free bowl for whipping egg whites. If you do a lot of baking, an extra bowl is indispensable. Also, there is an optional splash guard attachment that will keep dry ingredients from flying out onto your counter. It's not essential, but very nice to have.

Other Standing Mixers and Hand Mixers

I have used other standing mixers and hand mixers to make many of these recipes and you can use them, too. At least for the smaller cake layer sizes. For larger sizes and the full-size batch of buttercream, I do not recommend it. Also note that the mixing times will not be the same and, in the case of a hand mixer, be prepared to stand over the mixing bowl for an extended period of time! It is not that these machines make the recipes impossible, but it might feel that way!

Food Processor

I tested the recipes with a KitchenAid 11-cup model, but any food processor with a metal blade attachment will work. I use my processor often for grinding nuts and making purees.

Microwave Oven

It is hard to standardize recipes using microwaves as they come equipped with various wattages. My microwave has 1100 watts, which is considered powerful. I have given approximate levels of power for microwave usage in the recipes.

I use my microwave for melting dark chocolate, defrosting cakes and frozen ingredients, and, most often, for softening buttercream and butter, readying them for creaming.

Scales

While most of the ingredients in this book are measured with cups and spoons, some are best weighed, such as chocolate. I prefer electronic scales, which are more precise. Spring-loaded scales, while inexpensive, are not as accurate and do not hold up as long as electronic scales. I suggest investing in a high quality scale, which will give you a lifetime of use. Qualities to look for are the ability to measure ounces as well as grams and a long shut-off window, so that it doesn't shut off automatically while you are still in the middle of weighing ingredients. A tare feature is usually standard, but important. This allows you to place a bowl on the scale, reset it to zero so the bowl is not being weighed, and then place your ingredient in the bowl, such as chopped chocolate. This lets you weigh the 2 ounces (or whatever) of chocolate that you need.

Magi-Cake Strips

These strips are a must-have; they ensure that cake layers bake evenly.

There is simply nothing else on the market that accomplishes what Magi-Cake Strips do. They are fabric strips, lined with aluminum fabric, that are soaked in water and wrapped around the sides of cake pans before placing in the oven. They are fixed in place with a "T" headed pin that comes with them. They keep cake edges moist by helping them to bake more slowly than the center, yielding a more evenly baked cake, without peaking in the center. This makes your job easier when it comes time to level your layers and tiers before frosting. One boxed set has strips to fit 8- and 9-inch cakes, the other set has strips to fit 10-, 12-, 14-, and 16-inch cakes (I don't use them for 6-inch layers). They can be found in cake decorating stores and through certain mail-order sources. I always use Magi-Cake Strips when baking wedding cake layers and these recipes were tested with them in use.

Cake Pans

To bake beautiful, even cake layers, you need to start with sturdy, heavy, undented cake pans. I like heavy aluminum cake pans with straight sides with a 2-inch depth (such as Magic Line) that are sold in cake decorating stores or through catalogs such as Parrish's, who manufacture these pans. Beryl's also carries excellent pans and Wilton carries a line called Decorator Preferred, which are well made. The thinner gauge ones do not hold up and are not a worthwhile investment.

A comment on dents: it might seem obvious that a dent-free pan would be preferable, but I cannot stress enough how important this is. Dents will not only leave divots in your cakes, but they can sometimes make unmolding your cakes difficult by encouraging sticking. Sometimes, if a cake refuses to come out of the pan, it is tempting to turn the cake upside down and rap the edges of the pan on the counter. This can dent your pan and ruin it for future use. (This will not happen if you prep pans correctly and use pans in good condition.) Also, when I wash my pans, I dry them immediately and put them away, lessening the chance of a heavy pot being placed upon them, which could also dent them. Cake pans can and should last a lifetime if you handle them carefully.

Always make sure that the larger sized pans fit in your oven before you start! The largest sized pan I call for in this book is 14 inches in diameter and this is because it is the largest size that fits in most standard ovens, while still allowing the needed air-space around the pan's edges for proper air circulation and even browning.

If your oven is too small to hold the larger-sized cake pans (you'll need at least 2 inches of free space on either side of the pan for the cake to bake properly), there is still a way to proceed. Many supply houses, such as Sweet Celebrations, have half pans for the larger sizes. Picture a circle that is cut in half to make a half-moon shape. This way you pour the batter in each half, bake, and, upon assembling, just lay the pieces side-by-side to make a whole round. No one will know the difference once the buttercream is applied and the cake is assembled.

Cooling Racks

The texture of your cakes will be at their best if they are cooled properly, and to do this you need cooling racks. I like large ones (that are able to support large pans) with wires that are set very close together and run both vertically and horizontally.

Icing Spatula

This might tie with a turntable for most important wedding cake baking tool. The proper icing spatula will go a long way toward helping you frost your cakes with the most professional finish. Icing spatulas are comprised of flat metal blades with rounded tips affixed to a (usually) plastic or wood handle. They come in a variety of sizes from about 5 inches to over 14 inches for the blade length alone. They can also be perfectly straight or they can be offset. Offset icing spatulas, which have a zig-zag bend in them, are great for icing broad flat surfaces, such as the tops or middle of tiers.

That said, some bakers like to use offset spatulas to ice the sides of their cakes and this brings up an important point. Just as there is a huge variety of icing spatula shapes and lengths, so is there no one spatula for the job. It all depends on you: on the size of your hand, the flexibility of your wrists, and your general decorating style. I suggest you try out a few different kinds to find the one that becomes "your" spatula. I own and use several, but for me, I find a very flexible, straight 8-inch to be the one I use the most. I have decorated hundreds of wedding cakes and yet I could not decorate one with a very stiff blade. They just don't work for me. So, if you have never had much success decorating cakes, maybe it is that you haven't had the proper tools! They are inexpensive, so go get a few and get to work for some practice!

Another important tip is that the blades of your icing spatulas should be perfectly smooth. NEVER use one to pry open a can! Any kind of dent, ripple, crack, or bend along the edge of the blade will show up as a streak, groove, or impression in your icing as you apply it with the offending spatula. Take care of them. Wash and dry them immediately and store them carefully, as well.

Slicing Knife

Although a serrated knife will work well enough for leveling cakes, it can make a lot of crumbs and crumbs are the bane of the cake decorator's existence. They make a mess when you are trying to frost a cake. I think a straight-edge slicing knife with a very long, flexible blade is perfect for the job. The knife blade should be at least 14 inches long, if not 16 inches or more.

Baking Core

I love, love, love this little tool. It looks like a little metal drinking cup not more than 4 inches tall, with the smaller end being closed and the wider end being open (see page 24). To use it, you fill up your cake pan with batter (I most often use them for 12-inch and 14-inch layers), reserving a tiny bit. You coat the inside and out of the baking core with nonstick spray and then you press the baking core down into the center of the batter, wider open end up. Then you halfway fill the core with the extra batter.

During baking, the metal baking core attracts heat to the center of the cake, which, in turn, encourages the center of the cake to bake evenly along with the edges where the heat normally hits first. After cooling, you remove the core, pop out the little piece of cake and use it to plug up the hole in the tier. After you frost the cake, no one will be the wiser and you will have an evenly baked cake.

Measuring Cups and Spoons

For dry ingredients, I use high quality stainless steel cups that are sturdy enough not to dent. Dents make for inaccurate measurements. A good set is more expensive, but will last for years. The same goes for measuring spoons. Both my cups and spoons come from Williams-Sonoma, whose brand offers precise measurements. Along with the standard 1/4-cup, 1/3-cup, 1/2-cup, and 1-cup measuring cups, I also find it handy to have 1/8-cup, 2/3-cup, 3/4-cup, and 2-cup sizes on hand. You can find these in King Arthur Flour's The Baker's Catalogue (see Sources).

For liquid measurements, I use standard Pyrex measuring cups, available at most supermarkets and kitchenware stores. For the most accurate measurements, use a cup of similar size to what you are measuring. For instance, if you need 1/2 cup of liquid, use a 1-cup measurer, not a 4-cup. For the recipes in this book, it is handy to have 1-cup, 2-cup, and 4-cup sizes.

Decorating Turntable

A turntable is vital for decorating cakes. You could frost a cake without one, but it will not look the same, and I do not suggest that you attempt a special occasion cake without one. You can use an inexpensive, plastic lazy Susan, or invest in a heavy-duty one with a cast iron bottom and a stainless steel top if you are going to do a lot of cake decorating. I highly recommend you use the latter! If you do not want to buy one, consider borrowing one for your project. Once you have one, though, you will see that they make frosting and decorating even a simple 9-inch layer cake easier, and your results are that much better.

Thermometers

Oven thermometers play an important role in any baking project. Your baked goods can only come out their best if they are baked at the proper temperature, and an oven thermometer will tell you if your oven is calibrated properly or not.

A chocolate thermometer is used during tempering. This type of thermometer has 1° increments (usually ranging from 40°–130°F), which allows you to accurately judge the temperature of the chocolate—crucial during this procedure.

Parchment Paper

Parchment is available in rolls, like aluminum foil, from kitchenware stores, mail-order sources, and now, thankfully, in more and more standard supermarkets. Cut out circles to fit pan bottoms (place the pan on parchment and trace around the bottom edge), and use to line baking sheets. When it is used in conjunction with a greased pan, your cakes will release effortlessly. Parchment can also be cut into triangles to make paper cones (see page 104 for instructions on making a parchment cone).

Cardboard Rounds (and Squares and Ovals)

I cannot stress enough the importance of purchased and sized cardboard rounds. They come in a variety of shapes and sizes, so you will be able to find what you need. For a 6-inch cake, you use a 6-inch cardboard. They are used as guides for your icing spatula to help make a smooth, clean side and to allow you to maneuver your tiers around, which is necessary during the wedding cake preparation process. Cutting your own will not give you standardized shapes—buy them. They are inexpensive and I consider them necessary.

Cake Drums

These are stiff, strong round or square boards that typically come covered with gold or silver foil. They are about 1/2 inch thick, but will hold the weight of most cakes. They can be purchased in cake decorating stores or through mail order. Use these as an inexpensive base for cakes.

Cake Bases

You can use any sturdy, appropriate platter to support your cakes, such as the cake drums described above. If you have silver, fine china, pottery, or glass platters that are large enough, by all means use them. The problem is that you need a perfectly flat surface and most platters are either curved or not broad or strong enough. You need a base that is at least 2 inches and preferably 4 inches wider than your bottom tier.

Beryl's and Parrish's both carry Masonite boards, which are very sturdy, flat boards. They can be purchased precut in the sizes suggested in this book, and are ready for you to cover with the decorative foil or covering of your choice. You can also have glass rounds cut to fit from a store specializing in glass and mirrors. You can have any size round or square cut fairly inexpensively and they will even polish the edges. Tell the glasscutter what size cake you are making and they can make recommendations as to the proper thickness of glass to support your creation. I used glass bases for many of the photographs. You can use clear glass or you can paint the underside of the glass any color you like. I often spray paint them gold or silver.

Pastry Bags

You will need pastry bags to decorate many of these cakes. I like the polyester ones made by Wilton called Featherweight Decorating Bags. They come in sizes ranging from 8 inches to 18 inches (2-inch increments). The openings are trimmed to allow a large decorating tube to fit, or to fit a coupler, which allows you to change small tips easily. I use the 14-inch size most often.

To clean them, they may be boiled, or simply washed well with hot, soapy water. Do not store in a drawer with loose tips or other sharp objects. These can pierce the bags and ruin them for future use.

Decorating Tips

Decorating tips provide a cheap and easy way to add a visual dimension to your cake. They are usually just a couple of dollars and can help you make shell shapes, bead borders, leaves, and more out of buttercream on your cake. A good place to start would be to purchase a range of round and star tips, as well as one for a basket weave and a couple of tips used to

make leaves. Ateco makes great tips and they are numbered for convenience. Note that while many companies number their tips, they are not necessarily the same numbers as their competitors. The tips I refer to in this book are all Ateco. I suggest you start out with Ateco #2, #8, #10, #18, #22, #47, #67, and #69. Make sure you practice using them before working on the final wedding cake (see pages 43–46).

Cookie Cutters and Gum Paste Cutters

You have probably used cookie cutters to shape cookies, but they come into use for wedding cake decorations as well. For instance, after rolling out your chocolate plastic (using your pasta maker, perhaps—more on that later on page 156), you will use petal-shaped cutters to make the basis of roses and leaf-shaped cutters for, well, leaves! An assortment of cookie cutters will come in handy, as will gum paste cutters, which are essentially the same thing. Sometimes the gum paste cutters come with a textural pattern as well that embosses the plastic. Or, veiners can be used after you cut out your leaf shape to imprint texture (see below). For the chocolate plastic roses in this book, I used cutters manufactured by a company called FMM and they are available through Beryl's (see Sources). They make a set of rose petal cutters in various sizes and a set for rose leaves.

Leaf Veiners

These are soft, flexible mats (often silicone or other plastic) that come in various leaf shapes. A vein pattern specific to that leaf appears as raised lines on the mat. Soft chocolate plastic or marzipan is pressed onto the mats and the vein pattern is transferred, resulting in a very realistic "leaf."

Blue Magic

This is a small device that absorbs moisture. It is a little larger than a walnut with a clear glass bottom and metal perforated top. Inside is a dry chemical that absorbs moisture. I use these inside storage containers holding crystallized flowers and chocolate plastic shapes.

Baking, Frosting, Assembling, and Decorating Your Cake

This hands-on chapter guides you through the basic steps of baking, frosting, assembling, and decorating celebration cakes of all types. I encourage you to start here to gain a foundation: all of the cakes in this book follow these steps, as do any large celebration cakes you may make of your own design. Read this chapter through at least once to familiarize yourself with what techniques go into making a wedding cake, then use it later whenever you want to refer back to a particular step.

The 6-Inch Sample Cake

The basics of baking a wedding cake share many steps and stages with those of smaller special-occasion cakes, but—as wedding cakes are larger in size and scope—they do involve some extra steps.

The first extra step is very important. After you've planned your cake, but before you begin making it, make a sample 6-inch cake. Once you have chosen what cake, syrup, filling, buttercream, and decorative elements that you would like for the wedding cake (and these could come from one of the complete cakes in the book, or components from various cakes that you have mixed and matched), I strongly suggest that you make a 6-inch version of your cake to sample. In this way, you will be able to assess the ease or difficulty of the project, practice many of the techniques involved in making the full cake, and, most importantly, decide whether you like the taste and look of the finished cake.

This is when you can make adjustments and eliminate guesswork. Do you like the amount of syrup that you added? Would you like to add more chocolate shavings to the batter than I originally called for? Or, maybe you thought you'd like the white cake but now think the slightly richer yellow cake is what you are looking for. By completely baking and assembling a 6-inch cake, you will be able to make notes and then tailor the actual wedding cake to your specifications.

You will note that I have broken down the essential cake recipes by tier sizes, so it's easy to just make a 6-inch cake.

Please do not skip this step! This is your "dating" period where you are trying the cake on for size before committing to the whole shebang. If you have ever dyed your hair at home, you know that the directions on the box suggest that you do a "strand-test" first, where you are supposed to try the dye on a tiny piece of hair to see what the outcome will be. I called the Clairol hotline and they said, unfortunately, the greater percentage of calls are from people who have experienced an unpleasant result because they went ahead with the whole coloring process without testing first. Undesirable results could have been avoided if the "strand-test" had been done! You see the analogy here? Please make a small cake first and then there will be no surprises.

After you have made your sample 6-inch cake (which, of course, can be done as far ahead of time as you like), the next step is to figure out the schedule for making the actual cake. Refer to the basic schedule (see pages 49–50) for an idea of how to approach this, but make sure to also take into consideration any details unique to your cake and your situation. For instance, if you are going to be using your neighbor's extra refrigerator, coordinate when you will need access to it. Also, look through individual recipes to check which design elements (such as chocolate flowers) can be made way ahead.

Baking Basics for Wedding-Sized Cakes

Assembling a delicious wedding cake begins with the layers of cake. A moist, buttery cake acts not only as the textural base for a towering wedding cake, but as its taste center as well. This section details the techniques needed to make the best-tasting and -textured cakes.

Why Your Choice of Pans Matters

I bake a lot of cakes, so I own many cake pans and expect them to perform perfectly. To me, this means that the pans conduct heat evenly, the cakes unmold with nice, straight sides, and the pans remain sturdy for a lifetime.

In fact, your choice of cake pan will affect your baking time and cake results dramatically—I don't mean size and shape of cake pan, but the brand and construction. I have done side-by-side baking in various brands of pans with the same cake batter and the differences have been noteworthy. For instance, when I baked the Essential Chocolate Cake in a 9-inch Magic Line pan, the cakes baked in 40 minutes, baked uniformly, did not peak, and had an even texture throughout. When I used a thin, dark metal supermarket-brand cake pan, the cake baked in 30 minutes, peaked terribly, and turned out lopsided with hard, overcooked edges.

The cakes baked in this book were tested with Magic Line pans. I love the Magic Line brand of cake pans because they perform on all accounts (see Sources). If you use different pans, your baking times and results may be different. Also note that I always use pans with a 2-inch depth. If you use 3-inch deep pans, again, the results will vary.

Pan Preparation

Pan preparation is key to ending up with the most perfect, even cake layers possible. First, make sure that your pans are free of dents. Then, coat the entire inside of each pan with nonstick spray. (Many cake recipes suggest buttering and flouring pans, but I find that nonstick spray is more convenient and easier to apply, and that it gives excellent results. Also, I find flouring pans gives a "floury" coating to the cakes that I find undesirable.) Cut a parchment round to fit the bottom of the pan, then spray the parchment as well (spraying the bottom of the pan first ensures that the parchment will stick in place). To cut an exact size of parchment, I place the pan on top of a sheet of parchment, trace the shape around the bottom of the pan, then cut it out. It should fit perfectly. If your parchment is not wide enough, simply cut two overlapping pieces.

Cake Batter Preparation

The cakes in this book are all butter cakes and all begin with beating together, or "creaming," butter and sugar. Use butter at room temperature, which creams most easily. This stage is very important to the cake's structure and flavor. Sugar crystals are actually quite rough and create air pockets within the butter as you cream them together. When properly creamed, the mixture will have lightened in color because of the incorporation of air, which is exactly what you want. The air pockets create lightness within the baked cake layers. So do not rush this step. It might take several minutes to reach the appropriate light and creamy stage. To cream, use the flat beater attachment to your mixer, which is meant for this purpose. As you cream, scrape the bowl down once or twice for even mixing (more for larger layers).

After creaming, I like to add any flavorings, such as vanilla extract, citrus zest, etc. The butter, which is a fat, is an excellent carrier of flavor, and I find adding flavorings at this point gives great results.

Measuring and Weighing Ingredients

Baking is a precise art. While making your mom's pot roast, you might decide to add some red wine, an extra bay leaf, or less garlic. Any which way, it will come out fine, within reason. But with baking, you must follow ingredient amounts exactly. These recipes are formulas and they work as written because there is a proper balance between the leaveners, the eggs (which provide structure), the moistness from butter, and what have you. While some of the amounts called for might sound odd, such as "³/₄ teaspoon," or even "³/₄ egg," please take care to use what is requested. You will be rewarded with spectacular results. (The odd measurements are a result of breaking down the recipes into so many sizes.)

The proper measuring tools are also essential. Refer to the Equipment section in the first chapter, Dreaming and Planning Your Cake, for details about the actual tools. For proper measuring procedures, here is how I measured ingredients. I suggest you do the same.

For dry ingredients: I store flour in a large airtight container and always stir first with a whisk (in its container) to aerate it. That is because flour compacts as it sits and, without stirring, you will end up measuring more flour per cup than is appropriate. Having aerated it, use the proper-sized measuring cup (e.g., ¹/₂ cup to measure ¹/₂ cup of ingredients) and dip it into the flour. Do not shake it down, tap it down, or manipulate it in any way. Just dip, measure out a heaping amount, and use the dull edge of a knife to scrape off the excess, leaving the flour level with the top of the cup. This is the proper amount. (Because this is the technique I employ, I am a huge advocate of odd-quantity measuring cups, such as those representing ²/₃ or ³/₄ cup. They can be purchased from King Arthur Flour's The Baker's Catalogue—see Sources.) Measure granulated white sugar in the same way. Baking powder and baking soda are similarly measured with the proper spoons. Brown sugar is lightly packed into the appropriate sized cup.

For liquid ingredients: Use measuring cups designed for measuring liquids, such as Pyrex cups. Use cups as similar in size to the necessary amount as possible (don't measure ¹/₄ cup in a 4-cup measure). To measure, place the cup on a level surface, fill to the right level, then view so that you are eye-level with the cup to read the measurement. The liquid level should meet the desired line on the cup.

Weighing ingredients: Most of the ingredients in these recipes are measured by volume, but sometimes I call for weighing. Better quality chocolate, for instance, is sold in bulk and must be chopped. The chopped pieces will be of varying size and shape and cannot be accurately measured; they are best weighed. A scale is therefore required (see page 16).

Whole eggs and/or yolks go in next, and should be added one at a time, and the batter mixed so that each egg is absorbed before adding the subsequent one. Scraping down the bowl once or twice is helpful.

Dry ingredients should be sifted to make your cake as light as possible. Leaveners, such as baking powder and baking soda, must be fresh in order to help the cake rise properly (see page 12). Dry ingredients are often added alternately with wet ingredients, such as milk, which gives the best textural results. Begin and end with your dry mixture. Beat after each addition, scraping the bowl down once or twice (more for larger layers), but do not overmix or the protein in the flour will develop and your cake will be tough. Mix just until the batter is smooth.

Filling the Pans

Most of these cake recipes are meant to fill 2 pans of the same size. When making wedding cakes, it is especially important to split the batter evenly between both pans so that the layers will be exactly the same height. To do this, I suggest first filling each by eye as evenly as possible. Then, weigh each pan and add or remove batter as needed to make both pans exactly the same weight. I am assuming you will own a scale. If you do not, I suggest just using your eye and best guesswork. Any uneven layers can be trimmed later. I do not suggest scraping batter in and out of measuring cups as you will deflate the batter, altering the final texture, and you will lose some batter clinging to the cups.

One More Step for Even Layers

If you are baking a wedding cake, chances are you are pretty comfortable baking typical 8- and 9-inch cakes and, for the purposes of making simple layer cakes, you can get great-looking layers using quality cake pans alone. However, when baking layers for wedding cakes, it is so important to have the cakes bake evenly that I take the extra step of wrapping my cake pans with Magi-Cake Strips for every size except 6-inch. Magi-Cake Strips are strips of padded aluminum fabric that come in sizes to fit cake pans from 8 inches on up. (Check the boxes, as they come in various sizes to fit various sized pans and some sizes are sold together as a set.) You soak the strips in water, lightly wring them out, and then wrap them around the outside of each cake pan, holding them in place with a special pin or a paper clip. What they do is keep the outside edges of the cakes from baking too quickly, something that larger tiers are especially prone to do. This gives you a more evenly baked cake, without crusty sides, and allows the layers to rise more evenly, which means less cake will have to be cut off when you level them!

Technique close-up: perfectly level, baked using Magi-Cake strips

A Tip for Baking the Largest Tiers

For 12-inch and 14-inch tiers, I have one more tool and technique to suggest: the use of baking cores. These are small, hollow metal cones with flat bottoms. You pour the required amount of batter into your cake pan, reserving just a bit (maybe 1/2 cup) for the core. Then you coat the baking core, inside *and* out, with nonstick spray and nestle it down into the center of the cake. Place enough extra batter inside the core so that it is level with the batter outside of the core; now you are ready to bake.

While Magi-Cake Strips retard the baking of the edges, baking cores (see page 17) help speed the baking of the center: The metal of the baking core draws heat to the center of the cake, helping it to bake at a rate similar to that at the edges, where the heat naturally hits first. When the cake has cooled briefly on a rack, remove the baking core and pop out the little cakelet. Unmold the cake and cool the cake and cakelet on a rack. Once they are completely cool and you are ready to assemble your tier, first trim the cakelet, if necessary, to make it the same height as the cake. Then use it to plug the hole in the center of your cake. You can just press it into the hole. No buttercream is needed at this point as it will stick just enough. After you have torted, filled, and frosted the tier, no one will know the cakelet is there. It will become part of the whole. I love baking cores and use them all the time. They aren't expensive, so consider buying two (since you will typically bake 2 layers at a time).

 Baking Tiers At-a-Glance

✳ Use Magi-Cake Strips or equivalent on any cake larger than 6 inches

✳ Use baking cores for 12-inch and 14-inch cakes or for smaller tiers when the batter is heavy

Technique close-up: baking core inserted and filled with batter

 Homemade Magi-Cake Strips

You can make a homemade approximation of Magi-Cake Strips if you don't have them on hand. Take a string and wrap it around the cake pan you will be using; this will give you the circumference. Use the string to measure out a length of aluminum foil, adding 4 inches. Lay the length of foil flat on the counter. Take 1-foot lengths of paper towel and fold lengthwise several times to make a layered strip about 1½ inches wide. Soak this paper towel strip in cool water and place it on the foil, near one of the long edges of the foil. Repeat with lengths of paper towels until you have made a continuous strip of wet paper towels all the way along the length of the foil. Fold the foil up and around the towels so that the paper towels are completely encased in foil. You should have a strip of foil about 1¾ inches wide, filled with wet paper towels. Wrap this around your cake pan and affix in place with a paper clip placed over the overlapping ends. These homemade strips are disposable and should be used one time only.

Caution: Make sure no paper towels are exposed or they might catch fire. Dampened well and completely encased in foil, they will be fine and do the job.

When Is It Done? Making Sense of Baking Times

My recipes give approximate baking times, such as "bake for about 30 minutes." This means that if your batter is prepared properly, you have used the correct pans, and your oven is calibrated correctly, then the layers will bake in the approximate baking time. You should always begin checking a little beforehand, however: given the vagaries of ovens, even a properly prepared cake might take less or more time to bake, but it will be close.

To confirm doneness, I like to use the toothpick test. Take a wooden toothpick or skewer and insert it into the center of the cake. If it comes out with wet batter clinging to it, the cake is quite a ways from being done. If a few moist, but not wet, crumbs cling to it, the cake is pretty much done and still moist. My cakes are done at this point. Some cake recipes will say the toothpick should "test clean"—it should come out with no crumbs attached—but I believe most cakes are over-baked at this point.

Wood works better than metal as a cake tester because it allows crumbs to cling to it more easily. The metal ones will often test cleanly too soon and do not always allow the nuance of a few moist crumbs to cling to their surface.

Other visual cues that indicate doneness include the edges of the cake just shrinking away from the sides of the pan, and a golden color (for yellow and white cakes) along the edges and on top. Use your sense of touch as well. When you gently press the center of the cake, it should spring back and not leave an indentation. But press lightly!

Proper Cooling

Once your cakes are baked, they must be cooled before proceeding. Proper cooling will leave you with delicately textured cakes. Improper cooling can thwart all the effort you have put into your cakes up until this point and leave you with gummy cake layers. You need cooling racks and, since you will be working with large-sized cake pans, I suggest using cooling racks wide enough to accomodate the largest tiers you will be working with. At the very least, the racks should be no more than 2 inches narrower than your largest cake layer. I find the ones that have both horizontal and vertical bars to be the strongest; they will give you years of use. When the cakes are done, remove them from the oven and immediately place them on racks still in the pans. Leave them to cool a bit until the pan is barely warm to touch, around 5 minutes for small tiers and up to 20 minutes for larger ones (see individual recipes).

For 6-inch, 8-inch, and 9-inch sizes, I then unmold the cakes directly onto the racks, peel the parchment off the cakes if it has stuck, and allow the cakes to cool completely. The cakes will be upside down from their previous orientation, which is OK. For 10-inch cakes and larger, I place a cardboard round (square, oval, etc.) of the same size on top of the cake, flip it over, unmold, and then gently slip the cake from the cardboard onto the rack. The larger cakes need this support to prevent cracking. If the cake seems very fragile, leave it on the cardboard and place the cardboard on the rack. If you do not have a rack wide enough to support your tiers, then leave the cake on the cardboard round to offer support. This is not ideal, as the cardboard prevents the heat from dispersing evenly, but it is better than having edges of the cake hang too far over the sides of the rack and risk breaking off. Always make sure to

---

 Testing Doneness At-a-Glance

* Use approximate baking time as a guide, but always check a little early, just in case
* Insert a wooden toothpick or skewer into the cake; a few moist crumbs should cling to the tester
* Use your eyes! Look for color and texture changes
* Use your sense of touch! The cake should spring back under light pressure

---

Cooling Techniques At-a-Glance

* Allow cakes to cool in pans briefly, until the pans are barely warm to the touch (the larger the cake, the longer the layers should cool in the pans)
* Unmold cakes on cooling racks: directly for small tiers, supported by cardboard rounds for larger tiers
* Peel off parchment paper if it has stuck to the cakes
* Allow cakes to cool completely before filling, frosting, or wrapping

remove the parchment so that the cake can throw off heat and cool properly (this is also why I leave them upside down; it is where most of the heat is retained at this point).

PROPER STORAGE

When the cake layers are completely cooled, you may proceed with filling and frosting your cake, or you may wrap and store the layers. (I often make the cakes 1 day before I assemble them.) Place all cake layers on cardboard rounds of the same size—this prevents breakage—and double-wrap in plastic wrap. If you are frosting the cake the next day, you can now simply leave the layers at room temperature.

The schedule that I suggest has you baking the cakes 1 day before frosting them and 2 days before the event. If you cannot accommodate this timeline, then bake the cake layers ahead and freeze them. I do think that freezing causes the cakes to lose some moistness, but if the only way you can make a large celebration cake is to bake the cake layers ahead

and freeze them, then by all means, do it. (Or see my advice for freezing whole tiers.) Just give them an extra brushing of moistening syrup during assembly.

To prevent as much moisture loss as possible when freezing, wrap the cakes in foil after wrapping in plastic, then slip the layers into ziplock plastic bags, removing as much air as possible, and freeze. (You probably won't find ziplock bags large enough for your larger tiers, but the companies keep coming out with larger styles, so you might as well check.) When you place your cakes in the freezer, make sure they don't get crushed by any 4-pound chickens! I often slip the cakes back into cake pans (sometimes you need a slightly larger pan) to protect them from getting crushed by errant hunks of frozen food.

You can freeze cakes for up to 1 month. To defrost, remove them from the freezer and place in the refrigerator overnight, still wrapped. Do not bake the cake layers 3 to 5 days ahead and refrigerate as that will rob them of the most moisture. Your best choices are to bake either exactly 2 days prior, or a week or more ahead and freeze.

Storage Tips At-a-Glance

* Cool cakes completely
* Place cakes on cardboard rounds
* Double-wrap in plastic wrap
* Leave at room temperature, if assembling the next day
* If freezing, follow with a wrap in aluminum foil; then slip wrapped cakes in ziplock bags, if they fit
* Make sure nothing crushes cakes in the freezer
* If you can, slip the cake layers into cake pans to protect them

Freezing Whole Tiers

If you must make the cake layers way ahead of time, a different and, I think, better option—though a bit more involved—is to freeze whole tiers already filled and given a thin crumb coat, the initial coat, of butter-cream (see pages 27–32 for instructions on assembling tiers and applying crumb coats). The buttercream will form a moisture-proof seal around the cake to help prevent it from drying out. (This technique works only for cakes frosted and filled with buttercream; other frostings and fillings, such as Sour Cream Fudge Frosting or Lemon Curd, will not freeze well.)

To do this, immediately after the cake layers have cooled, proceed with subsequent directions to torte them (to split them horizontally), moisten them well with moistening syrup of choice, and then fill them with the chosen buttercream. Smooth a nice crumb coat of buttercream all over each cake tier, making it a little thicker than normal. Make sure that the entire surface of the cake tier is covered with buttercream, even though it is fairly thin and you might be able to still see cake beneath. Place the tiers in the freezer (they will already be on cardboard rounds) and freeze until the buttercream is firm to the touch. Then wrap and freeze as above, slipping each tier into a larger-diameter pan for protection, if you can. You can freeze cakes up to 1 month this way.

Defrost overnight in the refrigerator but try to unwrap while the buttercream is still cold so that it remains on the cake after unwrapping and does not completely peel away with the wrapping materials.

Leveling, Layering, Filling, and Frosting: Assembling Perfect Tiers

The term "assembling" should hint as to what this process is all about. As on a classic assembly line, all of the parts and pieces that you are about to work with must have been brought to the point where they are ready to use. Putting your cake together is the fun part—where you see your creation coming together. It is not about scrambling last-minute to prepare buttercreams or fillings—so please make sure that all your components are ready to go. Here's a checklist:

- Cake layers are baked and cooled
- Moistening syrup is prepared and cooled, with any flavorings added
- Any fillings are prepared and ready to use
- Buttercream or frosting is prepared and ready to use
- Anything made ahead and refrigerated or frozen has been brought to room temperature

Level Your Layers

When the time comes to begin assembling your cake tiers with fillings and frostings, there are some preparatory techniques you must attend to first. The first step is to make your cake layers level and all the same height. Some cake layers may peak during baking, or, at the very least, dome slightly—this is not unusual. Even if you use Magi-Cake Strips and produce wonderful, even-looking layers, you may still have to trim a little to produce a perfectly level cake. This is a very important step because each layer is sandwiched with another layer to make a tier, so even slightly uneven layers can add up to assembled tiers with a pronounced slope. Needless to say, the final filled tier must be level, as a tier with a rounded top could throw off the aesthetics at the very least, and literally throw off the sturdiness of the construction at the very worst! Also, even if the cake does not look particularly peaked, it might be subtly lopsided, and that must be corrected.

Start with baked and cooled cake layers; they should be at room temperature. Examine the top of each cake layer: if it is rounded at all, it must be leveled. To trim off any rounded portions from the tops of your layers, I suggest using a long, thin bladed slicing knife, such as a fish slicing knife. (This kind of knife has smooth, rounded indentations along the blade, which reduce drag and make for a clean cut.) A serrated knife will work, but can create crumbs, which are the bane of the cake decorator's existence. A knife that has a longer blade than the diameter of your cake will be best, but might not be possible for larger tiers. Use the longest knife you can find.

I use my turntable to aid this process. Place your cake layer in the center of the turntable. Get down to eye level with the cake and gently spin the turntable. You should be able to see the high spots of the cake pretty easily. Gently slice those away—always cutting conservatively. You can always cut more off later.

You also want to measure the depths of your layers. You want to end up with layers that are all the same height. Since you will have taken care with dividing the batter evenly between the pans, chances are they are even. But sometimes one cake will rise a little more in the oven than the other. Trim every layer so that it is the same height—most likely about 1 1/2 inches. Make sure to note the height so that all the subsequent cake layers of other sizes can be trimmed to the same height.

After leveling them, I usually flip the cakes upside down so that the cake's bottom is now the nice smooth, flat top.

TORTE YOUR LAYERS

Most of the cake tiers in this book are made up of 4 layers of cake. But you may have noticed that every recipe calls for only two 6-inch pans, two 10-inch pans, etc. There is nothing wrong with the math. You are going to cut each layer in half,

 A Carpenter's Level in the Kitchen?

In the early days of my cake decorating career, I kept ending up with uneven cake layers and I just couldn't figure out why. I was taking every precaution I could think of, but the cakes would always come out a little off. (The worst thing was that I usually didn't find this out until I was stacking the tiers and the saw that the entire cake looked lopsided!) Then, one day, a light bulb went off in my head . . . I took a carpenter's level and placed it on my work table. Sure enough, it turned out that my table was off-kilter! No wonder my cakes were, too! So, make sure your work surface is level. And while you're at it, check your oven. If your oven isn't level, you have no hope of baking a level cake.

leaving you with 4 layers of cake per tier. The technique of cutting a cake layer in half horizontally is called "torting." (Among other things, a torte refers to a many layered cake, and that is what we are talking about here.)

The key to torting is to split the layers evenly to yield 2 equal halves. You could try and do that by eye, but it is hard to do. One easy technique is to put the cake on a cardboard round and cut a small vertical line into the cake's side, from top to bottom—just deep enough to see (you'll be using this mark later to line the split layers back up). Now, hold a ruler vertically against the cake, placing the ruler against the top edge of the cardboard to get the true halfway mark, and right at that point make a small hole, just large enough to see, with a toothpick. Make this halfway mark with the toothpick at intervals all the way around the circumference of the cake moving the ruler around the cake as you go to help you mark the proper measurement. Place your cake in the center of your turntable and place your knife horizontally against one of the holes.

Technique close-up: "torting" a cake layer

There are many ways to get the syrup into the layers. I have tried them all, from squeezing out of needle-nose plastic bottles to spooning it on. Some chefs even use a spray bottle and mist it on! I have come full circle and now rely on that old standby: the pastry brush. Use a clean brush, not a brush you used to baste your chicken with a curry marinade! A soft bristle texture is best as it won't dredge up crumbs like a stiff brush. Look for the new silicone brushes on the market. They are soft and clean up especially well.

Using the brush takes a little finesse since you don't want to bring up crumbs. Dip the brush in the syrup. Then, instead of brushing it back and forth on the cake, just dab it over the cut surface of each layer. By gently dabbing the syrup where you want it, you also best control the amount applied. The cake will darken a bit where the syrup has been added, allowing you to see which parts you've already moistened. The aim is to add an even layer of syrup. Don't be skimpy. Remember, you want to get it into the layer so that it moistens the whole cake, not just deposit it on top. The cake will soak up the syrup pretty readily.

N O T E : *Some bakers have told me that they have trouble telling how much is enough. This is why I strongly suggest that you make your 6-inch sample cake; you will be able to actually taste whether you are applying the correct amount of syrup.*

Start gently cutting into the cake, spinning the turntable slowly, cutting all the while, and always making sure that the blade is level (horizontal) and hitting the right spots. Continue until the cake is cut evenly all the way through. Slide the top layer onto another same-sized cardboard round and set both layers aside. Keep the 2 half layers from the same cake together, because you will want to line them back up together to keep the full tier as even as possible and you don't want to confuse them with the other 2 half layers.

Torte all your cake layers before going on to the next step.

MAKE IT MOIST

All the cake recipes in this book are moist and delicious. However, I often brush cake layers with moistening syrup when I am making large celebration cakes. This is because the layers are generally worked on over the course of a couple of days, at least, and will most likely go in and out of refrigeration a few times, and all of these factors can dry out even the moistest cake. A moistening sugar syrup can add moistness, as well as extra flavor, since it often contains some kind of liqueur, extract, or juice.

 Liqueur-Enhanced Cakes

Many of the cakes in this book feature a moistening syrup enhanced with a liqueur, such as rum or raspberry eau de vie. Liqueurs provide a singular flavor, but if you prefer not to add alcohol to your cake, I suggest you use one of those flavored syrups that you find in coffee bars—the ones that turn your java into a hazelnut, raspberry, or vanilla drink. They have no alcohol, but carry lots of flavor (see Sources).

The chart below gives approximate syrup amounts per layer, however, of all the measurements in this book, this is the most variable. You will have to judge how much a particular cake needs, assessing its inherent moistness or dryness. For instance, if a cake is a tad overbaked, it will most likely need a larger quantity of moistening syrup. If there is a lot of humidity in the air, the cake might need a little less. Also, in the case of syrups with added alcohol, use your judgment. Some liqueurs are stronger tasting than others and you should let taste be your guide. And, as I have mentioned earlier, you might like the cake with no syrup at all. This is a highly personal decision and is why I suggest making a 6-inch sample cake first; you can assess your syrup amount with the test cake.

 How Much of Everything Should I Make?

I think it is important to retain a balance between cake, syrup, and filling. The balance I have striven for is so that each layer of cake is moistened, but not soaked, and that the layers of filling are rather thin. As with syrup, too much filling and the entire creation becomes overly sweet. In general, I use about a $1/4$-inch-thick layer of filling, less for some of the strongly flavored, non-buttercream fillings, such as Lemon Curd. But these are my preferences. Some bakers prefer thinner or thicker layers of filling. Please feel free to adjust to your own tastes.

The following chart gives you amounts for moistening syrup, filling, buttercream, crumb coat, final coat, and enough buttercream for very simple decorations. It is my hope that you will use this chart to develop your own combinations for your very own wedding cakes. The amounts are very generous, so will never run out in the middle of a project. Note that with some cakes, you will be using the same component for filling and buttercream (such as a Vanilla Buttercream used inside and out). In this case just add the filling and outer buttercream amounts together to determine what you need. Leftover moistening syrup and buttercreams may be saved for other cake projects. I have erred on the side of generosity, so you may very well have leftovers.

How to Use the Chart: Remember, most of the wedding cake tiers in this book consist of 2 cake layers that have been split in half to yield 4 cake layers. All 4 layers will be moistened with syrup; the bottom 3 will be spread with filling. So if the chart calls for 1 cup of syrup for every 6-inch tier, you would use $1/4$ cup syrup for every layer of cake. For a filling, again, you would divide the whole quantity among the 3 layers needing to be filled. The chart is written this way so that you know how much to prepare and have on hand for your project.

Syrup, Filling, and Frosting Amounts

Round Tiers

For each 6-inch round tier use 1 cup of moistening syrup

For each 8-inch round tier use 1¼ cups of moistening syrup

For each 9-inch round tier use 1½ cups of moistening syrup

For each 10-inch round tier use 2½ cups of moistening syrup

For each 12-inch round tier use 3 cups of moistening syrup

For each 14-inch round tier use 4 cups of moistening syrup

For each 6-inch round tier use 1 cup of filling

For each 8-inch round tier use 2¼ cups of filling

For each 9-inch round tier use 3 cups of filling

For each 10-inch round tier use 3¾ cups of filling

For each 12-inch round tier use 5¼ cups of filling

For each 14-inch round tier use 7½ cups of filling

For each 6-inch round tier use 3 cups of buttercream for crumb and final coat, and simple decoration

For each 8-inch round tier use 4½ cups of buttercream for crumb and final coat, and simple decoration

For each 9-inch round tier use 5½ cups of buttercream for crumb and final coat, and simple decoration

For each 10-inch round tier use 7 cups of buttercream for crumb and final coat, and simple decoration

For each 12-inch round tier use 9 cups of buttercream for crumb and final coat, and simple decoration

For each 14-inch round tier use 11 cups of buttercream for crumb and final coat, and simple decoration

Oval Tiers

For 5⅝ × 7¾-inch oval tiers prepare same amounts as for 8-inch rounds

For 7⅝ × 10¾-inch oval tiers prepare same amounts as for 10-inch rounds

For 9⅞ × 13-inch oval tiers prepare same amounts as for 12-inch rounds

Square Tiers

For 6-inch square tiers prepare same amounts as for 8-inch rounds

For 10-inch square tiers prepare same amounts as for 12-inch rounds

For 14-inch square tiers prepare same amounts as for 6-inch plus 14-inch rounds

Rectangular Tiers

For 13 × 9 × 2-inch rectangular tiers prepare same amounts as for 12-inch rounds

For the most popular sizes of our cakes you will need:

For a 6-inch, 10-inch, 14-inch round cake you will need 7½ cups syrup, 12¼ cups filling, 21 cups buttercream

For 6-inch, 9-inch, 12-inch round cake you will need 5½ cups syrup, 9¼ cups filling, 17¼ cups buttercream

Filling and Assembling the Layers

Once the layers are moistened with syrup, you can fill and assemble the layers of your cake tiers. Here is where the complete cake begins to take shape—where the flavor combinations come together and the choices you have made of cake, moistening syrup, filling, and frosting first converge.

All of the cakes in this book have one or more fillings, ranging from frostings, like Vanilla Buttercream or Sour Cream Fudge Frosting, to spreads like Lemon Curd and Nutella. In general, I like my filling to be about 1/4-inch thick.

It is important for the layer of filling to be even, and the best way to accomplish this is to use an offset spatula. Place a quantity of filling on the center of your layer (about 1/2 cup for smaller tiers and 1 cup for larger) and use the offset spatula to gently spread it back and forth evenly over the cake. Turning the cake on a turntable can help this procedure. Spread the filling almost to the edges, leaving about 1/4 inch border of cake all the way around. Some of the recipes will have exceptions to this rule, but this is the basic approach, and you will use this technique again and again. You want to leave the edges open because if the filling is a different flavor or color from the exterior buttercream frosting, it might peak through and mar the final appearance of the cake.

When you're ready to place the second (corresponding) layer of cake on top of your first filled layer, locate the vertical line that you cut on the bottom cake layer and make sure the top layer aligns with the one below. Then you add another layer of filling and another layer of cake. After the next and last layer of filling, you should once again line up the final layer of cake with the layer below (layers 1 and 2 came from one cake, layers 3 and 4 came from the other cake). Lining up each cake couplet will help you achieve as perfectly level a tier as possible.

I like the last layer (which is the top of the tier) to be the bottom of one of the original cake layers. The bottom of a baked cake is smooth and flat and, flipped upside down, makes the perfect uppermost layer, the bottom now facing up. This way, when you go to frost it, you will have the smoothest surface possible.

When the tier is assembled, bring your eyes down to cake level and slowly spin the cake around on the turntable. The top should look level. If one part is higher, gently press it down. Sometimes that is all you need. If it is really off, remove the top cake layer, add more filling where needed, replace the cake, and check again. You can also do some patch-up work with buttercream when you apply the crumb coat.

The All-Important Crumb Coat

I wish there was a better term for the "crumb coat." The term sounds strange, but actually does describe its purpose. Once your cake is filled, you might think you are ready to frost your cake, and you are, but not with the final coat. First you apply a crumb coat, or first coat, of buttercream to the outside of the cake, completely covering the top and sides, which seals in any crumbs that might be on the surface. It readies the cake for a smooth final coat of buttercream. The crumb coat makes a huge difference in how the final coat goes on and, in turn, how professional and smooth it looks. It sets the stage for the entire look of your final cake. Do not skimp on this step. It is easy, but it takes time, because you have to chill the tiers between applying the crumb coat and the final coat.

First, make sure that your buttercream is the right temperature. It should be very smooth and easy to spread. (See page 70 for information on buttercream.) To apply the crumb coat, place a filled tier on your turntable (that is already on a cardboard of the same size, of course). Using an icing spatula (I like to use a straight edge at this point) place a small quantity of buttercream on the top of the cake. Spread it around thinly; you want to create a smooth but thin layer of buttercream all over the top and then also on the sides. It does not have to look pretty; you will see the cake beneath the thin veil of buttercream. Just make sure to cover the tier completely.

This is also when you should rectify any unevenness in the cake. Spin the tier around on your turntable and if one section dips down a bit, then add more buttercream to that area to build it up and create a level surface. Place the cake tier in the refrigerator at this time (you did make sure you were going to have room, didn't you?) and allow it to chill until the buttercream is very firm to the touch, about 2 hours. Repeat with all of your tiers and chill them well before proceeding with your final coat of buttercream.

NOTE: *Make sure you have room in the refrigerator to store all of the tiers at once! During the winter here in the Northeast, I use the screened-in porch as my walk-in refrigerator!*

 Bowls and Bowls of Buttercream!

The chart on page 31 shows you how much buttercream you will need to fill and frost every size tier. With certain flavors of buttercream, such as coffee, it is vital that you make *all* the buttercream you'll need all at once because the buttercream can vary widely in color from batch to batch and you want your whole cake to match! (For some reason, even if you add the exact same amount of instant espresso powder to two batches of buttercream, they often end up being slightly different shades and this will show up on your cake.) To prevent this from happening, make the total number of batches suggested and then beat them together, batch by batch, until the buttercream is all of the same shade.

The amounts that I suggest are generous and will work in almost all situations. I always err on the side of having extra because, for instance, in the case of chocolate cakes covered with Vanilla Buttercream, the dark-colored cake will show through the light-colored buttercream without a good solid layer of crumb coat and final coat of buttercream. (Actually, in this particular case, I often end up doing a sheer second final coat, if not all over, then at least in spots that still need some covering.)

FROST IT

If you have taken the time to apply your crumb coat evenly, then this step will be a breeze. The approach is largely the same as applying the crumb coat, with a few exceptions. I like to start with my largest tier as it gives me a sense of accomplishment when it is finished and the rest follow easily.

Before you begin, make sure the crumb coat on the tier you are about to frost is chilled and firm. Then make sure your buttercream is perfectly smooth (it should be as soft as mayonnaise) and ready to use. Place your tier on the turntable and place a quantity of buttercream on the top of the cake.

Icing the Top

Now, for the next step, you use a technique that is different from the one you used for the crumb coat. Take your icing spatula and glide it over the buttercream, gently pushing the buttercream around the top of the tier (see photo, page 35).

Do not let the spatula touch the crumb coat layer where it might dig into it and release crumbs. You do not have to press down hard, just gently smooth it around. For small tiers (10 inches or smaller), I like to use a straight edge spatula for this stage, both tops and sides. For the larger tiers, an offset is often helpful for spreading the buttercream on the top. Some folks like to use an offset for the sides as well. Experiment.

To smooth the top, it is helpful to hold the icing spatula at different angles to see which works for you. Sometimes holding it very flat, just slightly angled, as you draw it across the cake will help create a smooth surface. Don't worry if the buttercream still has ridges and creases, just keep going over it. The whole process is one of adding buttercream and smoothing it away and adding and smoothing again and again until you get it right. You just have to keep working that buttercream back and forth.

To make the top as smooth as possible, draw your spatula of choice over the buttercream from the edges toward the center. In other words, the center of the cake is where you will and is pressed against the cardboard round beneath the tier, while holding it at a slight angle, but almost flat against the cake (see photo). The perfect shape of the cardboard keeps the spatula steady and helps you guide it around the cake in an even manner, creating smooth sides. This is one reason why I do not cut out my own cardboards—they would never be perfectly round, oval, or square, and so could not be used as an accurate guide for my spatula. (Making them is also time consuming, and the purchased ones are inexpensive and readily available.)

Start to turn the turntable, holding your icing spatula still. As the tier spins, the spatula will smooth the buttercream on the cake. You will need to stop constantly to add more buttercream, just like when you apply buttercream to the top of a cake—again, it is all about adding buttercream, then smoothing it out, removing some, adding some more, spinning and smoothing. By keeping the spatula vertical and still, pressing it against the cardboard and spinning the turntable, the buttercream on the sides of the cake will smooth out.

Whether you frost the tops or the sides first doesn't really matter. Different bakers develop different approaches. The one constant is that you will be adding buttercream, removing some as you smooth it out with your icing spatula, then adding more buttercream and repeating the process until the entire tier is covered, tops and sides, with a smooth coat of buttercream. This is a multi-step process.

For square cakes, you will use square cardboards and the straight edges of the boards will guide your spatula. The edges of square cakes are very hard to make clean. Just be patient and you will get it. (Because corners are so hard to frost well, the square cakes in this book have "camouflage"— they are decorated in such a way as to help disguise the corners.) Ovals are worked similarly to rounds.

lift the icing spatula off of the cake and risk leaving a mark. The centers of the cakes will be covered by smaller tiers and decorations, so concentrate on getting the edges as smooth as can be, not the center.

Icing the Sides

There is a special technique that I employ when applying buttercream to the sides. Pick up some buttercream on your icing spatula and sort of wipe it off onto the side of your tier. Then, position your spatula so that the tip is touching the turntable

More Helpful Techniques

Having a variety of icing spatulas comes in handy. A large offset might help smooth the top. Then you might want to change to a straight edge for the sides. When the cake is almost done and has just a few areas to be smoothed, try switching

Technique close-up: applying crumb coat

Technique close-up: spreading buttercream across top of tier

Technique close-up: adding buttercream to the sides

Technique close-up: final coat of buttercream

to a very small offset and/or straight edge to take care of the last bits of smoothing. There are even small offset spatulas that are triangular in shape and have a very narrow tip for touching up hard-to-reach areas. Remember, these are the techniques that work for me—feel free to experiment with different spatulas.

Almost any wedding cake you make will need a smooth final coat of buttercream. The exceptions in this book are when

Frosting Cakes At-a-Glance

* Make sure your crumb coat is chilled and firm before applying final coat of buttercream

* Your buttercream should be very soft—like mayonnaise

* Glide your icing spatula on top of the final coat of buttercream so as not to touch the crumb coat and dredge up crumbs

* Use plenty of buttercream on the tops and sides— it's all a process of adding and removing buttercream to make the final coat as smooth as possible

* Warm your icing spatula to help attain a smooth appearance

* Try different spatulas (longer, shorter, flexible, stiff, straight or offset)—what works for you might be different from what works for me

* Remember, perfection is not the goal—a lovingly prepared delicious cake is!

 Using a Pastry Bag and Tip to Fill and Frost Your Cake

I like to use icing spatulas to apply buttercream, but some bakers get good results using other techniques, and I wanted to point out to you one of the most popular, which is to use large tips. The tips apply a layer of buttercream, either on the tops of tiers for the filling or on the outside of the cake. Icing spatulas then smooth the piped buttercream out, but the tip makes for a quick way to get the buttercream in and on the cake.

To fill a cake, use an Ateco #804 round pastry tip (about ³/₈ inch) to gently squeeze out the filling in a spiral to cover the entire layer. (Remember to leave ¹/₄ inch of the edge free of filling.)

To frost the tops and sides, use a broad, flat tip (such as an Ateco #789 or #790 used on the nonserrated side) to apply ribbons of frosting to the tops and sides of cakes for either the crumb coat or final coat.

you are going to pipe on a pattern with decorating tips or are creating swirls in the fudge frosting. For the former, you pipe buttercream directly onto the crumb coat.

Even if you have followed the above recommendations, you might still not have perfectly smooth tiers. You know what? That's OK! I don't go for perfection. I like to see that the cake was made by the human hand. A few ridges here and there are just fine. Chances are they can be somewhat masked by decorations to come. However, there are a few more techniques to share that will help you get the buttercream to a point where it is as smooth as can be.

The technique I use the most is to dip my spatula in very hot water, shake off the excess, and then run it over the buttercream while it is still warm and damp. The heat will slightly melt and smooth the buttercream. Any moisture actually helps it glide and will evaporate. I do this repeatedly when I am applying a final coat.

Another technique involves a special kind of triangular-shaped spatula. I find that most folks have particular problems smoothing the sides. A large, broad, triangular-shaped spatula, such as one used for applying spackle to a wall (yes, go to the hardware store) can help. I look for one that has a flexible blade that is at least 4 inches wide: you want one as wide as your tier is high, at the very least. This way, there is a broad flat edge to swipe over the edges, which can help eliminate ridges of buttercream made from the edges of a narrow-bladed spatula.

Last but not least, I cannot stress enough the importance of buttercream that is at the right temperature. If it is too cold, it will not smooth out properly. It should be satiny smooth and spreadable, like mayonnaise.

Now, before you can stack the layers, the cake needs to go back into the refrigerator to chill. (If you tried to stack them at this point, you would end up smearing the buttercream.) However, if you are covering the sides with chopped nuts, chopped chocolate, or anything you want to adhere, you should press these ingredients directly into the sides while the buttercream is still soft and *then* place in the refrigerator.

A Wedding Cake Built to Last*:
Constructing Your Cake
(at least until the wedding!)

The cakes in this book are either stacked, which means that the tiers rest directly on top of one another, or separated to varying degrees by pillars. While stacked cakes are, by some estimations, less formal, these days people are deciding that formality is as much about the decoration as the pillars.

Either way, this is the point in your cake's assembly where aesthetics are temporarily placed to the side and the safety (and stability) of your creation take a central role. Your tiers need a strong structure supporting them in order to stay at their best and most beautiful all the way to the display table. Here's what you need to know.

At this point you have multiple tiers resting on cardboards and they have received their final coat of buttercream. Whether you are stacking the tiers or separating them with pillars, get them into the refrigerator to firm up while you complete the next step.

Prepare the Cake Base

While the tiers chill, you can ready your final platter or whatever the cake is going to be resting on. If you can find, rent, borrow, or buy a very large, sturdy, and perfecly flat platter,

then by all means do. You need something that is 2 to 4 inches larger than the largest tier. This will give you room for decorations. It must be completely flat. These are very hard to find. Do check your local rental company, though. They might have a silver platter you can use; or you can purchase one from Beryl's. (See page 154 for an example of this; to order one by mail, see Sources.)

Another excellent option is to have a piece of tempered glass cut to specifications, or you can even use heavy mirror. Glass is strong and attractive and goes with most cakes, and having it cut to order means you can specify the exact size

 Making Your Cake Base Prettier At-a-Glance

* Cover the cake base with heavy-duty colored foil from a craft store to match your decor (just cut a piece larger than your board and tape onto the bottom of the board where no one will see)
* Cover with pretty fabric; affix as for foil
* Use a glue gun to affix a decorative ribbon to the edge
* Use a glue gun to attach a strand of beads or pearls to the edge or top edge
* Give the look of a ribbon-covered board: You only have to cover the outer 3 inches, as the cake will be covering the rest. Buy 30 feet of 1-inch ribbon to cover a 16-inch board. Tape one end about 3 inches in from edge on bottom. Bring ribbon around edge to top of board and tape it again 3 inches in. Double back, slightly overlapping the first ribbon back onto the bottom and tape again. Repeat until board is covered. The cake will cover the center area

you want. (I used a glass base for almost all the cakes photographed in this book.) You can leave the glass as is, or spray-paint the bottom. It is elegant and inexpensive. A custom cut piece should cost you less than $20.

A third option is to buy what is called a "cake drum" from a cake decorating supply store (see Equipment section, page 18). They come in many different sizes and shapes. Cake drums are sturdy, disposable boards that usually come covered in gold or silver foil and are ready to use. You use them as you would a real silver platter.

A fourth option is to buy a Masonite board from the hardware or lumber store (either they can cut it or you can at home). This is an inexpensive, sturdy board, but it is unattractive. You will need to cover it with foil, which can be purchased at cake decorating stores. This is not just thin aluminum foil. It is heavy, usually embossed with swirls and pretty patterns, and comes in a variety of colors from silver and gold to pink, green, and everything in between.

Whatever you use, make sure it is sturdy. When you move your cake, such as from refrigeration to a car, you need a sturdy, inflexible base to keep the cake safe and to make sure it won't bend. If the base flexes, the buttercream is prone to crack.

Stacking Tiers

Stacked tiers are tiers that rest directly on top of one another.

Chill the individual tiers until the final coat of buttercream is firm, about 2 hours. Have your chosen cake base ready. To affix the bottom tier to the base, spread a bit of soft buttercream on the center of the base. I spread enough to cover about half to ensure that the tier will attach. Center the bottom tier (still on its cardboard) on top of the buttercream "glue." Press it down well to help it adhere. (Press the center of the cake; if you leave fingerprints, they will be covered by subsequent tiers.) After it is chilled, this buttercream "glue" will firm up and hold the tier in place.

Now, here comes the part that might seem odd, but is vitally important. You must provide an infrastructure to support your tiers so that the finished cake is sturdy and will not collapse. (Cake itself is not strong enough to support the weight of two cakes on top of it without getting squashed.)

Technique close-up: using cake pan from tier above to determine dowel placement

Technique close-up: submerging wooden dowels

The support comes from dowels inserted into the tiers which hold the weight of the tiers above. If your tiers will be centrally stacked (as most are), then take the pan from the next smallest tier (if the bottom is the 14-inch, you need the 10-inch pan for this next step), hold it open-side up, and center it on top of the lower tier; press gently to make a faint impression—very faint! This is your guide for placing that next tier (see photo).

Now you add the dowels for support. Take a long 1/4-inch-thick wooden dowel from a hardware or cake decorating store (they often come in lengths of a yard or more) and sink it into the cake at one point within the faint markings (see photo). Press it down all the way so that it touches the cardboard underneath the cake. With a pen, mark the exact level at which the dowel meets the top of the cake. Remove the dowel and cut it along this mark with a large serrated kitchen knife. Using the first dowel as a template, cut more dowels: I use 5 dowels for the bottom tier, and 1 less for each successively smaller tier.

Press the 5 dowels into the cake, spaced apart, but within the marked area. They should be flush with the top layer of buttercream. Spread a bit of buttercream over the marked area for "glue," then place the next tier on top, centering it using the faint markings as guides. Its cardboard will rest on the dowels, leaving the cake below free of pressure from above. Repeat with the subsequent tier; do not place dowels in the top tier as it will not be supporting anything very heavy. However, if you are going to use a heavy glass figurine or vase as top-tier décor, go ahead and press a dowel or two into the top tier.

If your tiers are to be offset, which means that they are lined up along one point along an edge, then place the dowels accordingly—they just need to be underneath where the next tier is placed.

The final step to assure sturdiness is to insert 1 long dowel all the way through the center of the cake. Take a very long dowel and make sure that it is at least 4 inches taller than the stacked cake. Sharpen one end to a point with a paring knife or in a pencil sharpener. Press the pointed end into the center of the top tier and press it straight down and into the cake. It will hit the cardboard that the top tier is resting on. Gently pound it through the cardboard by tapping the end with a mallet or hammer; it will go through. Keep pressing the dowel all the way through until it reaches the bottom cake base. About 4 inches will be sticking out of the top; that's OK. This vertical dowel will prevent any horizontal shifting of the tiers during transportation. You can also use the exposed

---

✿ Choosing the Front of the Cake

Once you have smoothed your final coat of buttercream, something will become apparent. Each tier will have a "front"—the best-looking side or section of the cake. When you assemble your tiers, you want all the "fronts" to be aligned so that the resulting cake has a proper "front" as well. When placing any subsequent decorations (buttercream or fresh flowers, for instance), do it with the "front" in mind. You might want to put the nicest decorations on the front to show them off; for example, save the most gorgeous flower for the front of the cake. On the other hand, you could strategically place decorations to cover up the other sides of the cake, and leave the better-looking front more plain to show off its beautiful smooth sides.

Some cake tables are out in the middle of a room, but for safety reasons—you don't want to be the one to bump into the cake table, do you?—it is best if the table is near a wall. This way, the cake can be placed with the "front" facing outward. This is the side of the cake that you photograph! If your display table is in the center of the room, then the cake must be equally gorgeous all the way around.

dowel to help steady the cake when you are moving it. Then, when you are ready to present the cake, you simply remove the dowel before you place decorations on top. If you like, you can have some soft buttercream and an icing spatula handy to patch up the little hole.

Separating Tiers with Pillars

For a more elaborate presentation, you can separate your tiers—or just one of your tiers—by raising them on pillars. There are any number of ways to do this, from elevating tiers high in the air for an impressive look, or just a few inches in order to fit flowers and other decorations in between the tiers. The instructions here relate to the ways I've raised the cakes in this book. (See pages 000, 000, 000, and 000 for examples of cakes using pillars.)

The usual way to separate tiers involves some form of plastic pillar. The primary two types of pillars that I employ are spiked and hollow pillars, which sink right through the cake tiers. They are the easiest to use and offer the most stability, due to the fact that the pillars are pressed right down into the cake. You can find them in cake decorating stores and catalogs; they usually come in white or clear plastic and in a variety of lengths.

Solid pillars that sink into the cake are sometimes called spiked pillars, because they are often tapered, or "spiked," in shape; but other times they have a uniform width and simply "spike" into the cake.

❀ Embellishing Your Pillars: Paint, Ribbon, and Frosting

Pillars are usually clear or white plastic, which does not necessarily enhance a cake's look. I often paint them with nontoxic paint in antique gold, silver, or sometimes even a bright color—depending on what the total cake design suggests. Always make sure the paint is nontoxic. You can find many types, both spray and liquid, in craft or hardware stores. I usually do not paint the part of the pillar that sinks into the cake. Measure the final height of your tiers. If they are 3$\frac{1}{2}$ inches, then leave about 3$\frac{1}{4}$ inches of the bottom of the pillars unpainted. If you paint pillars, you should paint the separator plates too. I have never had a problem with paint chipping.

Another decorative idea is to wrap pillars with ribbon. This is most successfully accomplished if you use the straight, trimmable, hollow type of pillar (see pages 41–43). I usually use ribbon that is at least $\frac{3}{4}$ inch wide and always need more than I think, so buy enough! To attach, I tape a piece of ribbon near the top, or inside the pillar, if I can, and then start wrapping round and round the outside, angling it as I go down and overlapping enough so that no plastic pillar pokes through. You obviously need to know where the "end" or bottom of your pillar is, because you will only wrap the part that is exposed between cakes, not the part that sinks into the cake. Sometimes I finish off the end cleanly with another bit of tape, and sometimes I make a pretty bow with an extra length of ribbon, so that the ribbon really becomes part of the design.

You can also cover the pillars with piped frosting decorations. In this case, first have your cake assembled on its display table, with pillars in place. Have some buttercream ready in a pastry bag with your tip of choice and pipe up and down the length of the pillars. This gives the pillar width and texture. I often like to do this with Ateco #18 tip.

Trimmable columns, called "hidden" or "hollow" pillars, also sink into tiers. They are called "hidden" because they are not meant to be seen (they are a ridged thin white plastic) and are cut to provide whatever size separation you desire—if you want a 2-inch separation, cut each pillar two inches longer than the height of your tier. Their round shape makes them perfect candidates for wrapping with ribbon or covering with frosting (see sidebar), and their softer material makes them easy to cut to a custom length. Don't worry—they are sturdy enough for the job!

Trimmable pillars are great for when you want "hidden" pillars that rise up only an inch or two from the cake's surface (see Hazelnut Praline and Apricot Cake, page 119). The result is that the guests do not see them, but they create enough space in which to place fresh flowers or other decorations. It makes it seem as though the tiers are floating above one another and can give quite an elegant effect.

Some pillars are contemporary looking and some resemble Roman or Grecian columns. Some are available with a loose plastic "base" that matches the solid pieces at the top of the column. It slides onto the column like a ring and then, after the pillar is put into place, settles to rest on the cake. It will look like the column has a top and a base, instead of the bottom just disappearing into the cake.

There also are more decorative items that you might come across, such as a pillar candle holder; a small sculpture with a flat top and bottom might also work. Not only can these act as separators for your tiers, but they can lend a highly individual look to your cake. But, please make sure they are sturdy enough to support the tiers above them, and use dowels within the cake tiers to support them.

Separator Plates

All columns, or pillars, are used in conjunction with separator plates. These are matching plastic plates that attach to the pillars and support the tier above. The bottom of the plates have little knobs or feet that jut out and these are what the pillars snap onto. You use 4 pillars per tier and 1 separator plate for every tier that you want to elevate. Sometimes I use the same size separator plate as tier, like a 6-inch plate for a 6-inch tier; other times, when I want a little extra space around the base for decoration, I use a separator plate that is 1 inch larger, such as a 7-inch plate for a 6-inch cake tier. Luckily, most manufacturers make both even- and odd-sized plates, so you have a choice. Wilton makes a wide array of pillars and plates.

Assembling a Cake with Pillars

Once you have chosen the sizes of separator plates to use, you need to mark the individual tiers for placement of the pillars. Don't be put off by the length of these instructions—marking the tiers for proper pillar placement sounds more difficult than it is. If you follow my instructions step by step with the cakes in front of you, it will make sense. If you have 3 tiers, all to be separated by pillars, then you will be using 2 sets of 4 pillars and 2 separator plates. Once your tiers are chilled, place your bottom tier on the cake, "gluing" it with buttercream spread across the center of the base.

Take the separator plate that will support the middle tier and center it over the bottom tier. Make sure that it is in the true center. Precision counts here. You can do this by eye, or use a ruler to make sure that the same amount of cake is exposed all the way around the separator plate. Lightly press the plate onto the cake so that the knobs on the bottom of the plate leave marks, which will show you where to press in the pillars. Remove the plate. Repeat with the other tiers using the separator plate from the tier above to make the marks (see photos on the following page).

The next step is to "glue" the chilled cake tiers to their plates using soft buttercream. This is also when you can apply any final buttercream decorations: some of the decorations, such as piped borders, will partially rest on the plates (individual instructions are given in specific recipes). Chill well so that the cake's glue firms up and any buttercream decorations also harden, about 2 hours, but a rest overnight in the refrigerator is preferred and suggested in every instance.

Technique close-up: using separator plate to mark cake for placement of pillars

Technique close-up: submerging pillars into tier

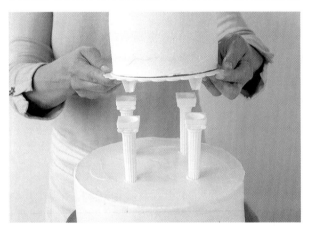

Technique close-up: placing top tier on pillars

Technique close-up: submerging "hidden" pillars into tier

Technique close-up: placing top tier on "hidden" pillars

At this point, transport the tiers separately and assemble with pillars at the reception site. (Pictures above are to be used as general guides.)

At the reception site, use the marks as guides to sink the pillars into the cake tiers all the way through to the cardboard beneath each tier (see photo). If the pillars have square tops, make sure that these are squared off with one another, then simply place the upper tier on top of the pillars by lining up the plastic knobs on the bottom of the separator plates with the holes inside the pillars (see photo). Some knobs snap into place, others simply rest within the holes, depending on brand and style. If you have more than one pillar separation within one cake, make sure that the pillars on each tier are all aligned in the same direction.

Make It Gorgeous, Make It Yours

This section discusses basic decorating procedures for wedding cakes. There are certain basic design details that are applied to almost every cake in the book and these are described here. I have divided them into decorations applied in the kitchen (Preliminary Decorations) and those that are applied when the cake is on its display table at the reception site (Final On-Site Decorations). Individual decorations for particular cakes can be found with the individual cake recipes.

PRELIMINARY DECORATIONS

These decorations are applied in the kitchen before the cake chills in the refrigerator overnight. Most of these are piped buttercream decorations that should also chill; others include chocolate curls or nuts that must be applied to soft buttercream. If the cake is to be stacked, you will apply these decorations to the completed, stacked cake. If the cake will be separated with pillars, you'll apply the decorations to the finished tiers on their separator plates.

Piping Buttercream Decorations

For most of the cakes in this book, you will want to apply some kind of decoration with buttercream using a pastry bag—at the very least you will probably want to pipe a decorative border along the bottom of each tier, both for aesthetics and to camouflage any visible cardboards or plastic plates. In general, if the tiers are to be stacked, they are stacked before borders are piped on. If you are assembling a cake with separations, then you will affix the tiers to their separator plates before you pipe any borders (the plates will support parts of the borders).

Using a Pastry Bag

To pipe borders, you will need a pastry bag, couplers, and decorating tips. I like using a 14-inch or 16-inch bag and a coupler intended for the smaller, more frequently used tips. When the bags are new, their narrow openings are too small to fit a coupler and have to be cut to allow its insertion. Cut it just so the coupler's ridges emerge through the opening.

> ### 🌹 "Before" and "After" Decorations At-a-Glance
>
> Here is quick overview of decorations you'll be applying while you're still in the kitchen (Before) and once the cake is on its presentation table at the receptions site (After).
>
> | Before | After |
> |---|---|
> | * Embellish sides with nuts | * Pipe decorations on pillars |
> | * Paint or be-ribbon pillars | * Top with fresh flowers |
> | * Affix chocolate curls or tiles | * Add glacéed fruits, whole nuts, or other decorations unless embedded in buttercream border |
> | * Pipe borders and decorations | |
> | * Embed decorations in still-soft buttercream border | |

You want the hole large enough to allow the cap that comes with the coupler to screw on tight after the tip is put into place—but not so big that the coupler pops out under pressure!

Once the coupler is inserted, choose your tip (see below) and place it on the coupler; then screw the coupler ring into place. Using a rubber spatula or icing spatula to press the buttercream into the base of the bag, fill the bag about halfway with soft buttercream. Do not overfill. Heat from your hands can overly soften the buttercream in the bag and half a bag's worth is about as much as you can pipe before it gets too soft (you also do not want to have so much buttercream that there is a backflow out of the top). Twist the top of the bag closed, letting out all the air and firmly pressing the bag against the buttercream. Hold the tip of the bag gently with one hand, which will be the guiding hand, and use the other hand to hold the twisted part closed tightly against the buttercream; this hand will squeeze out the buttercream.

Individual recipes will give specific instructions, but here are some basic piped borders. All of these borders will be applied after tiers are stacked or affixed to separator plates.

Know that, whatever tip you are using, the slightest change in angle of tip and bag will produce a different result. Varying pressure will also alter the look of what comes out of the tip, so practice, practice, practice!

Basic Decorative Borders

To Make a Shell Border—use star tips Ateco #16–#22. Often I will use smaller tips (Ateco #16–#18) for smaller tiers and the larger tips (Ateco #18–#22) on the larger tiers. You make shells by pressing buttercream out of the bag against a point on the cake's surface and then pulling away while gradually lessening the pressure, to form a shape like an elongated scallop shell with a tail (see photo). The next shell overlaps with the "tail" of the previous shell. Done repeatedly, you can make a chain of "shells."

To Make a Beaded Border—use a round tip, such as Ateco #6–#12, depending on the size bead you would like. Basically you are piping out little balls of buttercream right next to one another, creating a "beaded" look. You begin by pressing gently on the decorating bag so that a small round shape emerges from the tip. Pull the tip a little to the side while easing the pressure. You should have a modified teardrop shape. Simply begin the second "bead" over the "tail" of the first. In this way, what is left is a border of round "bead" shapes (see photo).

Round tips can also create a simple border that looks like a rope (see page 45 for an illustration of this).

To Make a Ribbon Border—use Ateco tips # 44 through 48, 895, and 897. Ribbon borders can be a simple, yet effective, border for the top and bottom edges of cakes. Ribbons can be made in a tight regimented fashion or in a more loose, casual style. Hold tip perpendicular to edge of cake (and either flat against cake top or vertical against cake side). For a tight ribbon, place tip just on the cake's surface and pipe buttercream, moving bag slightly away from you. You can determine the size of the ribbon with this first movement, but most likely you will pipe a length of between 1/2 inch and 2 inches. Lift bag slightly and pipe back down and over your first piping,

---

 Practice Makes Perfect—or, at Least, Better

If I haven't picked up a pastry bag in a while, my technique gets rusty. But like riding a bike, it does come back. Practice is worthwhile. You can practice with buttercream, or even pure vegetable shortening. Fit the coupler with the tip you want, fill the bag, and use an upturned cake pan as your practice surface. You can practice piping shapes along the upper edge and lower edges, then scrape up the buttercream (or shortening) and practice some more! You can even practice on a piece of parchment or foil, but the cake pan gives you a more realistic situation. After some practice, when you actually pipe onto your cake, your piping will be as neat as possible.

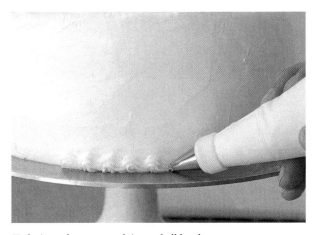

Technique close-up: applying a shell border

Technique close-up: applying a beaded border

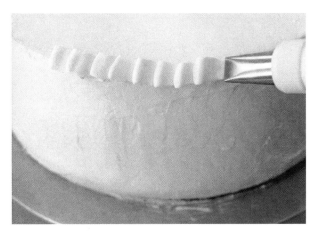

Technique close-up: applying a ribbon border

Technique close-up: applying a leaf border

this time coming toward you; this makes the first ripple of ribbon (see photo). Repeat to make a border of ribbons.

To Make a Leaf Border—I love leaf tips and use them often to make a border of overlapping leaves. There are two basic sets of leaf tips. Ateco #65–#70 tips make a more traditional looking leaf, and Ateco #349, #350, and #352 make a more streamlined contemporary looking leaf. You can make a leaf border orderly by having the leaves overlap symmetrically

(see photo), or have them somewhat hodgepodge, as real leaves would be, varying in size, shape, and angle. To make a leaf shape that starts out wide and tapers into a point, begin by applying more pressure, then lessen the pressure on the bag as you pull away.

To Create a Basket Weave Effect—you have three choices. You can either use a round tip (such as Ateco #8 or #10) for the vertical and horizontal bars; you can use the Ateco #8 or

Understanding Decorating Tips

Many bakers have cake pans and a mixer but pastry bags and decorating tips are often believed to be in the realm of the serious cake decorating enthusiast. They can intimidate people who have never used them or have only minimally dabbled. Really, there is nothing to fear. Creating lovely shell shapes or rounded bead borders on your cake does take some practice, but that's it! And it's easy to practice piping since you can reuse practice frosting again and again.

As far as understanding tips are concerned, there are a few things to know. First of all, the cakes in this book were decorated with Ateco tips. Not only does this company make high quality tips, but it is necessary to stick within one company's numbering system as tip numbers do not always correspond to other companies' numbers. In general, the lower the number, the smaller the tip. For instance, an Ateco #2 round tip has a smaller round opening than an Ateco #8 round tip. Also, shapes are grouped together, so Ateco #1–#12 tips are all round, and all the standard leaf tips are grouped from #65 to #70. Most of the tips suggested in this book are standard size and use a standard sized coupler, which allows you to change tips without removing buttercream from the bag. However, some of the recipes use large tips which will be directly inserted into the bags without a coupler. Tips are inexpensive, so indulge in a selection and get down to practicing!

#10 for the vertical ridged tips and Ateco #47 or #48 for the horizontal bars; or you can use the #47 and #48 for both vertical and horizontal bars. (See page 146 for detailed instructions on piping basket weave pattern.)

Decorating the Sides While the Buttercream is Soft

Some kinds of decoration that are applied to the cake's sides must be done right after frosting, while the buttercream is still soft, so that the decorations to adhere to it. For covering all or part of the sides with chopped nuts, shaved chocolate, or grated coconut, the basic technique is to hold the cake (on its board) in one hand, and scoop up the chopped nuts with the other and press them on to the sides of soft buttercream so that they adhere, letting the excess spill onto a tray below. You can use this method to cover the entire side, just half, a third, or to create a bottom border (see page 118). For more structured adornment of the sides, you can place on decorations piece by piece, such as in the Marzipan and Orange Essensia Cake (see page 107) or the Chocolate-Covered Caramel Cake (see page 155).

Patterns made in the frosting must also be done while the frosting is soft. To make patterns in the soft buttercream or frosting, there are a few options. There is a tool called a decorator's comb that has ridges of various widths along its edges. One of the edges can be dragged along an extra thick layer of buttercream and will leave a ridged pattern on the sides of the cake. Or you could create a swirled texture as we did with the Swirled Marble Cake with Sour Cream Fudge Frosting, using the back of a teaspoon or icing spatula (see page 87 for photos of technique).

FINAL ON-SITE DECORATIONS

These are decorations that will be applied to the completed cake after it is placed on the display table. In this book, that will mostly be fresh flowers, but there are a few cakes where glacéed fruits and certain whole nuts are added as well

One reason for applying these decorations on-site is that, regardless of what decorations you plan in advance to place on your cake, you will come up with creative ideas for using them as you move along and see your design taking shape. While you do need to have a rough idea of what you are doing beforehand—so that you can order the right number of fresh roses, or make the correct number of chocolate leaves—use this information as a guideline. You might have thought that five flowers would look good on the top tier, but once you start putting them in place, allow the individual character of the cake to help guide your decoration. Three might be enough.

I firmly believe that every cake begins to take on a life of its own once it is set on its display table and is in its reception environment. The light, the size of the room, the music to be played, the color of the display tablecloth all set a mood. Once you start placing your decorations here and there, allow the personality of the cake to come through. Maybe you thought you would not use any of the flower's greenery, but then, as you are placing roses, you see that dark green leaves tucked about might enhance the look. Go with the flow. You might have seen a cake in a magazine and wanted to do the exact same thing, but as you go, the placement of the decorations just doesn't seem right. Make changes you feel are right to get the results you want! Every cake is unique and I believe every cake will speak to you at this time. Let its singular beauty shine!

NOTE: *At this point, I strongly suggest you have some soft buttercream on hand to fix any smudges that might have appeared during transport. I usually bring buttercream, a couple of icing spatulas, a decorating bag, and any tips used on the cake with me to the reception site. Better safe than sorry!*

Placing Flowers and Other Decorations on Your Cake

Many of the cakes in this book have fresh flowers as adornment, and others use chocolate flowers, leaves, and what have you. You will not find fondant-covered cakes in this book, as I do not like how fondant tastes. Likewise with royal icing: I find it unbearably sweet, so I do not use it much. You will also not find any pastillage or gum paste flowers as I find them to be difficult for most people to master and, frankly, I do not like their artifice. They are meant to mimic real flowers and I would rather use the real thing. In the case of my chocolate flowers, they are not meant to be exact approximations of anything in nature, just a newly made creation that happens to be pretty and tasty.

When you are placing fresh flowers on a cake, you can place them directly on the cake if the cake is not going to be on display for an extended period of time. Or you can use accessories called flower spikes, which are small white plastic tubes that can be inserted into a cake tier, filled with a bit of water, and then the flower stems can be inserted into those. They can be purchased from Wilton or many cake decorating supply stores.

For flowers that are merely decorative, I do not generally worry about whether they were commercially grown as I have satisfied myself with current research about potential effects from pesticides, but this is a decision that you should make for your own cake. You can certainly request organic flowers if this concerns you. Or ask your purveyor for flowers that are "low spray." Another alternative is to lay a piece of parchment or waxed paper along the tops of the tiers and place flowers or fresh petals on top of that.

If you are going to crystallize your own flowers with the intent of them being eaten, you want unsprayed flowers and want to make sure that the flowers are edible. Refer to the next page for a list of popular edible flowers.

Popular Edible Flowers

Remember, not all parts of each plant are edible. For instance, a tulip blossom is edible, but the bulb is not! Please read up on this subject before embarking on an edible flower project of your own. Also, edible does not necessarily mean tasty. It just means that they can be eaten without causing any digestive problems. I think the most palatable are roses, pansies, Johnny-jump-ups, and violets.

Angelica

Apple blossom

Bee Balm

Borage *(Borago officinalis)*

Calendula *(Calendula officinalis)*

Carnation

Chive blossom *(Allium schoenoprasum)*

Chrysanthemum

Citrus blossom

Cornflower

Cymbidium

Dandelion

Daylily *(Hemerocallis* species and cultivars)

Dianthus *(Dianthus* species and cultivars)

Elderberry flower *(Sambucus nigra)*

English daisy

Fuchsia

Gardenia

Geranium *(Pelargonium* cultivars)

Gladiolas

Herb flowers: rosemary, basil, mint, sage, etc.

Hibiscus *(Hibiscus rosa-sinensis* cultivars)

Hollyhock

Honeysuckle

Hyssop

Iceland poppy

Impatiens

Lavender *(Lavandula officinalis)*

Lemon verbena *(Aloysia triphylla)*

Lilac

Marigold

Nasturtium *(Tropaeolum majus)*

Pansy

Passionflower *(Passiflora* species and cultivars)

Petunia

Rose

Safflower *(Carthamus tinctorius)*

Sunflower *(Helianthus annuus)*

Tuberous begonia *(Begonia tuberosa)*

Tulip *(Tulipa* species and cultivars)

Viola: pansy and Johnny-jump-up (Viola tricolor)

Violet *(Viola odorata* or English violet)

Yucca *(Yucca elephantipes)*

Zucchini blossom *(Curcurbita pepo* species and cultivars)

Why Perfection Is Not the Point

The last thing I ever want to hear is, "That cake is too beautiful to eat!" To me, that says that the person is treating my creation as a visual showpiece, not a luscious, tempting dessert. When I design my cakes, I take all the senses into consideration, but flavor and taste are always first and foremost on my mind. Because of this, I do not aim for perfection with buttercream or decorations. I do not expect my cakes to look airbrushed or seamless. I want them to be real and accessible, to hint at their food origins and spark your appetite.

When I go into a bakery and I see all the cookies lined up, or all the cakes in the display case, and they all look the same, I am disappointed. It is almost as if I can see and hear the mechanized approach that made each one. To me, a cookie-cutter approach to celebration cakes is not appropriate. I want the cake to have soul, to be its own creation. So don't worry if you cannot get that last bit of buttercream smoothed out. The mark on the cake will be your mark, telling the guests that this cake was made by hand, with love, that time and effort was poured into it, and that it is being presented in all of its peerless glory. Revel in each and every unique design accomplishment and flaw equally as they are what makes this cake yours and yours alone.

Baking and Assembly Schedule

OK, you've read through all the key steps from beginning to end. It's time to bake! The schedule that I usually follow is to bake the cake component 2 days ahead. So, for a Saturday wedding, I bake the cake layers on Thursday. While the initial cake layers are baking, I prepare the subsequent cake layers. Once the last batches are in the oven, I work on fillings and buttercreams. This does make for a very full day. If you have time earlier in the week, you can prepare many of the fillings in advance, and buttercream can be made as far as a month ahead and frozen.

Wedding cakes by their very nature demand time and effort, so set aside entire days to devote to the project. You might even want to make sure that no one else has any plans for the kitchen the 2 days before the wedding (order out for pizza for dinner) and double-check that you have the space you need in the refrigerator. Every recipe will tell you how far ahead you can prepare the components, so use those guidelines—and take advantage of the do-ahead steps! If I tell you that something can be made 4 days ahead, it really can, and you don't have to worry about it not keeping well. One of my pet peeves is when a recipe tells you it serves 12 and can be made ahead and it turns out that it really serves 8 and becomes stale before you know it. Trust that what I tell you is the real deal.

The day before the event is the day I reserve for filling, frosting, and decorating the cake. This way, the oven is off, the kitchen stays cool, and I can just concentrate on my assembly and design.

Baking and Organizing Schedule

1 Month Ahead

- Make buttercream, if you have the freezer room
- Make moistening syrup base

2 Weeks Ahead

- Shop for specialty ingredients or necessary equipment. Shop locally or use mail-order sources and double-check on delivery status (for instance, are they in stock?)
- Check with florist, greenmarket purveyor, or specialist (such as grocer, for kumquats) about any flowers, fruit, or greenery you may want and need to order ahead

1 Week Ahead

- Shop for basics, such as butter, sugar, flour, etc.
- Double- and triple-check that you have (or have ordered) everything that you need

2 Days Ahead

- Bake your cake layers
- If you've frozen anything, don't forget to defrost overnight in the refrigerator!
- Make fillings and buttercream, if you haven't already. Use the time while the cake layers are baking to make these other components
- Pick up any flowers that will need time to open up

1 Day Ahead

- Fill and assemble the cake; apply the crumb coat early in the day so that it has time to firm up in the refrigerator
- Apply the final coat, stack the cake or place on separator plates, and apply any decorations suggested at this stage
- Refrigerate overnight

Day of Event

- Keep the cake refrigerated until time to transport
- Transport the cake, bringing with you extra buttercream and any tools or ingredients you will (or might) need
- Assemble the cake on-site, if needed
- Apply any final decorations to the cake once it is on the display table

  NOTE: *Many decorations and certain fillings can also be made ahead of time, depending on what they are. (For instance, chocolate roses can be made way ahead, but chocolate leaves lose their pliability and must be made within 2 days of the event.) Refer to individual recipes for specific make-ahead information.*

Get It There on Time and Intact: Storing and Transporting Your Cake—Safely!

I hate to be the bearer of bad news, but just because your cake is basically finished, that doesn't mean your job is done. You must store it and, usually, transport it to a reception site. A stacked cake will already be stacked and assembled in your kitchen, which means it will be stored and transported in that state as well. Cakes that will be ultimately set on pillars will have the tiers affixed to their separator plates in the kitchen, and will be stored and transported that way.

Storage

Almost all of the cakes in this book use a meringue-based buttercream, and this means they should be refrigerated until shortly before they are served. If your cake is stacked, then it will be in one large piece, and it is fairly easy to determine what space you need to clear in your refrigerator. If you have a side-by-side refrigerator, you are going to have a problem as the refrigerator side may be narrow, so enlist a very good neighbor with a suitable fridge. Measure the size of your cake base and then the height of the finished cake. The largest bases I use are 16 inches in width, and these will fit in most non-side-by-side refrigerators. Take anything smelly out of the refrigerator, like garlic and olives or pungent cheeses. Your cake will pick up odors and, therefore, flavors as well.

If your cake is separated, each tier is on its own separator plate, and the bottom is on a large base, so you need even more room because you have to accommodate all of the individual tiers.

If it is cold outside (for a fall or winter cake), you might be able to place the cake on a screened-in porch or somewhere like that. If you have a very cool basement, consider that as an option. Or, if you have a small room where you can crank up the air-conditioning for the overnight period of time, then try that. You will know it is cool enough if the buttercream remains firm enough that if you touch it, your finger does not make a bad smudge. It should feel almost as firm as a cold stick of butter.

Also, depending on when you are delivering the cake in relation to when it will be served, you might also need to check on sufficient refrigeration at the reception site. However, I try to time my deliveries so that the cake can go right out onto its display table.

 What to Bring At-a-Glance

I suggest that, along with the cake, you bring some extra items to the reception site. Some are necessary, like the fresh flowers for the cake (if using). Others are part of an emergency kit, like extra buttercream and icing spatulas. There are also some notes about the vehicle used for transportation.

* Unless it is below 40° outside, make sure the air-conditioning is working in the car
* Make sure the car has a large enough flat area on which to place the cake
* If you are using fresh flowers, make sure to transport and keep them in water until needed. Make sure their container will not spill in the car
* Bring extra buttercream that is the same flavor and color as the buttercream on the exterior of the cake, for touch-ups
* Makes sure the buttercream is soft and ready to use (you won't be bringing a mixer!)
* Bring a couple of icing spatulas
* Pack any decorating tips you have used and a pastry bag and coupler
* If you have used chocolate-dipped nuts or curls (like on the Nutella cake), bring extras of those
* If your cake is to have separated tiers, make sure to pack the pillars—all of them!

Transportation

Every time I have to drive a cake from here to there I get a lump in my throat and a pit in my stomach. There is no way to get around the fact that it is a stressful endeavor. Through years of using various types of vehicles and techniques for safety, here are my suggestions.

First, you need a reliable car with a large flat space to accommodate the cake. Use the measurements taken from when you were figuring out storage to help you figure out how much space you need in a car. Station wagons are best. Sometimes you don't even need the middle seat down, sometimes you do. If you do, check to make sure it lays flat. Not all cars work this way.

Then, you have to decide what to put the cake on. If it is a stacked cake and you can find or buy a large commercial-style baking sheet, this is a good bet. Just make sure your cake base fits on it. Another way to go is to find a very large box or boxes, in the case of separate tiers. Cut the sides down to about 12 inches and use them to protect the cake(s).

In either scenario I like to also use a rubber mat to prevent sliding. You can purchase this at a hardware store. Cut it to fit the bottom of the pan or box and place the cake on top of that to minimize slippage. A very large piece on the bottom of the car's flat surface will then also help the pans/boxes not to slip and slide around in the car. You have spent hours creating your cake. Don't be fooled into thinking, "It's only a 10-minute drive, what can happen?" Better safe than sorry! I have also used a large thin piece of foam placed under the boxes to help cushion the cakes. You can buy 1- to 2-inch thick foam at a fabric store.

I also suggest driving with a friend, who can lean out the passenger side window and wave people on or give other signals.

Then, as my last, but very important, piece of advice, make a sign that says "CAUTION: WEDDING CAKE ON BOARD." Make it on a computer or handwrite it in broad letters on at least an 8½- × 11-inch piece of paper. Have it printed on bright yellow or other color paper and then have

The Old Sharpened-Dowel-Through-the-Center-of-the-Cake Trick

I went over this previously, but it bears repeating, as it will make your cake safer during travel. If you have a stacked cake, please use the additional technique of inserting a long dowel vertically through the entire cake before taking off in the car (see pages 39–40 for more explanation).

it laminated. Place it in the back window before you take off. Then, put your flashers on and drive slowly and carefully. People love this! If you just drive slowly with flashers and no sign, people get crabby and even drive more horribly than usual around you. When they see the sign, they give you the right of way; they wave and smile. Believe me, it makes the ride much, much better. PS: Even if you have "only" made a very large birthday or anniversary cake, nothing says special like "wedding cake." Use the sign!

MY TWO TRANSPORTATION DISASTERS: ONE MINOR, ONE NOT SO MINOR

I consider myself very lucky. I have been making and transporting wedding cakes for over 20 years and I have had only two bad incidents. The first was minor. I was catering the whole shebang, from appetizers to cake, and it poured in sheets that day (and we were grilling outdoors!). But the disaster came before we even got there. We had a refrigerated truck, as well as a bunch of cars carrying staff, and we were in a caravan traveling about 1 hour away to the reception site. The sun was out at the time and I had the driver's window open, and I was enjoying the ride. That is until the ONLY set of directions and contact information flew out the window! I pulled over (very slowly, of course, because I had the cake in the back), as did everyone else, and we all ran down the road trying to find the piece of paper, which, luckily, we did. Lesson learned—always have more than one set of directions!

OK, I am sure you want to hear about my real disaster, and I will tell you in all its gory detail, just so you can see that you can (and must, for the bride's sake) rise above any problem. I was driving a 3-tiered stacked cake about 1 1/4 hours away and I was 10 minutes from my destination. The cake was on a large baking sheet in the back of my air-conditioned mini-van, from which I had removed the seats. I was carefully driving along, when a car pulled out in front of me from a drive-way. I had to slam on the brakes, and the entire pan shifted and slid toward the sliding door, where there is a well for the step into the van. The pan reached the step and tipped over at an angle so that the cake slid to the side of the pan, smoosh-ing itself against the sliding door.

I stopped the van, righted the cake, surveyed the damage, and continued on my way. I got to the reception site, politely told the caterer that there was a problem with the cake but that all would be well and the bride would never know.

I called my friend and told her to bring me extra buttercream, pastry bags, tips, icing spatulas, etc. and to get there ASAP! I fixed the cake by re-applying buttercream, smoothing the sides and repiping borders with plenty of time to spare, so it was not such a fatal disaster after all.

Here are my suggestions in the event of a cake transportation emergency:

- Do not panic

- Assess the situation and calmly, but quickly; deal with it

- Always carry extra buttercream, necessary tips, and an icing spatula or two

- Always give yourself time at the reception site to fix up any smudges

- If worse comes to worse, cut it up and serve it from behind the scenes

- If all else fails, know that this will make for one hell of a story for the grandkids! It is, after all, just a cake!

Add a Little Pizzazz!
Presenting Your Cake

Your cake will be beautiful in and of itself, just like the bride. But just like the bride, a little embellishment can enhance the beauty even further. There is the table itself, the tablecloth or cloths covering it, any flowers or other items that might be placed on the table, and the cutting implements. All of these should be carefully chosen to add to the final presentation.

Cake Tables

When it comes to tables, sturdiness is a must. After that, there are many shapes and sizes. A "cake table" by most caterers' estimations will most likely be a 30-inch round table, and this is a great size to use. It is large enough so that the cake can be centered with space around it, but small enough so that the cake doesn't look like it is lost on top of it, or that something else should be sharing the space. I do tend to like round tables, but if you have a square cake, a square table can echo its shape nicely. I do not like putting a cake on the end of a banquet table as it has a greater chance of being jostled, since guests will most likely be getting items off the other end of the table. Best-case scenario is that the cake has its own table in an appropriate size—and it is not in the center of the room, where, again, it might be bumped.

How Long Can I Display My Cake?

Some weddings last for many, many hours. Some are outside in a field under a tent and some are indoors in a climate-controlled environment. All of these logistics will affect where and for how long you can display your cake. Most of the cakes in this book are butter cakes frosted with Italian meringue buttercream. This means that they are best eaten at room temperature, but, also, that they will not last long in a very warm environment.

I have delivered cakes into many less-than-ideal situations, including the aforementioned outdoor affair, and it can be in the high 90s with high humidity. This is the extreme; and even with this situation, the cake can last for almost 2 hours, if in the shade, such as under a tent. (If you are indoors in a climate-controlled room, there is no problem at all.) If the reception site presents such an extreme situation, I simply tell the bride that the cake will not be able to be displayed for the length of the reception.

 When to Arrive At-a-Glance

Timing the cake arrival will depend on many things. Will the cake be refrigerated on-site overnight before the wedding? Is there refrigerator room? Are you going to the wedding, in which case you have to bring it before the ceremony? You must take these and any other unique and specific details into account. However, I most often time the delivery so that the cake arrives about 2 to 4 hours before it is to be served, so that it can go right out onto its display table. With this in mind, heed the following:

* Make sure you have directions to the site and are aware of any glitches, like construction, detours, etc.
* Know how long the trip will take you—and note that whatever anyone says, they are assuming you will be driving average speed, which you will not be. Give yourself extra time and take advantage of it and drive slowly
* Plan to arrive 2 to 4 hours before the cake will be served so it can go right out onto the display table
* Give yourself an extra 30 minutes to fix any smudges, prepare the table, and apply decorations to the cake—and to take a picture!

TABLECLOTHS AND COVERINGS

The table most likely needs some sort of covering. A few times I have delivered a cake to a home in the country where a beautiful, worn, wooden table has supported the cake without embellishment, or to a contemporary home where a glass table was put to use, but these are the exceptions.

I like tablecloths that reach the floor, as even at a casual wedding, a certain amount of effort in the presentation should be put forth. The full-length ones look most elegant. They can be white or any color, as long as they harmonize with the cake. Patterned fabrics are tricky, as you do not want to overpower the cake; the cake should be the star. You can rent cloths of all descriptions, or you might find one to purchase. If you are handy with a sewing machine, the sky's the limit! Overlays are nice, too. How about a pale green cloth with a sheer tulle overlay? Or a deep rose cloth with an antique lace overlay? The overlay might also be floor length, or it can be shorter. These are just a few ideas. The key is to make sure they don't detract from the cake.

NOTE: *Make sure you find out the size and shape of the display table so that you can purchase, rent, or sew the right size cloth.*

TABLE DÉCOR

Once you have a tablecloth (or cloths) you can go a few steps further, if you like. You could scatter real or silk petals over the tablecloth and around the cake. This works best if the petals were used on the cake as well. Or, scatter them on top of the cloth and then top them with a piece of glass cut to fit the table top; this might be rented as well. The result looks like pressed flowers under glass.

The same can be done with leaves, either with or without the glass. I once saw an entire tablecloth covered with broad, shiny dark leaves that had been stitched or stapled on, one by one, in an overlapping fashion for a spectacular natural,

woodland effect. It was like a carpet of leaves for the cake (see my mini version on page 118).

A glass topper is great for topping a table covered with ribbons. Have 2-inch ribbons crisscrossing over the tablecloth and falling down the sides, where the ends have been tied into "love knots." You can leave them at slightly different lengths and make them different colors, if you like. Cover the top with glass and they will stay in place.

Runners in bright colors can look great. Have one right under the cake coming out from under the front of the cake and flowing down the front of the tablecloth. It will give the cake a "red carpet" treatment even if the runner isn't red!

 Last-Minute On-Site Assembly At-a-Glance

You'll be putting on the final decorations at the wedding site, as well as assembling the tiers if you are separating them with pillars, so make sure to bring along any tools you might need, extra decorations in case some break, etc. (Remember, you want to let the setting inspire you as you put on your final decorations.) Additionally, I *always* bring extra buttercream, icing spatulas, and a pastry bag with appropriate tips to patch up any smudges or repair any damage that might occur.

* Insert pillars and stack cake tiers, if necessary
* Patch up any smudges with extra buttercream
* Apply fresh or crystallized flowers, greenery, whole nuts, or candied fruit as desired
* Using fresh buttercream as "glue," add any extra chocolate curls or nuts or other decor previously applied if any have fallen off or if you see holes needing to be filled

Cutting and Serving the Cake

I am often asked if it makes me sad to see one of my cakes sliced and served, as though my artful creation were being destroyed and the act of cutting it would be painful for me to watch. Nothing could be further from the truth! From the beginning, when I am designing a cake, I am thinking about how it is going to be enjoyed—I mean eaten! To me, those two things go together. My cakes are about taste, and so cutting them up is just part of the process. The end of the process, maybe, but an important part!

Usually you will be presenting your cake at a reception site where a caterer or banquet manager will handle the slicing and serving, but in case you are left with the responsibility, or need to pass the job onto someone else with instructions, here is what you need to know.

NOTE: *Serve cake at room temperature. This is key. These cakes have a large proportion of butter, both in the cakes and in the buttercream, so they will be unpalatably firm in texture if too cold. Also, the flavors will not be at their best if the cake is cold. It is so easy to make sure that the cake is at room temperature, but too many people overlook this all-important step.*

THE FIRST CUT

First of all, many brides and grooms like to make a ceremonial cut in front of the crowd—but not all of them do. If it's your cake, and you don't want to, don't worry about it! It's like that garter removal/tossing thing. It is far from necessary. If you (the baker) or the bride do want to cut the cake in front of the guests, make sure you have a sharp knife and a narrow spatula to remove the first piece. The first piece is always the most difficult to remove, so plan ahead. This tasting slice, which the bride and groom may share, will be sliced from the bottom tier. The actual cutting is handled a bit differently if you have a cake with the bottom tiers separated by pillars or if the cake is stacked. Diagrams are worth a thousand words, so refer to the proper diagram (see page 58).

 Serving Pieces

As I have said before, my cakes are not too pretty to eat—they are meant to be eaten—so the moment will come when it is time to cut the cake. Some couples like to make this fairly ceremonious and cut the first slice together and then feed each other a piece, either smooshing it into one another's faces, or with grace. Either way, they need the proper utensils.

To cut and serve a slice of cake it is good to have a sharp knife and a cake server, which is a triangular or blunt edged spatula-type tool. You can rent silver or silver-plated ones, or buy a new set. They often come in sets, which is handy. I love antique ones, so keep an eye out. Note to bridesmaids—these make great engagement gifts.

Some are so pretty they can be left as is. But you can wrap pretty ribbon around the bottom handles and even attach a few sprigs of greenery or flowers. This makes a nice, small touch. Just don't obscure the handle too much as these tools have a job to do.

For a cake with pillars: make cuts into the part of the cake closest to you. All cuts are in the bottom tier. Insert the knife tip about 3 inches from the edge of the cake. Press the knife all the way down to the bottom of the cake, where your knife will meet the cardboard, and cut a slice towards you, cutting from the insertion point you have chosen to the edge of the cake; your first cut is done. Now make a 2-inch-long cut parallel to the cake's edge starting from your initial insertion point and slicing to the left or right. Finish off with another cut joining the 2-inch-long cut with the cake's edge. Insert a narrow serving spatula under the cake slice, making sure to place it in between the cake and the cardboard (not under the cardboard). Give a wiggle and a lifting motion and the slice should come free, ready for you to taste. How delicately (or not) you feed one another is up to you!

For a stacked cake: the instructions are largely the same. This time insert the knife tip at the base of the tier that rests upon the bottom tier. You should be able to feel the cardboard with the knife tip. Steer clear of the cardboard and cut into the cake, slicing back towards you, cutting all the way to the edge of the cake. Insert the knife tip at the original insertion point and make a 2-inch cut right along the base of the cardboard from the next tier. Make the last cut from the cardboard back to the cake's edge. Serve as described.

GENERAL CAKE-CUTTING INSTRUCTIONS

Whether a cake is stacked or separated by pillars, it should be disassembled before slicing and serving. Also, after the ceremonial cut is made, I suggest slicing and serving the cake behind the scenes. It can be a messy affair and is best done in the seclusion of the kitchen.

If the cake is "pillared," simply lift the tiers, still on their separator plates, off of their pillars. Place them on the table. Insert the knife or spatula between the cake cardboard and the separator plate and lift the cake, still on the cardboard, off of the separator plate. Place the cake on the table, ready to be sliced. If you leave the tier on the separator plate, it might be tippy, since it is balanced on the little plastic knobs, making serving difficult. Remove the pillars embedded in the cake tiers and you are ready to serve.

If the cake is stacked, use a knife to locate the cardboards supporting the tiers. One by one, gently pry the tiers from one another and place them, now all separate, on the table, ready to slice. Make sure to remove any submerged wooden dowels before serving!

Now, you just follow the diagrams provided on page 58.

PLATES

After being sliced, the cake will be served to the guests on plates. Most likely they will be fairly plain and that's OK, but there are ways to embellish them, too. You can pipe the initials of the bride and groom in dark chocolate the day before and chill the plates so that the initials harden. Chocolate could even be used to make other designs such as leaves or a vine with leaves and flowers. You could also ask the caterer to do this. Even if it is just the plate for the bride and groom or the plates for the head table, it is a nice touch. You can dust the plates with cocoa or powdered sugar or ground nuts, always taking into consideration what would complement the cake. A dollop of whipped cream on the side might be appropriate, or a drizzle of raspberry coulis. Lemon or orange powder can be made by pulverizing dried zests and sugar in a food processor. This makes a sparkly powder to dust over the plates. Another easy decoration is to moisten the plate's rim with lemon juice and roll them in colored sugar. How about blue, for "something blue," or a shade to match the bridesmaids' dresses?

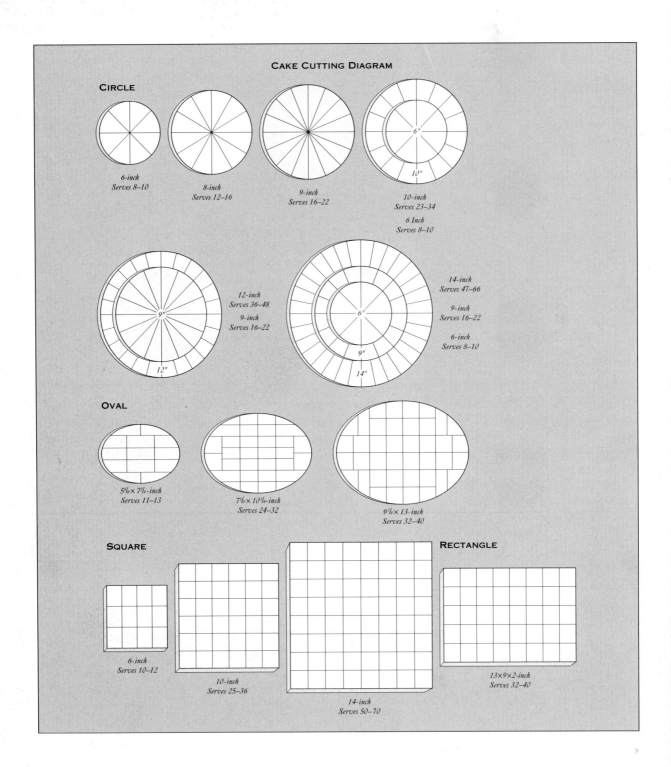

CAKE CUTTING DIAGRAM

CIRCLE

6-inch
Serves 8–10

8-inch
Serves 12–16

9-inch
Serves 16–22

10-inch
Serves 23–34

6 Inch
Serves 8–10

12-inch
Serves 36–48

9-inch
Serves 16–22

14-inch
Serves 47–66

9-inch
Serves 16–22

6-inch
Serves 8–10

OVAL

5⅝ × 7¼-inch
Serves 11–13

7⅝ × 10¾-inch
Serves 24–32

9⅝ × 13-inch
Serves 32–40

SQUARE

6-inch
Serves 10–12

10-inch
Serves 25–36

14-inch
Serves 50–70

RECTANGLE

13×9×2-inch
Serves 32–40

The Essential Recipes

All of the essential recipes for the wedding cakes in this book are here in this chapter: Essential Yellow Cake, Essential White Cake, Essential Chocolate Cake, Essential Moistening Syrup, and Essential Buttercream. All of these basic recipes have variations (see page 6 for a handy list), which are presented within the 16 individual wedding cakes. It is my hope that you first acquaint yourself with the basic recipes in this section, as you will then be ready to make any of the variations presented later on.

ESSENTIAL CAKES

Here are my three trustworthy cakes—the foundations of all my celebration cakes: Essential Yellow Cake, Essential White Cake, and Essential Chocolate Cake. The recipes are presented below, and I give you breakdowns for 6-inch, 8-inch, 9-inch, 10-inch, 12-inch, and 14-inch round tiers, as those are the most popular sizes used in wedding cake construction. In addition, the largest (14-inch) is not too large to fit in

---

 Cake Batter Preparation At-a-Glance

* Always use the best quality ingredients
* Have all ingredients at room temperature
* Take the time to measure ingredients as called for—so if the recipe asks for 3/4 teaspoon, do not eyeball it! Actually measure it
* If a recipe uses odd measurements, like 1/2 egg, please follow them! They are given for accuracy
* Make sure to use cake flour, not all-purpose Whisk your flour before sifting (to aerate it) and use a dip-and-sweep method to measure with accurate-sized measuring cups
* Beat the butter until smooth and creamy. It should also lighten in color. If your mixer pushes it to the sides of the bowl, scrape down the bowl's sides using a rubber spatula, bring the butter to the middle, and beat it some more until it is pale, smooth, and creamy
* Add sugar gradually with the mixer running. Once the sugar is all added, continue beating

until very light and fluffy, about 5 minutes (more for larger layers), until mixture is almost white in color, scraping the bowl once or twice
* Add whole eggs one at a time (scraping the bowl down after each addition), beating until well blended before adding the next egg
* Add dry ingredients and milk (or milk mixture) alternately, beginning and ending with the dry mix. Do not overbeat at this point, but do mix until well blended. Scrape the bowl once or twice or more for the largest tiers. The batter should be smooth, with no lumps or streaks of flour
* A little waste can't be helped with such a big production, but you can come up with lots of delicious uses for extra egg whites or yolks, or leftover buttercream!

---

most home ovens or refrigerators. While many professional cake bakers will dabble with 16-inch and 18-inch tiers and larger, they also have deck ovens and walk-in refrigerators and vans to transport the cakes in!

With all of the cakes, I suggest you use fresh unsalted butter, fresh eggs, pure vanilla extract, whole milk, cake flour, and Dutch-processed cocoa, where called for. Great ingredients make great cakes. You cannot make a great cake with inferior raw ingredients.

It is easy to say, "follow the recipe," but all too often bakers gloss over the particulars. Refer to "Baking, Frosting, Assembling, and Decorating Your Cake" (pages 20–50) for detailed instructions on baking particulars; then, while you mix the batter you can refresh your memory with the preceding box of the most important tips. Also, please note that all of these recipes were made using a 5-quart KitchenAid mixer, and the mixing times reflect its power and efficiency. Throughout, I have developed each recipe "batch" in line with what can be made in a 5-quart bowl. If you are using another type of mixer, use the visual cues to help assess whether a step has been completed properly.

 Cooling and Storing Cake Layers

Please refer to pages 25–27 where I detail proper cooling and storing of cake layers. Remember, there are some specific techniques for cooling and storing the larger sizes, so reacquaint yourself with those sections now before baking.

ESSENTIAL YELLOW CAKE

This cake is buttery tasting, and due to the whole eggs, a pretty pale yellow color. It goes well with a variety of fillings and flavors and is the most versatile cake in the book.

MAKES TWO 6 × 2-INCH ROUND CAKE LAYERS

1^1/$_2$ cups cake flour
1^1/$_2$ teaspoons baking powder
Pinch salt
^{1}/$_2$ cup (1 stick) unsalted butter, at room temperature, cut into tablespoon-sized pieces
^{1}/$_2$ cup sugar
^{1}/$_2$ teaspoon vanilla extract
2 large eggs, at room temperature
^{1}/$_2$ cup whole milk, at room temperature

1 Preheat the oven to 350°. Spray two 6 × 2-inch round cake pans with nonstick spray, line with parchment, then give the parchment a quick spray as well.

2 Sift together the flour, baking powder, and salt; set aside.

3 Beat the butter using the flat beater attachment until soft and creamy, about 2 minutes. Add the sugar gradually and beat until very light and fluffy, about 3 minutes. Scrape down the bowl once or twice, and then beat in the vanilla.

4 Beat in the eggs one at a time, scraping down after each addition, allowing each egg to be absorbed before continuing. Add the flour mixture in 4 additions, alternately with the milk. Begin and end with the flour mixture and beat briefly until smooth on low-medium speed after each addition.

5 Divide the batter evenly between the pans and smooth the tops with an offset spatula. Bake for about 22 minutes, or until a toothpick shows a few moist crumbs. The cake will be tinged with light golden brown around the edges and top and will have begun to come away from the sides of the pan.

6 Cool on racks in pans for 5 minutes. Unmold directly onto racks, peel off the parchment, and allow cakes to cool completely. Place on cardboards and double-wrap in plastic wrap; store at room temperature if assembling within 24 hours.

MAKES TWO 8 × 2-INCH ROUND CAKE LAYERS

2¼ cups cake flour
1 tablespoon baking powder
¼ teaspoon salt
¾ cup (1½ sticks) unsalted butter, at room temperature,
    cut into tablespoon-sized pieces
¾ cup sugar
¾ teaspoon vanilla extract
3 large eggs, at room temperature
¾ cup whole milk, at room temperature

Prep two 8 × 2-inch round pans with nonstick spray and parchment. Follow the instructions for 6-inch layers. With larger layers you will have to beat the butter and cream the butter/sugar mixture longer and scrape the bowl down a few more times during mixing. Take your time, and allow each step to reach the proper stage before continuing. Bake for about 23 minutes; cool in pans for about 8 minutes before unmolding.

MAKES TWO 9 × 2-INCH ROUND CAKE LAYERS

3 cups cake flour
1 tablespoon baking powder
⅓ teaspoon salt
1 cup (2 sticks) unsalted butter, at room temperature,
    cut into tablespoon-sized pieces
1 cup sugar
1 teaspoon vanilla extract
4 large eggs, at room temperature
1 cup whole milk, at room temperature

Prep two 9 × 2-inch round pans with nonstick spray and parchment. Follow the instructions for 6-inch layers. With larger layers you will have to beat the butter and cream the butter/sugar mixture longer and scrape the bowl down a few more times during mixing. Take your time, and allow

each step to reach the proper stage before continuing. Bake for about 25 minutes; cool in pans for about 9 minutes before unmolding.

MAKES TWO 10 × 2-INCH ROUND CAKE LAYERS

3¾ cups cake flour
1 tablespoon plus 1¾ teaspoons baking powder
½ teaspoon salt
1¼ cups (2½ sticks) unsalted butter, at room temperature,
    cut into tablespoon-sized pieces
1¼ cups sugar
1¼ teaspoons vanilla extract
5 large eggs, at room temperature
1¼ cups whole milk, at room temperature

Prep two 10 × 2-inch round pans with nonstick spray and parchment. Follow the instructions for 6-inch layers. With larger layers you will have to beat the butter and cream the butter/sugar mixture longer and scrape the bowl down a few more times during mixing. Take your time, and allow each step to reach the proper stage before continuing. Bake for about 30 minutes; cool in pans about 10 minutes before unmolding.

MAKES TWO 12 × 2-INCH ROUND CAKE LAYERS

Make the 9-inch recipe twice, once for each 12-inch layer. Prep two 12 × 2-inch round pans with nonstick spray and parchment. Preheat the oven to 325° and use a baking core; otherwise follow the instructions for 6-inch layers. With larger layers you will have to beat the butter and cream the butter/sugar mixture longer and scrape the bowl down a few more times during mixing. Take your time, and allow each step to reach the proper stage before continuing. Bake for about 30 minutes; cool in pans about 15 minutes before unmolding. Unmold cake onto cardboard, then slide onto rack.

Make the 10-inch recipe twice, once for each 14-inch layer. Prep two 14 × 2-inch round pans with nonstick spray and parchment. Preheat the oven to 325° and use a baking core; otherwise follow the instructions for 6-inch layers. With larger layers you will have to beat the butter and cream the butter/sugar mixture longer and scrape the bowl down a few more times during mixing. Take your time, and allow each step to reach the proper stage before continuing. Bake for about 35 minutes; cool in pans about 20 minutes before unmolding. Unmold cake onto cardboard, then slide onto rack.

 ### The Duncan Hines Conundrum

When I owned my own bakery, one of my specialties was wedding cakes. We also offered cakes in the refrigerated case for birthdays and for sale by the slice. In the early days, I used a genoise as the basic cake, which is a spongier, drier, European-style cake. The dryness is used to advantage by brushing the layers with flavored syrups, such as those flavored with Grand Marnier or Kahlua. I loved these elegant cakes, but, unfortunately, some of my customers complained that the cakes were not what they expected.

The fact is that they were very different from the Duncan Hines–style cakes with which the American public has become so familiar. The cake mixes on the market are incredibly moist, and they are also filled with preservatives and made with all sorts of ingredients that home bakers would never put in their own cakes. But their texture is what Americans have become used to and what they compare other cakes to. Many years ago, I switched to baking a more traditional American-style butter cake to satisfy my customer's tastes, and that is what these cakes are.

I love the taste and texture of a homemade butter cake, such as the ones presented here. In fact, I love them with fillings and buttercreams, without syrup brushed on the layers.

There are two problems with this approach when it comes to wedding cakes. First of all, wedding cakes are made over several days and are tinkered with quite a bit (torting, filling, crumb coating, sitting overnight in a refrigerator, etc.) and they can lose some inherent moisture. The other problem, which I have no control over, is that many Americans like a cake with an unusually high moisture content. To please the American palate, and my wedding cake customers, I brush the layers with Moistening Syrup.

The point is that the syrup is not necessary, but it may be desirable. It is up to you to decide whether to use it, and how much to use.

ESSENTIAL WHITE CAKE

This cake has no egg yolks, which is what gives it a delicate taste and white color. It, too, is a very basic cake, but less assertive than a yellow cake, so I suggest you use it with more delicate flavors or when you want the other flavors to be predominant.

MAKES TWO 6 × 2-INCH ROUND CAKE LAYERS

1³/₄ cups cake flour

2 teaspoons baking powder

¹/₄ teaspoon salt

3 large egg whites, at room temperature

³/₄ cup whole milk, at room temperature

¹/₂ cup (1 stick) unsalted butter, at room temperature, cut into tablespoon-sized pieces

³/₄ cup sugar

1 teaspoon vanilla extract

1 Preheat the oven to 350°. Spray two 6 × 2-inch round cake pans with nonstick spray, line with parchment, then give the parchment a quick spray as well.

2 Sift together the flour, baking powder, and salt; set aside. Whisk together the egg whites and milk in a small bowl; set aside.

3 Beat the butter using the flat beater attachment until soft and creamy, about 2 minutes. Add the sugar gradually and beat until very light and fluffy, about 3 minutes. Scrape down the bowl once or twice, and then beat in the vanilla.

4 Add the flour mixture in 4 additions, alternately with the egg white/milk mixture. Begin and end with the flour mixture and beat until smooth on low-medium speed after each addition.

5 Divide the batter evenly between the pans and smooth the tops with an offset spatula. Bake for about 25 minutes until a toothpick shows a few moist crumbs. The edges will be barely tinged with brown and will have begun to come away from the sides of the pan.

6 Cool on racks in pans for 5 minutes. Unmold directly onto racks, peel off the parchment, and allow cakes to cool completely. Place on cardboards and double-wrap in plastic wrap; store at room temperature if assembling within 24 hours.

MAKES TWO 8 × 2-INCH ROUND CAKE LAYERS

2²/₃ cups cake flour

1 tablespoon baking powder

¹/₃ teaspoon salt

4¹/₂ large egg whites, at room temperature

1 cup plus 2 tablespoons whole milk, at room temperature

³/₄ cup (1¹/₂ sticks) unsalted butter, at room temperature, cut into tablespoon-sized pieces

1 cup plus 2 tablespoons sugar

1¹/₂ teaspoons vanilla extract

Prep two 8 × 2-inch round pans with nonstick spray and parchment. Follow the instructions for 6-inch layers. With larger layers you will have to beat the butter and cream the butter/sugar mixture longer and scrape the bowl down a few more times during mixing. Take your time, and allow each step to reach the proper stage before continuing. Bake for about 30 minutes; cool in pans about 8 minutes before unmolding.

3¹/₂ cups cake flour

1 tablespoon plus 1 teaspoon baking powder

¹/₂ teaspoon salt

6 large egg whites, at room temperature

1¹/₂ cups whole milk, at room temperature

1 cup (2 sticks) unsalted butter, at room temperature, cut into tablespoon-sized pieces

1¹/₂ cups sugar

2 teaspoons vanilla extract

Prep two 9 × 2-inch round pans with nonstick spray and parchment. Follow the instructions for 6-inch layers. With larger layers you will have to beat the butter and cream the butter/sugar mixture longer and scrape the bowl down a few more times during mixing. Take your time, and allow each step to reach the proper stage before continuing. Bake for about 35 minutes; cool in pans about 9 minutes before unmolding.

4¹/₃ cups cake flour

1 tablespoon plus 2 teaspoons baking powder

²/₃ teaspoon salt

7¹/₂ large egg whites, at room temperature

1³/₄ cups plus 2 tablespoons whole milk, at room temperature

1¹/₄ cups (2¹/₂ sticks) unsalted butter, at room temperature, cut into tablespoon-sized pieces

1³/₄ cups plus 2 tablespoons sugar

2¹/₂ teaspoons vanilla extract

Prep two 10 × 2-inch round pans with nonstick spray and parchment. Follow the instructions for 6-inch layers. With

larger layers you will have to beat the butter and cream the butter/sugar mixture longer and scrape the bowl down a few more times during mixing. Take your time, and allow each step to reach the proper stage before continuing. Bake for about 40 minutes; cool in pans about 10 minutes before unmolding.

Make the 9-inch recipe twice, once for each 12-inch layer. Prep two 12 × 2-inch round pans with nonstick spray and parchment. Preheat the oven to 325° and use a baking core; otherwise follow the instructions for 6-inch layers. With larger layers you will have to beat the butter and cream the butter/sugar mixture longer and scrape the bowl down a few more times during mixing. Take your time, and allow each step to reach the proper stage before continuing. Bake for about 40 minutes; the edges will just be tinged golden brown; the top may be pale. Cool in pans about 15 minutes before unmolding. Unmold cake onto cardboard, then slide onto rack.

Make the 10-inch recipe twice, once for each 14-inch layer. Prep two 14 × 2-inch round pans with nonstick spray and parchment. Preheat the oven to 325° and use a baking core; otherwise follow the instructions for 6-inch layers. With larger layers you will have to beat the butter and cream the butter/sugar mixture longer and scrape the batter down a few more times during mixing. Take your time, and allow each step to reach the proper stage before continuing. Bake for about 45 minutes; the edges will just be tinged golden brown; the top may be pale. Cool in pans about 20 minutes before unmolding. Unmold cake onto cardboard, then slide onto rack.

ESSENTIAL CHOCOLATE CAKE

This is a luscious dark chocolaty cake. Make sure to use the Dutch-processed cocoa for best results.

MAKES TWO 6 × 2-INCH ROUND CAKE LAYERS

1 cup cake flour
$1/3$ cup Dutch-processed cocoa
$1/2$ teaspoon baking soda
Pinch salt
$1/3$ cup ($5^1/3$ tablespoons) unsalted butter, at room temperature, cut into tablespoon-sized pieces
$3/4$ cup plus 2 tablespoons sugar
$2/3$ teaspoon vanilla extract
$1^1/2$ large eggs, at room temperature
$2/3$ cup whole milk, at room temperature

1 Preheat the oven to 350°. Spray two 6 × 2-inch round cake pans with nonstick spray, line with parchment, then give the parchment a quick spray as well.

2 Sift together the flour, cocoa, baking soda, and salt; set aside.

3 Beat the butter using the flat beater attachment until soft and creamy, about 2 minutes. Add the sugar gradually and beat until very light and fluffy, about 3 minutes. Scrape down the bowl once or twice, and then beat in the vanilla.

4 Beat in the eggs one at a time, scraping down after each addition, allowing each egg to be absorbed before continuing. Add the flour mixture in 4 additions, alternately with the milk. Begin and end with the flour mixture and beat until smooth on low-medium speed after each addition.

5 Divide evenly between the pans and smooth the tops with an offset spatula, if necessary. Bake for about 35 minutes until a toothpick shows a few moist crumbs. The cake will have just begun to come away from the sides of the pan.

6 Cool on racks in pans for 5 minutes. Unmold directly onto racks, peel off the parchment, and allow cakes to cool completely. Place on cardboards and double-wrap in plastic wrap; store at room temperature if assembling within 24 hours.

MAKES TWO 8 × 2-INCH ROUND CAKE LAYERS

$1^1/2$ cups cake flour
$1/2$ cup Dutch-processed cocoa
$3/4$ teaspoon baking soda
$1/4$ teaspoon salt
$1/2$ cup (1 stick) unsalted butter, at room temperature, cut into tablespoon-sized pieces
$1^1/3$ cups sugar
1 teaspoon vanilla extract
$2^1/4$ large eggs, at room temperature
1 cup whole milk, at room temperature

Prep two 8 × 2-inch round pans with nonstick spray and parchment. Follow the instructions for 6-inch layers. With larger layers you will have to beat the butter and cream the butter/sugar mixture longer and scrape the bowl down a few more times during mixing. Take your time, and allow each step to reach the proper stage before continuing. Bake for about 35 minutes; cool in pans about 8 minutes before unmolding.

 Baking Times for Larger Layers

I suggest that you use a baking core (as described on page 17) for 12-inch and 14-inch tiers. This is a hollow, cone-shaped piece of metal that is inserted in the center of the cake. It draws heat to the cake's middle and helps these extra-large tiers bake as evenly as possible. It also shortens their baking times somewhat. (Sometimes, for heavier batters, which also take a long time to cook, I use a baking core for smaller layers as well.)

MAKES TWO 9 × 2-INCH ROUND CAKE LAYERS

2 cups cake flour

2/3 cup Dutch-processed cocoa

1 teaspoon baking soda

1/4 teaspoon salt

2/3 cup (10 2/3 tablespoons) unsalted butter, at room
temperature, cut into tablespoon-sized pieces

1 3/4 cups sugar

1 1/3 teaspoons vanilla extract

3 large eggs, at room temperature

1 1/3 cups whole milk, at room temperature

Prep two 9 × 2-inch round pans with nonstick spray and
parchment. Follow the instructions for 6-inch layers. With
larger layers you will have to beat the butter and cream the
butter/sugar mixture longer and scrape the bowl down a
few more times during mixing. Take your time, and allow
each step to reach the proper stage before continuing. Bake
for about 37 minutes; cool in pans about 9 minutes before
unmolding.

MAKES TWO 10 × 2-INCH ROUND CAKE LAYERS

2 1/2 cups cake flour

3/4 cup plus 2 tablespoons Dutch-processed cocoa

1 1/4 teaspoons baking soda

1/3 teaspoon salt

3/4 cup plus 2 tablespoons (1 3/4 sticks) unsalted butter,
at room temperature, cut into tablespoon-sized pieces

2 cups plus 2 tablespoons sugar

1 2/3 teaspoons vanilla extract

3 3/4 large eggs, at room temperature

1 2/3 cups whole milk, at room temperature

Prep two 10 × 2-inch round pans with nonstick spray and
parchment. Follow the instructions for 6-inch layers. With
larger layers you will have to beat the butter and cream the
butter/ sugar mixture longer and scrape the bowl down a
few more times during mixing. Take your time, and allow
each step to reach the proper stage before continuing. Bake
for about 42 minutes; cool in pans about 10 minutes
before unmolding.

MAKES TWO 12 × 2-INCH ROUND CAKE LAYERS

Make the 9-inch recipe twice, once for each 12-inch layer.
Prep two 12 × 2-inch round pans with nonstick spray and
parchment. Preheat the oven to 325° and use a baking core;
otherwise follow the instructions for 6-inch layers. With larger
layers you will have to beat the butter and cream the butter/
sugar mixture longer and scrape the bowl down a few more
times during mixing. Take your time, and allow each step
to reach the proper stage before continuing. Bake for about
40 minutes; cool in pans about 15 minutes before unmolding. Unmold cake onto cardboard, then slide onto rack.

MAKES TWO 14 × 2-INCH ROUND CAKE LAYERS

Make the 10-inch recipe twice, once for each 14-inch layer.
Prep two 14 × 2-inch round pans with nonstick spray and
parchment. Preheat the oven to 325° and use a baking core;
otherwise follow the instructions for 6-inch layers. With
larger layers you will have to beat the butter and cream the
butter/sugar mixture longer and scrape the bowl down a few
more times during mixing. Take your time, and allow each
step to reach the proper stage before continuing. Bake for
about 42 minutes; cool in pans about 20 minutes before unmolding. Unmold cake onto cardboard, then slide onto rack.

Essential Moistening Syrup

This is an extremely easy recipe. It consists of sugar, water, and vanilla. Its sole purpose in life is to bring added moistness and flavor to your cake layers. If you are using it as a vanilla-flavored syrup, then by all means use the vanilla bean. If you will be additionally flavoring it with a liqueur or some other flavor, then you may consider using the vanilla extract. A few recipes will suggest no vanilla flavor whatsoever, and those directions are given in individual recipes (such as for the Lemon Blackberry Cake, where you want a pure lemon syrup without vanilla).

MAKES 3 CUPS

2 cups sugar
2 cups water
1 vanilla bean, split and scraped, or 1 teaspoon vanilla
  extract

1 Place the sugar and water in a saucepan and stir to wet the sugar. Add the split vanilla bean and all the seeds, if using. Bring to a boil over medium-high heat, swirling the pan around once or twice to help dissolve the sugar.
2 Turn the heat down to medium and simmer for 1 minute. Make sure all the sugar is dissolved.
3 Remove from the heat and allow to cool to room temperature. (Whisk in the vanilla extract, if using, at this point.) Remove the vanilla bean, scrape any seeds into the liquid, and refrigerate in an airtight container until needed, up to 1 month.

 ## What Kind of Frosting Is That?

Wedding cakes come with many different kinds of frostings and outside coverings. There is a trend for many cakes to be covered in fondant, a thick sugary paste that can be rolled out in sheets and draped over cakes. Fondant offers an amazing look; in fact fondant cakes look like they are covered in satin or porcelain. However, I have never actually met anyone who likes to eat fondant; it has a very sweet taste and chewy texture that many find unpleasant. I believe cakes that feature fondant are mostly concerned with looks, and that is why you won't find any fondant in this book.

When it comes to frostings and buttercreams, there are a variety of textures and flavors available. Some bakers use a frosting made of vegetable shortening and powdered sugar that is not only extremely sweet, but its texture is half gritty/powdery and half greasy. Not what I want on a wedding cake, or any cake!

I prefer a buttercream based on a boiled sugar syrup (hence, the lack of grit), egg whites (for the white color they produce), and sweet butter (which gives it body and flavor). Italian meringue buttercream is my frosting of choice. It is as smooth as silk, takes on additional flavors endlessly, can be made way ahead and frozen, and is not too sweet. Its one downfall is that it does melt when exposed to high temperatures (due to the high butter content) so in very warm weather a cake featuring Italian meringue buttercream is not as stable as a fondant-covered cake or a cake frosted with a vegetable shortening–based icing. I believe the payoff in taste and texture outweighs these disadvantages. (For details on how long you can let one of my cakes be out on display, even in 95° heat, turn to page 54.)

ESSENTIAL BUTTERCREAM

This buttercream has a divine, silky texture, is slightly off-white in color (due to the butter content), and is not too sweet. A candy thermometer will be of great help when making this recipe, but I also give you visual cues, so it is not necessary. The instructions are lengthy, but after you make the buttercream a couple of times, you will not have to reread them in total.

This recipe is meant to maximize the capacity of your 5-quart mixer. For multi-tiered cakes you will have to make the recipe several times. You may make this up to 1 month ahead and freeze it.

MAKES 7 CUPS

1¼ cups plus ⅓ cup sugar
½ cup water
8 large egg whites, at room temperature
1 teaspoon cream of tartar
1½ pounds (6 sticks) unsalted butter, at room temperature, cut into small pieces

1 Place the 1¼ cups of sugar and water in a small saucepan. Stir to wet all of the sugar. Bring to a boil over medium-high heat, swirling the pan occasionally to help dissolve sugar. Dip a pastry brush in cold water and wash down sugar crystals from the sides of the pot once or twice. Turn down the heat so the mixture simmers gently. You want to be able to bring the syrup to a rapid boil when needed.

2 Meanwhile, place the whites in your clean, grease-free mixing bowl and whip until frothy on low speed using the wire whip attachment. Add the cream of tartar and turn the speed up to medium-high. When soft peaks form, add the ⅓ cup sugar gradually. Continue whipping until stiff, glossy peaks form. This is the meringue part of the buttercream.

3 Return the sugar/water mixture to a rapid boil and cook until it reaches 248° to 250°. The trick here is to have the syrup ready at the same time as the glossy meringue. If the meringue is done before the syrup, turn the mixer speed down to the lowest setting so that the whites are continuously moving, but not highly agitated. If the syrup is done first, add a bit of hot water to lower the temperature and continue to cook until the meringue is ready.

4 While the syrup is cooking at a rapid boil, there are many visual clues to use to see how it is progressing. It starts out thin with many small bubbles over the entire surface. As it cooks, the water evaporates and the mixture will become thicker. The bubbles get larger and do not rise to the surface so rapidly. The bubbles will become thick and sticky and pop open more slowly as well.

At this point, the syrup definitely looks thickened, but it has not begun to color, which would mean it is about to turn into caramel. The stage you want—called the firm ball stage—is right before the sugar starts to color. If you drop a bit of the syrup into a glass of cold water it will harden into a ball. When you squeeze the ball between your fingertips, it will feel firm.

5 When the syrup is ready, with the mixer running on medium-high speed, pour in the syrup in a steady stream, without getting any on the rotating whip or the sides of the bowl. If it does, the syrup will harden and cling and not make it down into the meringue mixture. Turn off the machine to add the syrup if you find it easier. You just don't want to let the meringue sit still for longer than a few seconds.

6 The meringue must be whipped until it cools, which may take as long as 15 minutes, depending on the ambient temperature. At this point, beat the meringue on high speed. Occasionally touch the outside bottom of the bowl; you should be able to feel it cooling down. When the bowl is no longer warm, stop the machine and touch the surface of the meringue with your finger to double-check that it is indeed cooled. If you add the butter while the meringue is

Whipping Egg Whites

Properly whipped egg whites are the basis for Essential Buttercream. They provide volume and structure and there are a few tips that will help you accomplish this successfully.

* Separate each egg into a small separate bowl before adding it to the larger bowl of egg whites, so if you get some egg yolk in your egg white, it will only be that one egg and you won't waste the whole bunch already in the main bowl
* Start with a grease-free mixing bowl. Any traces of grease will prevent whites from whipping.
* Use a wire whip or similar attachment to your electric mixer for maximum volume
* Start on slow speed to create a stable foam
* When the whites are foamy, it is at this point that you add cream of tartar, if suggested in the individual recipe
* Turn to medium-high speed and keep whipping until soft peaks form. If you pick up the beater, and a soft egg white peak is left behind, one that mostly stands up, but flops over a bit near the top of the peak, then you have soft peaks
* At soft peak stage you begin adding sugar. Add it slowly and gradually
* Continue to whip at medium-high speed until meringue looks glossy and smooth and stiff peaks form. When the beater is lifted the peaks will stand up straight
* Do not overwhip at this point. Whip just until stiff peaks form. (Overbeating produces whites that are cottony and lumpy looking and they will adversely affect your recipe.)

warm, the butter will melt and ruin the texture of the buttercream by turning it liquidy. It will also decrease the volume of the final product.

7 When the meringue is cool, turn the machine down to a medium speed and begin to add the butter, a couple tablespoons at a time. The meringue will change the moment the butter becomes incorporated; the texture becomes thicker, creamy, and smooth as it turns into buttercream.

Continue to whip the buttercream, adding the remaining butter. Keep beating until the buttercream is completely smooth. If at any time the mixture looks lumpy or separated, just continue to beat; it will come together. (For tips on saving buttercream that has separated or turned lumpy, see page 72.)

8 You may use the buttercream as soon as you make it. However, it is often more convenient to make it ahead. Refrigerate in an airtight container for up to 1 week, or freeze for up to 1 month. (Certain flavorings, like lemon curd, liqueur, and melted chocolate, taste most fresh when added to the buttercream at the last minute, so I generally recommend freezing the essential recipe and stirring in the flavor component when the buttercream is defrosted, softened, and ready to be used. In the buttercream variations that appear with the individual cakes, I indicate when a flavoring can be added in advance and frozen.)

TO SOFTEN CHILLED BUTTERCREAM

If the buttercream has been refrigerated for even a few hours, it will be very firm. It is not spreadable or usable at this point. If it is frozen, defrost in the refrigerator overnight and follow the same instructions.

Here are three ways to revive and soften your chilled buttercream. My favorite technique is to place a quantity of cold buttercream in the stainless steel bowl of my mixer and place it over an extremely low heat on top of the stove. Hold the bowl with one hand and constantly fold the pieces of buttercream over one another so that no one piece is ever on the bottom for very long receiving direct heat. You want to warm the buttercream, but not melt the butter out. Be careful.

Another technique uses the microwave. If the buttercream is stored in a microwavable container, place the container in the microwave and set it on a very low power and heat in 15-second spurts, checking the softening progress often. You want to bring it to room temperature uniformly without melting the butter. This technique will depend on your familiarity with your microwave and your ability to control its temperature and defrosting times.

Another technique is to place a quantity of buttercream in your mixer bowl and heat it with a warm hair dryer. Use the hair dryer to blow warmth directly on top of the buttercream as well as to the underside and sides of the bowl. Stop to whip the buttercream every now and then to see if it has sufficiently softened.

After you have warmed up your buttercream, whip it with the wire whip attachment until smooth and creamy. Heat again if it is still lumpy; chill if too soupy. It is best to be conservative and heat it slowly, rather then to melt the butter and end up with sweet soup. Your buttercream is now ready to use.

 Making Buttercream At-a-Glance

There are three parts to the buttercream recipe: a sugar syrup, a meringue, and the softened butter added at the end. The tricky part is getting the sugar syrup cooked to the proper temperature of 248° to 250° at the same time your meringue forms stiff glossy peaks. It does take some back and forth.

The timing is important and the instructions go on and on. That is because I have tried to explain every little detail for you so that you can really learn the techniques. Once you make it, you will understand the timing of it all. It will come together perfectly, and you won't have to reread the directions every time you make buttercream—just refer to the handy boxes to refresh your memory.

* Use a candy thermometer if you have one
* Begin whipping egg whites slowly so that you get maximum volume
* Use the cream of tartar; it helps to stabilize the egg whites, giving you more room to play around with your timing because the whites won't collapse
* If your egg whites are done before your sugar syrup is ready, keep the mixer on its very lowest speed; letting the whites sit still wreaks havoc
* Make sure to beat the egg white/sugar syrup meringue until there is no sign of warmth before adding butter; make sure your butter is at room temperature
* Add the butter a little bit at a time so that the meringue can absorb it gradually, ensuring a smooth end result

ALL THIS TALK ABOUT TEMPERATURE HAS ME SCARED!

Here's the deal. Making this buttercream is all about temperature. If the butter is too cold and you try and whip it, you will end up with buttercream that is chunky to the eye and the tongue. If the butter is too warm (this rarely happens—it is usually too cold), it will be thin and liquidy, you will have lost volume, and, heaven forbid, if it is really too warm, the melted butter will have separated from the rest of the mixture, and it will be a greasy mess. But guess what? None of the above scenarios is unsalvageable.

The good news is that you can manipulate the temperature and save your buttercream. Just keep chilling or warming the bowl, depending on what it needs. You can chill it effectively by placing the bowl over a larger bowl filled with ice water and beat until it comes together. Or, if it is too cold, simply allow it to stand at room temperature, or aim a hair dryer at the bowl while it beats until it smooths out. This is a great trick that really works!

If it is very warm and you see puddles of butter that have melted out, you can make another batch of perfect buttercream and then use bits of the good batch to bring the "bad" batch together. You might even just add half of the new batch to half of the old and end up with a batch of perfect buttercream. It is actually quite magical. There will be a moment when all of a sudden it goes from being out-of-whack to having its desirable creamy texture. You can watch the change right in the bowl. The mixer will sound different too as, all of a sudden, it is whipping up a silky creamy mass. You'll see! It will be fine!

NOTE: *The only buttercream that I couldn't save had been frozen for months, and I had rewarmed it and refrozen it several times. The only way I can describe it is that it seemed tired. It had no life left to it. The texture refused to cooperate. But the typical 1 month freeze is no problem whatsoever.*

The Wedding Cakes

ESSENTIAL VANILLA WEDDING CAKE

This simple, elegant cake is the most basic and straightforward wedding cake in the book. Consider it a master recipe for whatever cake you choose to make, be it directly from this book or from your own combination of recipes I have provided. This recipe takes you from the beginning to the end of putting together a wedding cake, without any variations or extra recipes. Read it through to get a sense of how all the wedding cakes in this book are laid out before you proceed to the more individualized cakes.

If you've designed your own cake, mixing various cake components from this book, or from elsewhere, you can use this to help plot out each step. Follow this recipe using any cake, frosting, filling, or moistening syrup in this book (see page 7 for suggested combinations), or go with the pure vanilla version, if vanilla is your favorite flavor.

This cake requires no special techniques beyond a basic bead border. To decorate it for the photograph, we went as simply and beautifully as we could, arranging fresh rose petals and an array of crystallized flowers whimsically here and there. You could add as many or as few as you like, and use whatever flowers you want—I promise the result will be beautiful. And another plus—you can use flowers to artfully conceal any imperfections in your buttercream!

Serves 100

RECIPE COMPONENTS

- Yellow Cake
- Vanilla Bean Moistening Syrup
- Vanilla Buttercream

DECORATION

- Assorted pastel fresh rose petals
- Crystallized Flowers

SPECIAL EQUIPMENT

- Two 6 × 2-inch, two 10 × 2-inch, and two 14 × 2-inch round pans with corresponding cardboard rounds
- Ateco #6 tip
- 16-inch round cake base (can be covered with pale pink foil)
- 1/4-inch-thick wooden dowels (1 yard)
- Creamy white or solid pastel tablecloth

TIMELINE

- **Up to 1 Month Ahead:** Make the Vanilla Buttercream, Vanilla Bean Moistening Syrup, and Crystallized Flowers (if making)
- **2 Days Ahead:** Make the Yellow Cake
- **1 Day Ahead:** Assemble the Cake
- **Wedding Day:** Decorate, Present!

Up to 1 Month Ahead

Make the Vanilla Buttercream: Make the Essential Buttercream (see page 69) 5 times with the following changes: beat 1 tablespoon vanilla extract into each batch.

Make the Vanilla Bean Moistening Syrup: Make the Essential Moistening Syrup (see page 68) 2¹/₂ times.

Make the Crystallized Flowers: If you are making your own crystallized flowers, follow the instructions on page 96.

2 Days Ahead

Make the Yellow Cake: Make the Essential Yellow Cake in 6-inch, 10-inch, and 14-inch sizes (page 61).

1 Day Ahead

Assemble the Cake: Before assembling, have all the components made and ready to use. Have all your tools and equipment on hand, and make sure there is space for the tiers in the refrigerator.

1 Level and torte the cake layers (see pages 27–29).
2 Moisten the cake layers, fill, and assemble each tier (see pages 29–32) as follows: cardboard, first cake layer, syrup, buttercream, corresponding second layer, syrup, buttercream, third cake layer, syrup, buttercream, corresponding fourth layer, syrup.
3 Apply the crumb coat (see page 32) with Vanilla Buttercream. Chill until firm. Meanwhile, prepare your cake base (see page 37).
4 Apply the final smooth coat of buttercream (see page 35). Chill again, if time allows. Place the 14-inch tier on the center of the cake base, using some soft buttercream as glue between the base and the cake tier's cardboard.
5 Center and stack the remaining tiers using dowels for internal support (see pages 38–39).
6 Fit a pastry bag with a coupler and Ateco #6 tip. Pipe a bead border along the bottom edges of each tier (see pages 44–45). Chill overnight.

Ingredient Tips:

↝ The vanilla bean for the syrup should be moist and plump. Tahitian vanilla beans have a floral flavor that I like. "Bourbon" vanilla beans, which are more common, are fine, too.

↝ Use high quality pure vanilla extract for the buttercream. I like Neilsen-Massey brand.

Decoration Tips:

🌀 Speak with your local greenmarket flower seller or florist ahead of time to see if they can provide you with rose petals, or see Sources for a great mail-order company called Fresh Petal, or you can pluck your own (see page 87).

🌀 For crystallized flowers, you may make your own (see page 96), or order them as I did from Meadowsweets (see Sources). Owner Toni Elling makes the most exquisite crystallized flowers I have ever seen, and they will enhance any cake you make.

Wedding Day

Decorate, Present! At the site of the wedding, place the cake in the center of a tablecloth-covered display table. Artfully place rose petals and crystallized flowers on the tops of the tiers and along the vertical sides of the cake. Scatter additional flowers and petals directly on the table, if desired. Serve the cake at room temperature.

LEMON BLACKBERRY CAKE

With its lighthearted look, this cake is perfect for an outdoor wedding, in a backyard, or a garden or lawn anywhere. This cake is simply (but beautifully) decorated with bright purple-blue cornflowers, Gerbera daisies in a color called Confetti, and blackberries. If you can find blackberries on the vine, that would be perfect; otherwise, perhaps you can find some wild vines and wind them around the tiers, as we did here. Creating this cake is simple. Basic yellow cake is enhanced with lemon zest, the moistening syrup made tangy with lemon juice. For fillings, each tier has alternating ribbons of lemon curd and fresh blackberry jam. Additional lemon curd is folded into the buttercream to give it a subtle lemon flavor and pale, creamy yellow color. The round tiers are offset for an asymmetrical look. This cake is best prepared when blackberries are at their peak, so make sure they are available. This cake is lovely if plated along with a scoop of blackberry sorbet.

Serves 75

RECIPE COMPONENTS

- Yellow Cake with Lemon Zest
- Lemon Moistening Syrup
- Lemon Curd Filling
- Fresh Blackberry Jam Filling
- Lemon Curd Buttercream

DECORATION

- Fresh blackberries on the vine
- Cornflowers
- Gerbera daisies

SPECIAL EQUIPMENT

- Two 6 × 2-inch, two 9 × 2-inch, and two 12 × 2-inch round pans with corresponding cardboard rounds
- Ateco #2 tip (round tip) and #67 tip (leaf tip)
- 14-inch round cake base (can be covered with deep blue foil)
- 1/4-inch-thick wooden dowels (1 yard)
- Pale periwinkle (lavender-ish) blue tablecloth is perfect

TIMELINE

- **Up to 1 Month Ahead:**
  Make the Buttercream base and Moistening Syrup base
- **Up to 1 Week Ahead:**
  Make the Lemon Curd Filling
- **Up to 4 Days Ahead:**
  Make the Fresh Blackberry Jam Filling
- **2 Days Ahead:**
  Make the Yellow Cake with Lemon Zest
- **1 Day Ahead:**
  Finish making Lemon Curd Buttercream and Lemon Moistening Syrup, Assemble the Cake
- **Wedding Day:**
  Decorate, Present!

Up to 1 Month Ahead

Make the Buttercream Base: While the lemon curd should not be added to the buttercream until you are ready to frost the cake, you can save time by making the buttercream base well in advance and freezing it. Make the Essential Buttercream (see page 69) 2^1/$_2$ times.

Make the Moistening Syrup Base: The moistening syrup can also be made ahead but should not be flavored with lemon juice until right before using. Make the Essential Moistening Syrup (see page 68) 1^1/$_2$ times, but do not use the vanilla bean or vanilla extract.

Up to 1 Week Ahead

Make the Lemon Curd Filling: Make the recipe for Lemon Curd Filling (page 97) 3 times. To save time, you can make 1 double batch and 1 single batch, but don't attempt all 3 batches at once! Set aside 3^1/$_4$ cups of this for the filling and 4^1/$_4$ cups to fold into the buttercream. Any extra is delicious spread on English muffins and scones. The lemon curd should be made at least 1 day before you fill and frost the cake.

Ingredients Tips:

⌇ Buy firm, heavy lemons. The firmness will make them easier to zest and the heaviness usually means they are full of juice. Figuring on 2 tablespoons juice per lemon, you will need about 18 lemons for the moistening syrup, and 12 more for the lemon curd.

⌇ Remember, the same lemons will provide zest for the cake and juice for the syrup (and curd, if you are not making it in advance).

Decoration Tip:

⌇ Finding blackberries on the vine might be tricky. If you are lucky, you might have blackberries in your yard, or a friendly neighbor might help. If not, speak with a vendor at a farmer's market. Or call Green Valley Growers (see Sources).

Up to 4 Days Ahead

Make the Fresh Blackberry Jam Filling: This is simply a mixture of berries, sugar, and water cooked until thick. A little lemon juice sparks up the flavor. The jam needs time to set in the refrigerator, so make this at least 1 day before assembling the cake. Make this recipe 2 times. (If you have a very large, wide pot, you may make it all at once by doubling the recipe. The cooking time will be almost twice as long; use the visual cues for best results when doubling.)

Fresh Blackberry Jam Filling

Makes 3 cups

4 cups blackberries
1/2 cup sugar
2 tablespoons water (optional)
1 teaspoon lemon juice

1 Pick over the blackberries and remove any stems or leaves. Place in a large nonreactive saucepan with the sugar and water (use water if they are dry; leave it out if they are juicy). Stir to combine. Place over low-medium heat and cook until the mixture comes to a simmer.

2 Simmer the mixture, stirring frequently, until thickened, about 30 minutes. The blackberries will have broken down and the mixture will resemble jam, although it will not be sticky. It will become sticky and spreadable as it cools.

3 Remove from heat and stir in the lemon juice. Allow to cool to room temperature, stirring occasionally to help release heat. When cool, refrigerate in an airtight container until needed, for at least 1 day.

2 Days Ahead

Make the Yellow Cake with Lemon Zest: Make the Essential Yellow Cake (see page 61) in 6-inch, 9-inch, and 12-inch sizes, with the following changes: When creaming the butter and sugar, add lemon zest: 1 tablespoon for the 6-inch recipe, 2 tablespoons for each 9-inch recipe (the 12-inch cake is made from two 9-inch recipes).

> **Technique Note:** Since you are zesting the lemons, scrub them with a vegetable scrubbing brush to remove wax and possible pesticide residue. Remember that lemon zest is the yellow part of the skin, not the white part right underneath, which tastes bitter. I use a microplane zester, which effortlessly removes just the zest (see Sources).

1 Day Ahead

Finish Making Lemon Curd Buttercream and Lemon Moistening Syrup: For the Lemon Curd Buttercream, simply beat the 4^{1}/$_{2}$ cups of the Lemon Curd Filling into the buttercream base until well blended. If you want to do this in batches, beat 1^{3}/$_{4}$ cups lemon curd into each 7-cup batch of buttercream and about ^{3}/$_{4}$ cup lemon curd into the half batch. (^{1}/$_{4}$ cup lemon curd for every cup of buttercream.)

For the Lemon Moistening Syrup, stir in 2^{1}/$_{4}$ cups freshly squeezed lemon juice to the entire batch (or to taste). If you are making the syrup now, do not add lemon juice until the syrup has cooled completely.

Assemble the Cake: Before assembling, have all the components made and ready to use. Have all your tools and equipment on hand, and make sure there is space for the tiers in the refrigerator.

1 Level and torte the cake layers (see pages 27–29).

2 Moisten the cake layers, fill, and assemble each tier (see pages 29–32) as follows: Cardboard, first cake layer, syrup, jam, corresponding second layer, syrup, lemon curd, third cake layer, syrup, jam, corresponding fourth layer, syrup.

3 Apply the crumb coat (see page 32) with Lemon Curd Buttercream. Chill until firm. Meanwhile, prepare your cake base (see page 37).

Piping vines on sides of tier

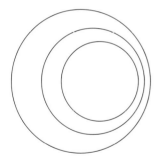

Making buttercream leaves

Align offset tiers along one side of the cake

4 Apply a final smooth coat of buttercream to each tier (see page 35). Chill again, if time allows. Place the 12-inch tier on the center of the cake base. Stack the remaining tiers in an offset manner (see photo, page 78, and diagram below), so that the tiers align at the "back" of the cake and then fan out from there, using dowels for internal support (see pages 38–39). Align dowels with the central position of the tier that will be resting on them.

5 Fit a pastry bag and coupler with Ateco #2 tip. Pipe vines on the sides of the cake (see photo). Switch tip to an Ateco #67 and pipe small leaves here and there along the vines (see photo). Using same #67 tip, pipe an overlapping leaf border along the outside top edges and bottom edges. (See page 45 for instructions on piping a leaf border.) Chill overnight.

Wedding Day

Decorate, Present! At the site of the wedding, place the cake in the center of the tablecloth-covered display table. Trim flower stems to about ¹/₂ to 1 inch. Arrange flowers, blackberries, and greenery on top of the cake and cascading down in tiers (see photo for inspiration). Serve at room temperature.

SWIRLED MARBLE CAKE WITH SOUR CREAM FUDGE FROSTING

This rich, "fudge-y" cake is aimed at dark chocolate fans. It is one of the simplest cakes in the book and—with its thick frosting swirls and petals tossed on like confetti—it's just right for an informal, youthful reception (even if you're an older couple). This icing is not a variation of our Essential Buttercream; instead it is a very simple, rich combination of chocolate and sour cream. The cake's marbled effect is achieved by adding melted unsweetened chocolate to half of the yellow cake batter, then swirling the two batters together. Basic vanilla bean syrup moistens the layers and the Sour Cream Fudge Frosting acts as both filling and frosting, so there are not a lot of extra ingredients involved. I call the cake "swirled" not only because the batters are swirled together but also because the frosting is casually swirled on the outside for an easy but attractive appearance. (No pastry bags or piping tips needed.) The result is easy, beautiful, and absolutely scrumptious!

Serves 100

RECIPE COMPONENTS
- Marbled Yellow Cake
- Vanilla Bean Moistening Syrup
- Sour Cream Fudge Frosting

DECORATION
- Pink and red rose petals from 16 roses

SPECIAL EQUIPMENT
- Two 6 × 2-inch, two 10 × 2-inch, and two 14 × 2-inch round pans with corresponding cardboard rounds
- 16-inch round cake base (can be covered with pale pink foil)
- 1/4-inch-thick wooden dowels (1 yard)
- A dark red tablecloth looks great, or try a contrasting color like lilac

TIMELINE
- **Up to 1 Month Ahead:**
  Make the Vanilla Bean Moistening Syrup
- **2 Days Ahead:**
  Make the Marbled Yellow Cake
- **1 Day Ahead:**
  Make the Sour Cream Fudge Frosting and Assemble the Cake
- **Wedding Day:**
  Prepare the Rose Petals, Decorate, Present!

Up to 1 Month Ahead

Make the Vanilla Bean Moistening Syrup: Make the Essential Moistening Syrup (see page 000) 2 1/2 times, using the vanilla bean.

2 Days Ahead

Make the Marbled Yellow Cake: Make the Essential Yellow Cake in 6-inch, 10-inch, and 14-inch sizes, with the following changes: For the 6-inch cake size, divide the finished batter in half. Fold 1 ounce melted and slightly cooled unsweetened chocolate into one half of the batter. Add the batters to the pans in alternating large spoonfuls of yellow batter and chocolate batter. Then gently draw a butter knife through the batters to marbleize. Do not over-marble the batter or you will lose the visual definition of the dark and light swirls. Bake the 6-inch layers for about 22 minutes.

For the 10-inch recipe, use 2 1/2 ounces of chocolate and bake the layers for about 27 minutes. For the 14-inch recipe, use 5 ounces of chocolate and bake the layers for about 35 minutes.

1 Day Ahead

Make the Sour Cream Fudge Frosting: For this cake, the filling and frosting are the same: a deep, dark, chocolate fudge frosting (this recipe is not based on our Essential Buttercream). It has a tang from the sour cream, which is unusual, but quite delicious. You will have to make the recipe a total of 5 times for both filling and frosting.

While the frosting can be made ahead, refrigerated for up to 4 days, and rewarmed, it is easiest to use when freshly made. That it is why it is suggested to make it fresh in the Timeline. In fact, I suggest literally using the frosting as it is made, preparing 2 batches, filling the cake, then making your next batch for crumb coat, applying crumb coat, and so on (see assembly instructions on page 87). This may seem like a hassle but don't worry because the frosting comes together really quickly.

Sour Cream Fudge Frosting

Makes 6 cups

30 ounces bittersweet or semisweet chocolate, finely chopped
3 cups sour cream, removed from refrigerator 1 hour ahead

1. Melt the chocolate in the top of a double boiler or in the microwave (see instructions on page 13); stir until smooth. Allow to cool until it is just warm to the touch.
2. Fold in the sour cream with a large rubber spatula just until no white streaks of sour cream remain. The frosting will become overly thick with too much folding, but will remain silky if not overworked. If it becomes too stiff, you may warm it gently over a pot of warm water. It is best if used right away.

Ingredients Tips:

- Find the plumpest vanilla beans you can for the syrup. This cake is about the harmony of chocolate and vanilla, so you want these flavors to shine.
- Use a high quality semisweet or bittersweet chocolate, such as Scharffen Berger Bittersweet. Also, make sure to use full-fat sour cream—the low- or non-fat kinds just won't do.

Decoration Tip:

- Pink and red roses come in many different shades, so speak to your supplier (gardener, greenmarket vendor, florist) ahead of time to choose the exact colors you want, and preorder if necessary. You can stick to one shade of red and one of pink, or go with several shades varying from pale pink to deep red.

Using an icing spatula to make swirls in frosting

Using a spoon to make swirls in frosting

Assemble the Cake: Before assembling, have all the components made and ready to use. Have all your tools and equipment on hand, and make sure there is space for the tiers in the refrigerator.

1 Level and torte the cake layers (see pages 27–29).

2 Prepare the first 2 batches of frosting.

3 Moisten the cake layers, fill, and assemble each tier (see pages 29–32) as follows: Cardboard, first cake layer, syrup, fudge frosting, corresponding second layer, syrup, fudge frosting, third cake layer, syrup, fudge frosting, corresponding fourth layer, syrup.

4 Make next batch of frosting at this time, if needed. Apply the crumb coat (see page 32). Chill until firm. Meanwhile, prepare your cake base (see page 37).

5 Prepare remaining batches of frosting and apply the final coat of frosting (see page 35). This is best accomplished by first spreading a thick layer of fudge frosting all over each tier. While the frosting is still soft, use an icing spatula or the back of a teaspoon to make swirls all over (see photos, left).

There is no one right way to do this. Just make pleasing shapes, ridges, and ripples. The frosting sets up quickly, so work briskly. If you need to fix a swirl, try warming your icing spatula or spoon in hot water, wiping it clean with a dish towel, then using it to fix the problem. (The warmth softens the frosting, allowing you to alter the shape.) The entire cake should be covered with chocolate swirls. Remember that there will be petals scattered on top, so perfection is not the goal. Chill again, if time allows.

6 Place the 14-inch tier on the center of the cake base. Center and stack the remaining tiers using dowels for internal support (see pages 38–39). Add more frosting, if necessary, to cover up cardboard rounds. Chill overnight.

Wedding Day

Prepare the Rose Petals: For each rose, simply peel off one petal at a time, taking care not to tear the petals, which is easy to do. Be particularly careful around the bases of the petals where they attach to one another and tear most easily. Peel your roses right before you want to use them.

Decorate, Present! At the site of the wedding, place the cake in the center of a table-cloth-covered display table. The cake should be at room temperature for the petals to best adhere. Scatter the rose petals over the cake, gently pressing them to adhere to the sides, if desired (see photo for inspiration). Scatter some petals around the base of the cake on the tablecloth as well. Serve at room temperature.

Technique Note: If the frosting is too firm for the petals to adhere, use a hair dryer aimed here and there to soften up sections where you want to affix petals. Yes, this means you have to carry a hair dryer to the display site, but it is a professional trick that is fairly easy to accomplish and will give you great results.

RASPBERRIES AND CREAM CAKE

The sight of a bride cutting the first slice of this charming White Chocolate Cake to reveal soft white layers with ribbons of pink Raspberry Buttercream is a scene out of a fairy-tale wedding. This image is enhanced by the decoration of white chocolate curls, with raspberries and crystallized flowers peeking out here and there, and it would not be going too far at all to add a pixie-dust sprinkling of powdered sugar over the top. The tart edge of the raspberries and raspberry liqueur harmonizes beautifully with the sweet creamy white chocolate. The cup-shaped chocolate curls and the berries echo the flavors within; the crystallized flowers add panache.

Serves 75

RECIPE COMPONENTS

- White Chocolate Cake
- Raspberry Eau de Vie Moistening Syrup
- Raspberry Buttercream Filling
- Vanilla Buttercream

DECORATION

- White chocolate curls
- Fresh, firm raspberries (3 cups)
- Crystallized flowers (about 25, preferably pink)

SPECIAL EQUIPMENT

- Two 6 × 2-inch, two 9 × 2-inch, and two 12 × 2-inch round pans with corresponding cardboard rounds
- 14-inch round cake base (can be covered with pale pink foil)
- 1/4-inch-thick wooden dowels (1 yard)
- Any pink-colored tablecloth
- Flat steel baking sheet(s) (see Equipment Tips)
- 3 to 4 sturdy, round, sharp cookie cutters, each from 1 1/2 to 3 1/2 inches in diameter (see Equipment Tips)
- Chocolate thermometer

TIMELINE

- **Up to 1 Month Ahead:**
  Make the Vanilla Buttercream, the Moistening Syrup base, and Crystallized Flowers (if making)
- **Up to 1 Week Ahead:**
  Make the White Chocolate Curls
- **2 Days Ahead:**
  Make the White Chocolate Cake, Finish Making the Raspberry Eau de Vie Moistening Syrup
- **1 Day Ahead:**
  Finish Making the Raspberry Buttercream Filling, Assemble the Cake and Cover with Chocolate Curls
- **Wedding Day:**
  Decorate, Present!

Up to 1 Month Ahead

Make the Vanilla Buttercream: Make the Essential Buttercream (see page 69) 4 times with the following changes: beat 1 tablespoon vanilla extract into each batch. You will use 9 cups of this buttercream as a base for the Raspberry Buttercream Filling; the rest will serve as the frosting.

Make the Moistening Syrup Base: The moistening syrup can be made ahead but should not be flavored with raspberry eau de vie until right before using. Make the Essential Moistening Syrup (see page 68) 2 times, but do not use the vanilla bean or vanilla extract.

Make the Crystallized Flowers: If you are making your own crystallized flowers, follow the instructions on page 96.

Up to 1 Week Ahead

Make the White Chocolate Curls: There are many ways to make chocolate curls, some more dramatic than others. These are on the formal end of the spectrum.

WHITE CHOCOLATE CURLS

3 pounds white chocolate couverture, such as Valrhona or Callebaut, finely chopped

1 Temper the chocolate according to instructions on page 13.
2 Pour some of the chocolate (about 4 ounces) out onto a clean, dry, scratch-free steel baking sheet. Use an offset spatula to spread it very thinly, but you shouldn't see the pan through the chocolate. If you have more than one pan, repeat with the additional pans.
3 Place the pan(s) in refrigerator briefly to allow the chocolate to partially firm up. If the chocolate is too cold, the curls will shatter; if the chocolate is too warm, the curls will not "curl." You will need to periodically make test curls to see whether the chocolate is at the proper temperature or not.

Ingredients Tips:

↝ You may substitute nonalcoholic raspberry syrup for the raspberry liqueur in the syrup, if you like.
↝ While I prefer this cake when fresh raspberries are available, you can use frozen to make the filling and just leave out the fresh ones from the decoration on the outside of the cake.

Equipment Tips:

↝ To make the chocolate curls you need steel baking sheets. Bits of the more common aluminum baking sheets would be scraped off if you used them for making curls. Steel pans can be purchased from La Cuisine (see Sources). One pan will do (you will just have to reuse it several times) or if you can find/borrow/purchase 3 or 4, the process will go more quickly.
↝ Ateco carries sets of nesting round cutters, which are perfect for this project (see Sources). These are a worthwhile investment, as you will find many uses for them beyond making chocolate curls, from cookies to biscuits and more.

This is a very easy cake to decorate. You don't have to make the sides ultra smooth, as they will be covered with large chocolate curls. The berries should be dry and nice and round. You can purchase crystallized flowers from Meadowsweets (see Sources), or make them yourself (see page 96). My choice would be to call Toni at Meadowsweets—her flowers are perfect!

4 When the chocolate is set, use a sharp, round cutter to make the curls. Place the far edge of the cookie cutter near the top of the chocolate spread on the pan. Holding the cutter at a very slight angle (it will be angled up toward you) scrape the chocolate by pulling the cutter toward you. The curl should form within the cutter. Keep pulling to make a complete curl that wraps around itself. Use various size cutters, ranging from 1 1/2 to 3 1/2 inches, to make various sizes of curls.

5 Keep making curls, using up all of your chocolate. Store the curls in an airtight container in the refrigerator until needed. Take care not to crush them!

2 Days Ahead

Make the White Chocolate Cake: Make the Essential White Cake (see page 64) in 6-inch, 9-inch, and 12-inch sizes, with the following changes: add 1 ounce of white chocolate shavings to the 6-inch recipe, and 2 ounces to each 9-inch recipe (the 12-inch cake is made from two 9-inch recipes).

> **Technique Note:** To create the proper-sized shavings, take a block of white chocolate and use a large chef's knife to shave off shards from an edge or side.

Finish Making the Raspberry Eau de Vie Moistening Syrup: Stir about 1 cup (or more or less, to taste) of raspberry eau de vie into the entire batch. If you are making the syrup now, do not add liqueur until the syrup has cooled completely.

1 Day Ahead

Finish Making the Raspberry Buttercream Filling (see next page): Part of the Vanilla Buttercream is used to make this vividly colored and fruity tasting raspberry filling. I like it seeds and all, but if you prefer you may puree the berries first, strain out the seeds, and then beat the puree into the buttercream. Beat the raspberries into the buttercream right before you are going to use it; the flavor and color will be brighter than if you add them ahead of time. In a pinch, unsweetened frozen raspberries may be used in the buttercream. However, if you want to add a layer of raspberries nestled in the center layer of buttercream, they need to be impeccably fresh, dry, and firm; frozen will not work.

RASPBERRY BUTTERCREAM FILLING

9 cups reserved Vanilla Buttercream, at room temperature

1½ cups raspberries (more or less to taste)

5¼ cups fresh, firm, and dry raspberries (optional)

1 Have the buttercream in the mixer's bowl. Add about ¾ cup raspberries to the buttercream and mix in on medium speed. The berries will break down and become incorporated into the buttercream. Add the remaining ¾ cup berries, adjusting for color and taste, mixing until well blended. The buttercream will be a bright pink with bits of berry here and there. There will be a point where the buttercream will not absorb any more berries; that's how you tell when you've added enough.

2 The buttercream is ready to use. If you also want to nestle fresh raspberries in the central buttercream layer of each tier, use the optional raspberries and follow the instructions in the assembly section below. You will use ¾ cup fresh raspberries for the the 6-inch tier, 1½ cups for the 9-inch tier, and 3 cups for the 12-inch tier.

Assemble the Cake and Cover with Chocolate Curls: Before assembling, have all the components made and ready to use. Have all your tools and equipment on hand, and make sure there is space for the tiers in the refrigerator.

1 Level and torte the cake layers (see pages 27–29)

2 Moisten the cake layers, fill, and assemble each tier (see pages 29–32) as follows: Cardboard, first cake layer, syrup, Raspberry Buttercream Filling (see note on page 93), corresponding second layer, syrup, Raspberry Buttercream Filling. Now pause and nestle fresh berries in this center layer of buttercream, if you like. Finish with third cake layer, syrup, Raspberry Buttercream Filling, corresponding fourth layer, syrup.

3 Apply the crumb coat with Vanilla Buttercream (see page 32). Chill until firm. Meanwhile, prepare your cake base (see page 37).

4 Apply the final coat (see page 35) of Vanilla Buttercream. While the buttercream is still soft, gently press and place white chocolate curls all over the sides of the tiers. Chill again, if time allows. Place the 14-inch tier on the center of the cake base.

5 Center and stack the remaining tiers using dowels for internal support (see pages 38–39). Place more chocolate curls on the tops of the tiers so that the entire cake is covered with chocolate curls. Mound the curls on the top tier to give a rounded appearance. Chill overnight. Bring extra curls with you to the reception site.

N O T E : *When you are spreading the raspberry buttercream on the layers as filling, do not go all the way to the edge of the cake. Leave about 1/4 inch bare. Then, when you apply the crumb coat on the tier's sides, press some of the Vanilla Buttercream into those gaps. This way, the pink Raspberry Buttercream Filling will not show on the outside of your cake, and the tiers will look completely white.*

Wedding Day

Decorate, Present! At the site of the wedding, place the cake in the center of the tablecloth-covered display table. Make sure your raspberries are fresh, firm, and dry. Place them here and there, along with the crystallized flowers (see photo for inspiration). Add more curls if necessary; the top of the cake might need more as the mounded curls might shift during transport. Serve at room temperature.

LEMON COCONUT CUPCAKE TOWER

This wedding-cake-shaped tower would be perfect for a shower (bridal or baby), a casual outdoor affair, or any wedding where whimsy might be appreciated. The cupcakes sit on graduated cake pedestals, which gives a unique look that is very easy to create. Different pedestals will hold different numbers of cupcakes, which is fine. If your set-up does not hold all 50, the remainder can be served from behind the scenes.

Unsweetened coconut in the cupcake batter provides coconut flavor without adding unnecessary sweetness. Lemon juice gives the moistening syrup a bit of a tang and creamy Lemon Curd is injected into the center of each cupcake. A thick swirl of Vanilla Buttercream crowns each cupcake, topped with a coating of long-shred sweetened coconut. Put it all together and you get a harmonious and luscious blend of lemon and coconut in a fanciful shape. Every cupcake is further adorned with a single, perfect crystallized flower. There is a healthy amount of buttercream on top of each cupcake because it is necessary to give them a pleasing domed appearance.

Serves 50

RECIPE COMPONENTS

- ✺ Coconut White Cupcakes
- ✺ Lemon Moistening Syrup
- ✺ Lemon Curd Filling
- ✺ Vanilla Buttercream

DECORATION

- ✺ Sweetened long-shred coconut (13 cups)
- ✺ Crystallized Flowers (50, plus extra in case of breakage)

SPECIAL EQUIPMENT

- ✺ Muffin tins (ideally enough to bake 25 cupcakes at once)
- ✺ Ateco large #802 tip, and Ateco large #885 tip
- ✺ A cake platter and 2 or 3 cake pedestals (see Equipment Tips)
- ✺ Any pastel tablecloth, to pick up colors from crystallized flowers
- ✺ Cupcake liners for 50 cupcakes

For making Crystallized Flowers:
- ✺ Cooling rack with horizontal and vertical bars
- ✺ Tweezers
- ✺ 2 soft, small artist's brushes

TIMELINE

- ✺ **Up to 1 Month Ahead:**
  Make the Vanilla Buttercream, Moistening Syrup Base, and Crystallized Flowers (if making)
- ✺ **Up to 1 Week Ahead:**
  Make the Lemon Curd Filling
- ✺ **1 Day Ahead:**
  Finish making the Lemon Moistening Syrup and Make the Coconut White Cupcakes, Fill and Frost the Cupcakes
- ✺ **Shower or Wedding Day:**
  Assemble, Decorate, Present!

95

Up to 1 Month Ahead

Make the Vanilla Buttercream: Make the Essential Buttercream (see page 69) 4 times; add 1 tablespoon vanilla extract to each batch.

Make the Moistening Syrup Base: The moistening syrup can be made ahead but should not be flavored with lemon juice until right before using. Make the Essential Moistening Syrup (see page 68) 1 time, but do not use the vanilla bean or vanilla extract.

Make the Crystallized Flowers: If you are making your own Crystallized Flowers, you must first choose edible flowers that are unsprayed. For these cupcakes, I suggest pansies, small roses, or rose petals (see page 48 for a list of other edible flowers).

Do not start working with the flower you like the best! Practice on a few until you get the hang of it. These must be made at least 2 days in advance so that the flowers can dry completely. Refer to Special Equipment list for tools you will need.

CRYSTALLIZED FLOWERS

50 pansies, small roses, or rose petals
3 large egg whites
2 cups superfine sugar

1   Make sure that the flowers are clean and dry. Place the egg whites in a small bowl and whisk gently to break them up. Fill a shallow bowl or plate with superfine sugar.
2   Place the cooling rack over aluminum foil or parchment to catch the extra sugar.
3   Pick up 1 of the flowers with the tweezers or your fingers holding the base, taking care not to bruise the petals. Now spread the petals apart gently with your fingers or with one of the brushes, allowing all of the surfaces to be exposed. Then, with the other paintbrush, apply a thin, even coat of egg white to the flower so that the entire surface is coated. You must coat the entire flower at this point as you cannot go back and patch areas after sugar is applied. Doing so makes for an uneven, thick, and unsightly layer of sugar.
4   Hold the flower over the bowl containing the sugar. Use a teaspoon to scoop up and sprinkle the sugar gently over the flower to coat evenly. You want one even coat. Place the flower on the rack to dry. Repeat with the remaining flowers. The flowers must dry completely before they can be used, which might take a day or longer. If you have a gas oven with a pilot light, place the rack on a tray in the oven with the oven off and leave overnight. The flowers will dry perfectly.

Ingredients Tips:

⋙ You need two kinds of coconut for this recipe. The unsweetened coconut in the batter, sometimes called desiccated coconut (which doesn't sound good, but is!) is sold in bulk sections of whole foods stores; it has a very fine shred.

The coconut used on top of the cupcakes is sweetened and has a long shred. You can find this kind in most any supermarket, sometimes labeled as "angel-flake."

⋙ If you crystallize your own flowers, you will need superfine sugar, occasionally called bar sugar. It will give the flowers a sparkly, velvety quality that regular sugar cannot duplicate. Do not buzz regular sugar in a food processor; it will turn powdery and lose its sparkle.

Decoration Tip:

⋙ While you are certainly welcome to make your own crystallized flowers, I highly recommend ordering the gorgeous flowers from Meadowsweets, as we did for the photo (see Sources).

5 Dry storage is important. Line shallow, airtight containers with several layers of paper towels and place the flowers in a single layer on top of towels. Put a Blue Magic device alongside the flowers before sealing the container to help keep them dry (see Sources). They can last for months, but they are very fragile. Make sure to gently move the container when placing it on and taking it off a storage shelf or counter.

Up to 1 Week Ahead

Make the Lemon Curd Filling: A tangy, creamy lemon curd serves as the moist filling for these cupcakes—piped into the center with a pastry bag. It must be made at least the day before the cupcakes are filled so that the curd is cold and firm. If you have any leftover, simply refrigerate it in an airtight container and spread on toast or stir into yogurt. A dollop on top of fresh fruit is nice, too.

LEMON CURD FILLING

Makes 3 cups

$^1/_2$ cup freshly squeezed lemon juice
4 large eggs
2 large egg yolks
1$^1/_2$ cups sugar
$^3/_4$ cup (1$^1/_2$ sticks) unsalted butter, at room temperature,
    cut into tablespoon-sized pieces
2 teaspoons finely grated lemon zest (optional)

1 Place all the ingredients except the butter and zest in the top of a double boiler or a heatproof bowl. Whisk together just enough to break up the eggs, and add the butter. Place over the bottom of the double boiler or a saucepan that is filled with enough hot water to just barely touch the bottom of the bowl. Place over medium heat and bring the water to a simmer.
2 Cook, whisking frequently, for about 25 minutes or until the mixture reaches 180°. (It might take longer; just use visual cues.) When done, the mixture will have thickened and will form soft mounds when dropped from a spoon. Remove from the heat and stir in the optional zest. Let cool to room temperature, scrape into an airtight container, and refrigerate overnight.

1 Day Ahead

Finish making the Lemon Moistening Syrup: Stir in 1$^1/_2$ cups freshly squeezed lemon juice to the entire batch (or to taste). If you are making the syrup now, do not add lemon juice until the syrup has cooled completely.

Make the Coconut White Cupcakes: Make the Essential White Cake (see page 64) 2 times in the 10-inch size and 1 time in the 8-inch size (enough batter for 50 cupcakes) with the following changes: prepare standard-sized muffin tins by coating the tops of the muffin tins with nonstick spray and lining them with paper liners. (If using silver foil liners, they may be used without muffin tins and simply placed on a baking sheet.)

Use only 1½ teaspoons vanilla for the 8-inch recipe and 1 tablespoon vanilla for each 10-inch recipe. Fold ¾ cup unsweetened coconut into the batter along with the flour mixture for the 8-inch recipe; fold 1¼ cups unsweetened coconut into the batter for each 10-inch recipe.

Bake the cupcakes for about 25 minutes, or until a toothpick just tests clean. Place the tins on a rack to cool for 3 minutes, then unmold and cool the cupcakes completely on racks. I like to bake cupcakes the day before serving. While most cake components in this book may be baked up to 2 days ahead, cupcakes are smaller and can dry out more quickly. They are best baked as close to the serving day as possible.

Fill and Frost the Cupcakes: Before assembling, have all the components made and ready to use. Have all your tools and equipment on hand.

1 Place the cupcakes on baking sheets to catch crumbs. Take a wooden skewer or toothpick and poke each cupcake about half-a-dozen times. Brush Lemon Moistening Syrup on top of each cupcake once; when you have finished the 50th cupcake, go back and apply syrup for a second soaking; you will still have some syrup leftover which you can use for other baking projects.

2 Take a pastry bag and insert Ateco large #802 tip. Fill the bag halfway with Lemon Curd Filling. Insert the tip into the center of the top of a cupcake and press into the center of the cupcake. Squeeze the bag to fill the cupcake with lemon curd. Apply pressure to the pastry bag gently; as soon as you see the top of the cupcake puff a little, you know you have filled the cupcake properly. If the top of the cupcake cracks a bit, that's OK; it will be covered with buttercream.

3 Once all the cupcakes are filled, fit a clean pastry bag with Ateco large #885 tip, and fill it halfway with buttercream. Each cupcake gets a hefty swirl of buttercream. Starting at the edge of the cupcake liner, begin piping a ring of buttercream around the outer edge of cupcake. When you come to the beginning/end of the circle, continue piping slightly inside the first ring for a much smaller second ring, and then finish off with a swirl on the top. The buttercream should be higher in the center. You want a nice large dome of buttercream (see photo).

Equipment Tips:

↝ Choosing cupcake liners is important, as it affects the visual presentation of your cake. You could go with white (as we did) or pastel, or liners with hearts, flowers, or some other design. Silver and gold foil are an option as well.

If you use foil, please test the cupcakes for doneness shortly before the suggested time, as they might bake a little quicker. The advantage of the silver foil liners is that they can be used without muffin tins. They are simply lined up on a baking sheet.

↝ There are a couple of ways to approach constructing your tower. You can use a platter with two pedestals. (I recommend a 12-inch platter or flat cake plate and 10-inch and 8-inch pedestals.) Or, for a taller look, as in the photograph, try three pedestals measuring approximately 12, 10, and 8 inches across. Make sure that the pedestals are at least 4 inches tall so that the cupcakes fit.

Every setup will be different and might hold anywhere from 30 to 50 cupcakes. Additional cupcakes can just be served from behind the scenes.

Crate and Barrel has lovely selections of glass and china pedestals that will all work beautifully (see Sources).

- To secure the pedestals on the display table, you can use something like UHU Tac, a removable adhesive putty found in art supply stores, that will hold the pedestal bases to the plates below them.
- Make sure you have enough airtight containers deep enough to hold all of the cupcakes in a single layer. Shoe-box-sized ones are perfect. After you decorate the cupcakes, you will store and transport them in these containers. You will also need containers to hold the crystallized flowers, if you are making your own.

4 Place the sweetened long-shred coconut in a bowl. (If you want, you can toast half of the coconut, both for color and increased flavor: spread it on a rimmed baking sheet and toast at 350° until light golden brown, about 5 minutes, shaking the coconut once or twice during baking. Cool completely before tossing with raw, white coconut and proceeding.) Take each cupcake and hold it over the bowl while you use your fingers to gently press coconut all over the surface of the buttercream. Alternately, you can try rolling the buttercream portion of the cupcake around in the coconut, then patch any bare spots using your fingers. Store in single layers in airtight containers.

Wedding Day

Assemble, Decorate, Present! At the wedding site, place the bottom platter in the center of a tablecloth-covered display table and arrange the pedestals on top. To secure the pedestals to one another and to the base, you can use sticky temporary glue such as UHU Tac (see Equipment Tips). Take a wad and place it on the center of the platter and affix the middle pedestal to it. Similarly affix the smallest pedestal to the middle one. This will minimize the chances of the tower tipping over. It won't damage your display items.

Gently, but firmly, press a crystallized flower on top of each cupcake. You need to press them through the coconut so that they can stick to some buttercream. Fill the open areas of the platter and middle pedestal with cupcakes. The top pedestal will hold about 7 cupcakes in one layer. Place 3 on top of that and then save the prettiest cupcake as the crowning touch on top. Different pedestals will suggest different arrangement; go with the flow and just arrange a pretty display. Any extra cupcakes can be served from the kitchen. Serve at room temperature.

STRAWBERRY SHORTCAKE AND MERINGUE CAKE

This cake looks and tastes like the summer. Ripe, luscious strawberries nestle between layers of Essential Yellow Cake and crunchy discs of Vanilla Meringue, with Vanilla Buttercream inside and out. The tiers are tall, due to the additional meringue layer, and raised slightly by embedded pillars. Vertical ribbons of piped buttercream accent the cake's height.

Any kind of delicate flower can peak out from between the tiers, but I chose sweet peas because I like how the frilly, casual-looking petals contrast with the tall, formal dimensions of the cake—an interesting play of up- and downscale. (Maybe the bride has a fancy dress but wants her dog in the ceremony!) A white chocolate monogram combining the bridal couple's initials may crown the top as an option. It can be covered with silver or gold leaf or left plain, showing off the creamy color of the white chocolate.

Serves 100

RECIPE COMPONENTS

- Yellow Cake
- Vanilla Meringue Discs
- Vanilla Bean Moistening Syrup
- Vanilla Buttercream

DECORATION

- Assorted pastel sweet peas (about 50 stalks)
- White Chocolate Monogram, 4 to 5 inches around (optional)

SPECIAL EQUIPMENT

- Two 6 × 2-inch, two 10 × 2-inch, and two 14 × 2-inch round pans with corresponding cardboard rounds
- Ateco #45, #806, and #895 tips
- 16-inch round cake base
- 7-inch and 11-inch separator plates
- 8 trimmable (hollow) pillars
- A pink and white striped silk tablecloth

For making White Chocolate Monogram

- Silver or gold leaf (most likely 3 sheets), optional
- Tweezers
- 2 small artist's brushes

TIMELINE

- **Up to 1 Month Ahead:**
  Make the White Chocolate Monogram (optional), the Vanilla Buttercream, and the Vanilla Bean Moistening Syrup
- **Up to 4 Days Ahead:**
  Make the Vanilla Meringue Discs
- **2 Days Ahead:**
  Make the Yellow Cake
- **1 Day Ahead:**
  Prepare the Strawberries for Filling and Assemble the Cake Tiers
- **Wedding Day:**
  Place Tiers on Pillars, Decorate, Present!

Up to 1 Month Ahead

Make the White Chocolate Monogram (Optional): To form the white chocolate monogram, you need a monogram template. Look for ideas in books that provide lettering and draw or photocopy a monogram on a piece of paper. Thicker, block-style lettering will be easier to copy (see photo).

Silver or gold leaf can be purchased from some cake decorating stores or art stores.

8 ounces white chocolate coating, such as Wilton Candy Melts, finely chopped
1 large egg white, optional

Making outline with melted chocolate in parchment cone

1 Melt white chocolate coating (see Ingredient Tips) in a double boiler or microwave. You will not need it all for one monogram, but I suggest you make multiple chocolate monograms in case of breakage. Meanwhile, place the traced monogram on a perfectly flat baking sheet and cover with parchment. You should be able to see the monogram beneath.

2 Place the melted coating in a parchment cone (see instructions on page 105) and snip a small opening. Begin by piping the outline of the monogram. Refrigerate for 5 minutes, or until the outline is firm. Now flood the center of the outline with melted chocolate; chill again. Do not peel the monogram off of the paper until you are ready to transfer it to the cake top. Repeat and make at least 2 more monograms.

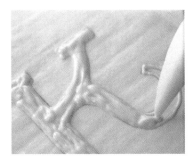

Flooding the outline with chocolate

3 To cover the monogram with silver or gold leaf, whisk egg white in a small bowl until frothy. Very lightly brush the chilled and firm monogram with the egg white using one of the brushes. You are just trying to lightly and evenly moisten the monogram. Pick up a sheet of silver or gold leaf with tweezers and allow it to fall on top of the monogram. Use the second dry brush to gently press the leaf onto the monogram and remove any excess around the edges. Gently blowing straight down on the leaf can also coax it to lie flat. Continue applying leaf to cover the entire monogram. Store at cool room temperature or in the refrigerator in an airtight container.

Make the Vanilla Buttercream: Make the Essential Buttercream (see page 69) 6 times, with the following changes: beat 1 tablespoon vanilla extract into each batch.

Make the Vanilla Bean Moistening Syrup: Make the Essential Moistening Syrup (see page 68) 2¹/₂ times.

Applying silver leaf to firm chocolate

Partially covered with silver leaf

Ingredient Tips:

- If you choose to make a monogram, which is not necessarily to eat, I suggest you use white chocolate coating as opposed to real chocolate, as it is easier to work with and does not need to be tempered. Wilton Candy Melts is one brand that is available nationally and through mail order (see Sources).
- Use strawberries that are ripe, but not too soft, or they will exude too much juice. Don't go by color with strawberries. Some that are tinged with green can actually be quite sweet. If possible, taste before you buy.

Up to 4 Days Ahead

Make the Vanilla Meringue Discs: Meringue is simply a mixture of stiffly beaten egg whites and sugar, and here it is formed and baked into crunchy discs, which will be layered within the tiers. The discs are made 1 inch smaller than the cake layers so that their brittle edges do not interfere with the smooth, round shape of the tier's sides. Because the largest disk is too big to fit in the sheet pans, you will make 2 half-round shapes. No one will know once the halves are assembled within the stacked tiers, and "glued" together with buttercream. (Alternatively, if you have an extra 14-inch cake pan, you may bake the largest disc within it.)

Making the meringue is easy. Forming the discs sounds more complex than it really is. Follow these instructions carefully and you will get great results.

Meringue Discs

4 large egg whites
1/4 teaspoon cream of tartar
1 cup sugar
1/2 teaspoon vanilla extract

1 Preheat the oven to 250°. Line 3 baking sheets with parchment paper. Draw one 5-inch circle and one 9-inch circle on 1 parchment paper sheet. (A compass is the easiest way to do this, unless you have pans of required sizes to trace.) Draw half of a 13-inch circle on another pan and another 13-inch half-circle on the last pan. The easiest way to do this is to cut out a 13-inch parchment round, fold it in half, and use that as a template. Flip the parchments over so that the pen or pencil does not transfer to the meringue.

2 Place the egg whites in the clean, grease-free bowl of a mixer. Whip on medium speed with the wire whip attachment until frothy, about 1 minute. Add the cream of tartar, increase speed to high, and whip until soft peaks form, about 3 minutes. Gradually add the sugar and whip until stiff, but not dry, peaks form, about 3 minutes. Beat in vanilla extract.

3 Fit a pastry bag with Ateco #806 tip (no coupler needed) and fill it with the meringue. Pipe concentric circles (or half-circles) of meringue to completely fill your disc shapes with a single layer of meringue. Alternatively, you can carefully fill in the traced borders with meringue by spreading with an offset spatula to a 1/2 inch thickness.

4 Bake for about 2 hours or until completely dry to the touch. Place pans on racks to cool completely. Meringue discs must be stored completely flat and dry in an airtight container at room temperature.

2 Days Ahead

Make the Yellow Cake: Make the Essential Yellow Cake (see page 61) in the 6-inch, 10-inch, and 14-inch sizes.

1 Day Ahead

Prepare the Strawberries for Filling: Prepare these less than an hour before using. Use 60 medium, ripe-but-firm strawberries (see Ingredient Tips). Very gently rinse the berries and dry with a cloth or paper towel. Hull the berries, then slice them vertically into 1/8-inch slices (thicker slices will cause the tiers to slide) and spread them out on a paper towel in a single layer, to blot up any extra juice.

Assemble the Cake Tiers: Before assembling, have all the components made and ready to use. Have all your tools and equipment on hand, and make sure there is space for the tiers in the refrigerator.

1 Level and torte the cake layers (see pages 27–29).
2 Moisten the cake layers, fill, and assemble each tier (see pages 29–32) as follows: Cardboard, first cake layer, syrup, buttercream, layer of berries, corresponding second layer, syrup, buttercream, meringue, buttercream, third cake layer, syrup, buttercream, layer of berries, corresponding fourth layer, syrup.
3 Apply the crumb coat with buttercream (see page 32), filling up the space left by the meringue discs, which are a tad smaller in diameter than the cake layers, making sure any air pockets along the cake's edges get filled with buttercream. Chill until firm. Meanwhile, prepare your cake base (see page 37).
4 Affix 6-inch and 10-inch tiers to separator plates. Apply the final coat of buttercream in a ribbon pattern to each tier as follows: Use an Ateco #895 tip (no coupler needed) to pipe overlapping vertical ribbons of buttercream, placing each ribbon as close to halfway over the last ribbon as possible (see Technique Note, below). End each ribbon so that it is just slightly higher than the tops of tiers. Don't worry about the tops being neat as they will be cleaned up and then covered by a ripple of ribbons circling the tier top.
5 Use a small offset spatula to even out the tops of the ribbons as follows: swipe the spatula over the peaks of each ribbon, moving from the outside of the cake toward the inside, so that the ribbons are even with the top of the cake. Chill, if time permits.
6 Place the 14-inch tier on the center of the cake base. Using Ateco #45 tip, pipe a ripple of flat, overlapping ribbons along the tops of each tier, covering the tops of the vertical ribbons (see instructions and photo, pages 44–45). If the bottoms of your vertical ribbons do not cover the cardboards, then pipe overlapping ribbons along the bottom edges as well. Chill overnight.

Equipment Tips:

↝ Make sure any equipment that will come into contact with the meringue, such as bowls, beaters, spatulas, pastry bags, and tips, are clean and grease-free. Any grease will prevent the egg whites from whipping into the volume that is needed.

↝ Make sure the baking sheets you use for baking the meringue discs are perfectly flat. I use sturdy, rimmed jelly-roll pans that have interior measurements of 11 3/4 inches by 16 1/2 inches. (Remember, if pans have rims, it's the interior measurements that count!)

Decoration Tip:

↜ I chose sweet peas for their frilly, pretty, feminine look. You could use other flowers, if these are not available, but obviously the look of the cake will change. Other flowers to consider are pansies, daisies, and nasturtiums, which all have a frilly appearance that would work with the cake's look.

As you can see in the photograph, the spaces between the tiers must be filled with flowers. Picture how the flower you choose would look. It isn't that you could not use tulips, but the look of the cake would be dramatically different from the photo—but if it is what you want, then by all means, use them! Whatever you use, make sure you buy plenty, so you're not caught short.

Technique Note: Piping the vertical ribbon pattern of buttercream on the outside of the cake is not difficult, but you'll want to practice getting the ribbons as uniform as possible. You can practice on an upended cake pan until you get the knack. Assemble a pastry bag with Ateco #895 tip and some buttercream.

Have the upended cake pan on a cake turntable. Bring yourself down to eye-level. Begin at the bottom of the pan and, holding the bag and tip directly in front of you at about a 45-degree angle to the cake, with the slit in the tip positioned horizontally, pipe a flat ribbon right against the pan, drawing the tip upwards as you go, releasing pressure as you reach the top. Don't worry if there are any peaks left at the top; you can fix them later as described in the recipe. If this movement feels awkward, try piping top to bottom; it might work better for you. To apply the second ribbon, repeat the motions as above, but begin this ribbon halfway overlapping the first ribbon. Obviously, any subsequent ribbons will not be flat against the cake, as half of their length will be propped up slightly from the previous ribbon. Just make them as flat as possible. Also, take care not to mar any previous ribbons, as it is hard to redo them.

Wedding Day

Place Tiers on Pillars, Decorate, Present! At the wedding site, place the cake base holding the 14-inch tier in the center of a tablecloth-covered display table. Trim the pillars so that there will be a 2-inch separation between layers when they are sunk all the way into the tiers. Attach the separator plates to the pillars, which have been sunk into the tiers (see pages 38–43 for instructions on working with pillars and separator places). Place the sweet peas so that they fill up the spaces between the tiers and peak out a bit; use your judgment as to how short to trim the flower stems. For the top tier, either form a mound of flowers, or place the monogram flat on the tier, if using. Serve at room temperature.

 To Make a Parchment Cone

Cut a triangle from parchment paper with two equal short sides and one longer side. The center of the long edge will become the point of the cone. Holding the triangle in front of you, with the long side facing left, place your left thumb and index finger at the center of the long side. Take the top corner and fold it down and under itself, pulling it toward the right, until it meets up with the corner that lies opposite the long side. Now move your thumb and index finger to hold these two new points together.

Take the other extended corner and wrap it around the entire outside of the cone so that it meets up with the first two—all three corners will be overlapping.

Jiggle the parchment back and forth so that the fit is perfect and the point is tight. Fold the three corners inward to secure the cone. The cone is ready to fill. (Never overfill.) Fill up about halfway, then fold the open edge over itself several times to make a seal. Snip off the point with sharp scissors. Make a very tiny opening for most uses. Discard bag when finished.

As an easy alternative, use a ziplock bag. Simply partially fill with melted chocolate or whatever you are piping, partially seal bag, then snip one of the bottom corners. Discard bag when finished.

MARZIPAN AND ORANGE ESSENSIA CAKE

This cake actually uses almond paste rather than marzipan (marzipan is sweetened almond paste often used in candy making), but marzipan sounded better in the title! Moist almond paste has a very distinct almond taste and it adds flavor and moistness to the cake. The syrup, flavored with Essensia, a sweet dessert wine made from the orange muscat grape, with flavors of apricot and orange blossoms, brings an elusive, elegant flavor. Tangy Orange Marmalade Buttercream fills the central layer, while a Vanilla Buttercream fills and frosts the rest. The décor is both textural and natural: the leaves and fruit provide a loose feel that is held in check and made elegant by the gold-brushed whole almonds and streamlined rows of sliced almonds along the sides. While the flavors and colors echo those found in Spain and the French Riviera, you don't have to have a destination wedding to indulge in this cake.

Serves 100

RECIPE COMPONENTS

- Marzipan Orange Cake
- Essensia Moistening Syrup
- Orange Marmalade Buttercream Filling
- Vanilla Buttercream

DECORATION

- Glacéed whole clementines or glacéed orange wedges, or a combination (2 dozen)
- Blanched, sliced almonds (16 cups; enough for you to choose the best ones)
- Gold-Dusted Whole Almonds (buy 1 dozen almonds in the shell)
- Whole kumquats (if they have nice leaves, use those too; 1 dozen)
- Small camellia or lemon leaves (2 dozen)

SPECIAL EQUIPMENT

- Two 6 × 2-inch, two 10 × 2-inch, and two 14 × 2-inch square pans, and corresponding cardboard squares
- 16-inch square cake base (can be covered with gold foil)
- 1/4-inch-thick wooden dowels (1 yard)
- Forest green or white tablecloth
- Small, soft artist's brush
- Gold Powder
- Vodka (optional)

TIMELINE

- **Up to 1 Month Ahead:**
  Make the Moistening Syrup Base, Orange Marmalade Buttercream Filling, and Vanilla Buttercream
- **2 Days Ahead:**
  Make the Marzipan Orange Cake and the Gold-Dusted Whole Almonds, Prepare the Sliced Almonds and the Other Decorations
- **1 Day Ahead:**
  Finish the Essensia Moistening Syrup, Assemble the Cake and Apply the Sliced Almonds to the Sides
- **Wedding Day:**
  Decorate, Present!

Up to 1 Month Ahead

Make the Moistening Syrup Base: The moistening syrup can be made ahead but should not be flavored with Essensia until right before using. Make the Essential Moistening Syrup (see page 68) 2 times, but do not use the vanilla bean or vanilla extract.

Make the Orange Marmalade Buttercream Filling: Make the Essential Buttercream (see page 69) 1 time. Take 5 cups of the buttercream and fold in 2¹/2 cups of orange marmalade. Add 1 teaspoon vanilla extract to the remaining 2 cups, and combine this with the Vanilla Buttercream (see below).

Make the Vanilla Buttercream: Make the Essential Buttercream (see page 69) 5 times, and beat 1 tablespoon vanilla extract into each batch. Combine with the 2 cups Vanilla Buttercream left over (see above).

2 Days Ahead

Make the Marzipan Orange Cake: Make the Essential Yellow Cake (see page 61) in 6-inch, 10-inch, and 14-inch square sizes: For the 6-inch square, make the 8-inch round recipe. Add 3 ounces almond paste by crumbling it and creaming with the butter and sugar. Use only ¹/2 teaspoon vanilla extract and add with it ¹/2 teaspoon almond extract and 1¹/2 teaspoons orange zest.

For the 10-inch square, make the 12-inch round recipe. Add 6 ounces almond paste. Use 1 teaspoon vanilla extract and add 1 teaspoon almond extract and 1 tablespoon plus 1 teaspoon orange zest.

For the 14-inch square, make the 6-inch round recipe once, and the 10-inch round recipe twice. For the 6-inch round recipe, add 2 ounces almond paste. Use ¹/4 teaspoon vanilla and add ¹/4 teaspoon almond extract and 1¹/4 teaspoons orange zest. For each 10-inch round recipe, add 5 ounces of almond paste. Use ³/4 teaspoon vanilla extract and add ³/4 teaspoon almond extract and 1 tablespoon orange zest. Baking times might be a bit longer than for round cakes of similar size.

Prepare the Sliced Almonds: Sort through the almonds and select the whole, unblemished, medium-sized ones. Uniformity is key for making perfect layers. Store the nuts in an airtight container at room temperature until needed.

Prepare the Other Decorations: To make the gold-dusted whole almonds, either brush on "paint" made by adding drops of vodka to a small bowl of gold powder (this will be vivid and shiny), or simply brush on dry gold powder (this will give a satiny, subtle effect)—or use a mixture of both techniques. After brushing, place the gold-dusted nuts on a work surface to dry for a few minutes. Store in single layers separated with with parchment paper in an airtight container at room temperature until

Ingredient Tips:

↪ Many well-stocked supermarkets carry two kinds of almond paste; one in a tube and one in a can. Use the canned, which has a better texture and flavor. The recipe will not work with the sweeter tube style. Check your local specialty store for high quality almond paste. American Almond makes a great product (see Sources).

↪ While you can use any dessert wine made from orange muscat grapes, Quady vineyards makes one called Essensia, which is exceptional and the one I used.

Equipment Tip:

↪ Square corners are notoriously difficult to make clean and neat when applying frosting. Try various offset spatulas to see which work best for you. Very small straight and offset spatulas work best for me.

Decoration Tips:

↪ Use blanched (skinned) sliced almonds for the sides. Make sure they are broad and flat (see photo), not the blanched slivered almonds, which look like splinters. The amount suggested in the recipe is a generous amount, which will allow you to sort out uniformly sized slices.

- Whole almonds in the shell can often be found in bulk sections of whole foods stores. Edible gold powder can be found at well-stocked cake decorating stores or ordered from Beryl's (see Sources).
- Whole glacéed clementines and glacéed orange wedges are specialty products and may be ordered from Fauchon, where they refer to them as "comfit" (see Sources).
- Fresh kumquats are in season during the fall and winter, and might have to be ordered from your produce supplier. To ensure they stay fresh, buy kumquats no more than 2 days in advance.

Applying sliced almonds to sides of tiers

needed. (Do this no more than 2 days ahead as the nuts lose their color as they roll around in storage.) Store the glacéed fruit in an airtight container at room temperature until needed. Kumquat fruits should be refrigerated until needed. Kumquat stems should be kept in water until needed. Just pluck off the leaves as you need them.

1 Day Ahead

Finish Making the Essensia Moistening Syrup: Stir in about 2 cups (or more or less, to taste) of Essensia wine. If you are making the syrup now, do not add the liqueur until the syrup has cooled completely.

Assemble the Cake and Apply the Almonds to the Sides: Before assembling, have all the components made and ready to use. Have all your tools and equipment on hand, and make sure there is space for the tiers in the refrigerator.

1 Level and torte the cake layers (see pages 27–29).
2 Moisten the cake layers, fill, and assemble each tier (see pages 29–32) as follows: Cardboard, first cake layer, syrup, Vanilla Buttercream, corresponding second layer, syrup, Marmalade Buttercream Filling, third cake layer, syrup, Vanilla Buttercream, corresponding fourth layer, syrup.
3 Apply the crumb coat with Vanilla Buttercream (see page 32). Chill until firm. Meanwhile, prepare your cake base (see page 37).
4 Apply the final smooth coat of Vanilla Buttercream (see page 35), taking special care with the corners. While the buttercream is still soft, affix the sliced almonds. Start at a right bottom corner and place an almond flat against the cake, with the long edge of the almond along the bottom of the cake and the point of the almond facing to the right. Place the next almond halfway over the first (see photo). Continue all the way around, completing the first row of almonds. Repeat until you have 3 rows. Chill again, if time allows. Place the 14-inch tier on the center of the cake base.
5 Center and stack the remaining tiers, using dowels for internal support (see pages 38–39). Chill overnight.

Wedding Day

Decorate, Present! At the site of the wedding, place the cake in the center of a table-cloth-covered display table. Place the glacéed oranges and kumquats here and there on the tops of the tiers, tucking the whole almonds and greenery alongside. Either place them in bunches, as I did, or arrange the fruit, nuts, and greenery any way you like (cascading, etc.). Serve at room temperature.

NUTELLA CAKE

I f the title of this cake caught your eye, it is probably because you are a Nutella fan! It used to be a specialty food product, but now you can find the jars right next to the peanut butter in most large supermarkets. It is creamy like peanut butter, but the chocolate hazelnut taste is sophisticated.

The filling in this round-tiered cake is Nutella itself; the rest of the cake was developed with flavors that would support the silky filling. This is a perfect example of how one aspect, in this case the Nutella, dictated the whole cake! It doesn't matter how you design a cake, as long as it is the cake that speaks to you. The cake is covered with a pale chocolate buttercream and curls of gianduja (hazelnut-flavored chocolate), as well as chocolate-dipped hazelnuts. The gianduja will have to be purchased at a specialty food store or mail-ordered. This cake has a very restrained look, which I think works well as a groom's cake or a second-wedding cake. I was inspired to offer you a cake that had lush, rich flavors but with a more restrained design—there is something for everyone!

Serves 100

RECIPE COMPONENTS

- Yellow Cake
- Light Chocolate Buttercream
- Frangelico Moistening Syrup
- Nutella Filling

DECORATION

- Chocolate-dipped hazelnuts
- Gianduja chocolate curls
- Dutch-processed cocoa (optional)

SPECIAL EQUIPMENT

- Two 6 × 2-inch, two 10 × 2-inch, and two 14 × 2-inch round pans, and corresponding cardboard rounds
- Ateco #10 tip (optional)
- 16-inch round cake base (can be covered with gold foil)
- 1/4-inch-thick wooden dowels (1 yard)
- A burgundy tablecloth would bring a masculine air. A bright pink cloth lightens up the deep chocolate tones.
- Toothpicks for dipping nuts in chocolate
- Styrofoam for holding chocolate-dipped nuts

TIMELINE

- **Up to 1 Month Ahead:** Make the Light Chocolate Buttercream and the Moistening Syrup Base
- **Up to 1 Week Ahead:** Make the Chocolate-Dipped Hazelnuts and the Gianduja Chocolate Curls
- **2 Days Ahead:** Make the Yellow Cake
- **1 Day Ahead:** Finish Making the Hazelnut Moistening Syrup, Prepare the Nutella Filling, Assemble and Decorate the Cake
- **Wedding Day:** Present!

111

Up to 1 Month Ahead

Make the Light Chocolate Buttercream: Make the Essential Buttercream (see page 69) 4 times with the following changes: add 14 ounces melted and cooled bittersweet chocolate to each batch. Just beat it in after the Essential Buttercream is done. Make sure that the color of each batch is as similar as possible; beat the completed batches together if necessary.

Make the Moistening Syrup Base: The moistening syrup can be made ahead but should not be flavored with Frangelico until right before using. Make the Essential Moistening Syrup (see page 68) 2 times but do not use the vanilla bean or vanilla extract.

Up to 1 Week Ahead

Make the Chocolate-Dipped Hazelnuts: Use 2 1/4 cups peeled hazelnuts and 2 pounds bittersweet couverture chocolate. Simply temper the chocolate as described on page 13. Insert a toothpick into the broad, rounded end of each nut, and dip the top, pointed end into the chocolate so that the chocolate covers half of the nut. Each nut should have a little cap of chocolate.

Stick the toothpicks in the Styrofoam (see photo) and chill the nuts until the chocolate has hardened. You can make these in batches. When the chocolate is firm, remove the nuts from the toothpicks and place them, chocolate-side up, in an airtight plastic container. Line the bottom of the container with paper towels so that the nuts don't roll around. Repeat with the remaining nuts. Store in the refrigerator until ready to use.

Make the Gianduja Chocolate Curls: Gianduja is softer than pure chocolate and very easy to make curls with. Use 2 1/2 pounds gianduja chocolate (in large solid blocks). Simply shave off curls from a block of gianduja with a sharp vegetable peeler (see photos). If your peeler doesn't seem to be doing the job, it might not be sharp enough, also, some of them do not cut at the right angle. Sometimes I get good results with a triangular, flat cheese plane to make curls. Try it, if you have one. You should have about 15 cups of curls of various sizes.

2 Days Ahead

Make the Yellow Cake: Make the Essential Yellow Cake (see page 61) in the 6-inch, 10-inch, and 14-inch sizes.

1 Day Ahead

Finish making the Frangelico Moistening Syrup: Stir in about 1 1/4 cups (or more or less, to taste) Frangelico to the entire batch. If you are making the syrup now, do not add the liqueur until the syrup has cooled completely.

Ingredient Tips:

- Frangelico is a lovely hazelnut-flavored liqueur and the brand I use; it is easy to find in wine and spirit stores.
- Buy peeled, toasted hazelnuts for the decoration, which will save you time.
- The gianduja can be found in specialty stores or through mail-order (see Sources); make sure to buy the kind made with milk chocolate, not dark chocolate. I use Callebaut brand.

Chilled chocolate-dipped hazelnuts set into Styrofoam

A curl beginning to form

Completing a curl

Prepare the Nutella Filling: The filling is simply Nutella spread onto the layers straight out of the jar. You will need 12¼ cups Nutella (thirteen 13-ounce jars). Make sure the Nutella is at warm room temperature, otherwise it will be hard to spread and will pull up crumbs. If it is hard to spread, warm it very gently in the microwave or set it in a pan of hot water until softened. (FYI: every 13-ounce jar of Nutella yields about 1 cup.)

Assemble and Decorate the Cake: Before assembling, have all the components made and ready to use. Have all your tools and equipment on hand, and make sure there is space for the tiers in the refrigerator.

1. Level and torte the cake layers (see pages 27–29).
2. Moisten the cake layers, fill, and assemble each tier (see pages 29–32) as follows: Cardboard, first cake layer, syrup, Nutella Filling, corresponding second layer, syrup, Nutella Filling, third cake layer, syrup, Nutella Filling, corresponding fourth layer, syrup.
3. Apply the crumb coat with Light Chocolate Buttercream (see page 32). Chill until firm. Meanwhile, prepare your cake base (see page 37).
4. Apply the final coat of buttercream (see page 35). While the buttercream is still soft, press the gianduja chocolate curls all over the sides of the tiers (see photograph for placement ideas). Carefully place the 14-inch tier on the center of the cake base.
5. Center and stack the remaining tiers using dowels for internal support, taking care not to smudge the soft buttercream (see pages 38–39). Touch up any buttercream, if necessary. Place additional curls in any leftover spaces, as needed. Place the chocolate-dipped hazelnuts, chocolate side up, all around the outer top edge of each tier, forming a decorative ring of nuts. If you like, fit a pastry bag and coupler with Ateco #10 tip and pipe a bead border along the bottom edges. (We did not for the photograph.) If the cardboard rounds under each tier are showing, this would be a good reason to pipe a border. Chill overnight.

> **Technique Note:** You will be handling the tiers quite a bit while the buttercream is soft, so take special care not to smudge them. You need the buttercream to stay soft so you can press the curls onto the sides and nestle the hazelnuts along the top edges.

Wedding Day

Present! At the wedding site, place the cake in the center of a tablecloth-covered display table. Additional gianduja curls may be placed on the tops of the tiers, if desired. For added visual interest, dust the cake with a light coating of cocoa sprinkled through a fine-mesh sieve. Serve at room temperature.

ORANGE MOCHA CAKE

range, chocolate, and coffee meld in this cake for a sophisticated blend of flavors. I can see this cake appealing to a more adult bridal couple, possibly even at a second wedding. It often appeals as much to grooms as it does to brides. The cake is our Essential Yellow Cake made with added orange zest. The syrup and exterior buttercream are flavored with Grand Marnier and orange juice concentrate; the filling is a deep, dark, rich espresso-flavored bittersweet chocolate ganache. The stacked round tiers are decorated with roses and tulips, in orange, russet, and apricot tones, and candied orange wedges, while the smooth, creamy sides are punctuated by little squares of candied orange peel and dark greenery.

Serves 100

RECIPE COMPONENTS
- Yellow Cake with Orange Zest
- Orange Moistening Syrup
- Espresso Ganache Filling
- Orange Buttercream

DECORATION
- Apricot-, orange-, and russet-colored roses and tulips (about 30 total)
- Candied orange wedges (about 1 dozen)
- Lemon leaves
- Diced orange peel (about 1 cup)

SPECIAL EQUIPMENT
- Two 6 × 2-inch, two 10 × 2-inch, and two 14 × 2-inch round pans with corresponding cardboard rounds
- Ateco #67 tip
- 16-inch round cake base (can be covered with bronze-colored foil)
- 1/4-inch-thick wooden dowels (1 yard)
- Orange or cocoa brown are good tablecloth colors

TIMELINE
- Up to 1 Month Ahead: Make the Moistening Syrup Base and the Orange Buttercream
- Up to 1 Week Ahead: Make the Espresso Ganache Filling
- 2 Days Ahead: Prepare the Flowers and Make the Yellow Cake with Orange Zest
- 1 Day Ahead: Assemble the Cake
- Wedding Day: Decorate, Present!

Up to 1 Month Ahead

Make the Moistening Syrup Base: The moistening syrup can be made ahead but should not be flavored with orange juice concentrate and Grand Marnier until right before using. Make the Essential Moistening Syrup (see page 68) 2 times, but do not use the vanilla bean or vanilla extract.

Make the Orange Buttercream: Make the Essential Buttercream (see page 69) 5 times with the following changes: beat 2 tablespoons defrosted orange juice concentrate and 3 tablespoons Grand Marnier into each batch.

Up to 1 Week Ahead

Make the Espresso Ganache Filling: Make the Bittersweet Chocolate Ganache (see page 151) 3 times with the following changes: add 2 teaspoons espresso powder to each batch—simply whisk it into the warmed cream to dissolve before pouring the cream over the chocolate. Refrigerate until ready to use.

2 Days Ahead

Prepare the Flowers: If you buy the roses a day or two ahead, they will have time to open and relax. You can also place the roses in warm water to encourage them to open a bit if they are closed and tightly furled. When they open sufficiently, they can be put in cold water in the refrigerator (if you have space) or a cool room. An open rose is more lush and romantic looking, but it is also nice to have them in various stages of bloom. The tulips usually come ready to go, so keep them in cool water in a cool room until needed or pick them up the day before or the day of the event.

Make the Yellow Cake with Orange Zest: Make the Essential Yellow Cake (see page 61) in 6-inch, 10-inch, and 14-inch sizes, with the following changes: add 1 tablespoon orange zest to the 6-inch recipe; beat it into the butter and sugar mixture. Beat in 2 tablespoons plus 1 1/2 teaspoons orange zest to each 10-inch recipe (the 14-inch cake is made from two 10-inch recipes).

> **Technique Note:** When you remove zest from citrus fruit, make sure to remove just the colored part of the peel and none of the bitter white pith underneath. I use a microplane zester, which effortlessly removes just the zest (see Sources).

Ingredient Tips:

↬ Use firm, thick-skinned oranges for orange zest, such as navel oranges. Scrub them well first to remove any wax.

↬ For the espresso powder for the filling, I like Medaglia D'Oro brand. Regular instant coffee will not give you the right flavor.

↬ Grand Marnier is an orange-flavored liqueur based on cognac, and it has a deep, rich flavor. Do not substitute the less expensive Triple Sec.

Decoration Tips:

↬ You can buy the flowers from a florist or direct from a local grower, but you should plan to preorder them. Now, you are probably thinking that no local grower is going to have roses in these exact colors, and you are probably right. However, the idea is that I have provided you with a color palette. Maybe they have other flowers of similar colors that will give you the look you want. Always feel free to experiment.

For the candied orange decorations, buy long elegant strips of candied orange peel and, if you can find them, glossy glacéed wedges. Strips are fairly easy to find and you can use them as-is or cut into dice. If you want to splurge and use glacéed orange wedges to nestle with the flowers, you will need to special-order them from Fauchon, where they call them "comfit" (see Sources).

1 Day Ahead

Finish making the Orange Moistening Syrup: stir in $1/2$ cup defrosted orange juice concentrate and $1/2$ cup Grand Marnier (or to taste) to the entire batch. If you are making the syrup now, do not add flavorings until the syrup has cooled completely.

Assemble the Cake: Before assembling, have all the components made and ready to use. Have all your tools and equipment on hand, and make sure there is space for the tiers in the refrigerator.

1 Level and torte the cake layers (see pages 27–29).
2 Moisten the cake layers, fill, and assemble each tier (see pages 29–32) as follows: Cardboard, first cake layer, syrup, ganache, corresponding second layer, syrup, ganache, third cake layer, syrup, ganache, corresponding fourth layer, syrup.
3 Apply the crumb coat with Orange Buttercream (see page 32). Chill until firm. Meanwhile, prepare your cake base (see page 37).
4 Apply the final smooth coat of buttercream (see page 35). Position the small dice of candied peel randomly or in a pattern on the sides of the tiers; press gently to adhere to the soft buttercream. Chill again, if time allows. Place the 14-inch tier on the center of the cake base.
5 Center and stack the remaining tiers using dowels for internal support (see pages 38–39). Fit a pastry bag and coupler with Ateco #67 tip. Pipe an overlapping leaf border along the bottom edges of the tiers (see instructions and photo, page 45). Scatter more diced orange peel on the tops of the tiers, if desired. Chill overnight.

Wedding Day

Decorate, Present! At the wedding site, place the cake in the center of the tablecloth-covered display table. Trim the flower stems to about $1/2$ to 1 inch. Arrange the flowers and candied orange wedges on tops of the tiers, and place greenery on the tops and sides of the cake tiers (see photo for inspiration). Serve at room temperature.

HAZELNUT PRALINE AND APRICOT CAKE

This sophisticated finale blends the soft white color of Vanilla Buttercream with the rich green of the "leaf" doily and the purples and lavenders of the lilacs and champagne grapes; you could imagine this lushly appointed cake being served anywhere from a Renaissance-inspired wedding to a soiree at the country club.

This cake features the basic yellow cake enhanced with ground hazelnuts. Frangelico, a hazelnut liqueur, adds flavor to the moistening syrup; the hazelnut flavor is further bolstered by a crushed hazelnut praline buttercream filling on 2 of the layers. The other layer sports a ribbon of whole-fruit apricot jam. The round tiers are covered with off-white Vanilla Buttercream and the sides are partially covered with additional crushed praline for visual and gustatory texture. The tiers are just slightly set off of one another to allow the fresh décor to appear to float in between and cascade about. While the leaf doily is optional, it looks smashing. It is easy to make, but takes a lot of time, so plan accordingly.

Serves 60

RECIPE COMPONENTS
- Yellow Cake with Ground Hazelnuts
- Frangelico Moistening Syrup
- Hazelnut Praline Buttercream Filling
- Apricot Filling
- Vanilla Buttercream

DECORATION
- Crushed hazelnut praline
- Purple and lavender lilacs (12 clusters of each color)
- Champagne grapes (12 clusters)

SPECIAL EQUIPMENT
- Two 8 × 2-inch and two 12 × 2-inch round pans with corresponding cardboard rounds
- 14-inch round cake base (can be covered with dark green foil if not using leaf doily)
- 9-inch separator plate
- 4 trimmable (hollow) pillars
- Leafy doily or pale sage green tablecloth
- Release nonstick aluminum foil

TIMELINE
- **Up to 1 Month Ahead:**
  Make Vanilla Buttercream, Moistening Syrup Base, Hazelnut Praline, and Hazelnut Praline Buttercream Filling
- **2 Weeks Ahead:**
  Order Lilacs, Grapes, and Leaves
- **2 Days Ahead:**
  Make Yellow Cake with Ground Hazelnuts
- **1 Day Ahead:**
  Finish Making the Frangelico Moistening Syrup and Prepare Apricot Filling, Make Leaf Doily (If Using), and Assemble Tiers
- **Wedding Day:**
  Place Tiers on Pillars, Decorate, Present!

Up to 1 Month Ahead

Make the Vanilla Buttercream: Make the Essential Buttercream (see page 69) 3 times, with the following changes: add 1 tablespoon vanilla extract to each batch. Four cups of this will be used to make the Hazelnut Praline Buttercream Filling (see below).

Make the Moistening Syrup Base: The moistening syrup can be made ahead but should not be flavored with Frangelico until right before using. Make the Essential Moistening Syrup (see page 68) 1½ times but do not use the vanilla bean or vanilla extract.

Make the Hazelnut Praline: The praline is an ingredient in the Hazelnut Praline Buttercream Filling, and is also used to decorate the sides of the cake.

Hazelnut Praline

Praline is a mixture of caramelized sugar and nuts, in this case hazelnuts, but you can substitute almonds, if you like. (Use either blanched or natural almonds.) For our purposes, part of the praline will be finely ground and added to buttercream for filling, and part will be more coarsely ground and used as décor on the outside of the cake. Store the praline in an airtight container with a Blue Magic insert—this is very important, as praline will become very sticky in humid weather or if not stored properly (see Sources).

3 cups peeled hazelnuts (or natural or blanched almonds)
3 cups sugar
¾ cup water

1 First, lightly toast the nuts. Peeled hazelnuts will already be toasted through their peeling process. For almonds, preheat the oven to 350°, spread the almonds on a rimmed baking sheet in a single layer, and bake until lightly browned, shaking once or twice during baking. Check after 5 minutes, and continue baking until done. Cool before proceeding.
2 Have 2 large pieces (each about 30 inches long) of nonstick aluminum foil on your work surface, or use pieces of regular aluminum foil spritzed with nonstick spray.
3 Combine the sugar and water in a large pot; stir to moisten. (A dark pot will make it hard to see when the caramel is done; I suggest using a stainless steel pot.) Bring to a simmer over medium-high heat, without stirring. Swirl the pot around a few times to help combine the sugar and water. Wash down the sides of the pot once or twice with

Ingredient Tips:

๛ Hazelnuts can be purchased already skinned—a great time saver. They will be more expensive, but when you make a wedding cake, time is at a premium. Also, make sure they are very fresh because if they are stale, they will impart an off flavor and aroma to your finished creation.

๛ The hazelnut paste can be found at specialty food stores and through mail order. You can find it both sweetened and unsweetened; both use roasted nuts. I like the unsweetened as the cake is sweet enough otherwise. The ingredients should just state "hazelnuts." Like nuts themselves, the paste should be impeccably fresh and smell like fresh roasted nuts.

↷ Lilacs are in season for a short time in spring, depending on where you live. If possible, use a blend of the dark purple French lilacs and lighter lavender colored ones.

↷ The champagne grapes are about $1/4$ inch in diameter and the clusters drape beautifully. They are alternately referred to as Black Zante or Corinth Zante grapes. You will most likely have to go to a specialty produce supplier for these and preorder them. They too have limited availability, so check in advance to make sure that you can get them. Regular grapes can work, but the effect will not be as fluid or delicate.

a wet pastry brush. Continue to cook until the caramel begins to color, about 12 minutes total. The caramel should be a golden brown color (see photo, page 128); the temperature will be between 330° and 360° if checked with an instant-read thermometer. As soon as the caramel reaches the desired color, remove it from the heat and immediately stir in the nuts with a few broad strokes.

4 Quickly pour the mixture onto the 2 sheets of of foil and spread it so that the nuts are in a single layer. Let it cool completely; the praline will harden. Break it up into chunks for storing.

5 To crush, add chunks of praline to a food processor fitted with a metal blade and pulse on and off (to prevent nuts from overheating, which would extract oils and create a paste) until coarsely ground for the decoration, or finely ground for the filling. For the coarse ground, you want chunks about $1/8$ to $1/4$ inch in size. The finely ground should be powdery. You need 1 cup of finely ground; the rest should be coarsely ground.

Make the Hazelnut Praline Buttercream Filling: Beat 1 cup unsweetened hazelnut paste into 4 cups of the Vanilla Buttercream. Then fold in the 1 cup finely ground Hazelnut Praline.

2 Weeks Ahead

Order the Lilacs, Grapes, and Leaves, if Using: See Decoration Tips for advice on selecting and buying these. You should pick them up the day before the wedding. Store grapes in refrigerator. (Don't forget to bring them to the wedding site!) Trim lilac bottoms and store in water in a cool, dark room. The leaves you will use the same day to make the leaf doily.

2 Days Ahead

Make the Yellow Cake with Ground Hazelnuts: Make the Essential Yellow Cake (see page 61) in 8-inch and 12-inch sizes with the following changes: For the 8-inch recipe, instead of using $2^{1}/4$ cups flour, use $1^{1}/2$ cups flour and $3/4$ cup finely ground hazelnuts (pulse nuts on and off in food processor to avoid releasing oils); bake for about 25 minutes.

The 12-inch recipe consists of the 9-inch recipe made 2 times. For each 9-inch batch, use 2 cups flour and 1 cup finely ground nuts; bake for about 35 minutes.

1 Day Ahead

Finish making the Frangelico Moistening Syrup: Stir in about $2/3$ cup (or more or less, to taste) Frangelico to the entire batch. If you are making the syrup now, do not add the liqueur until the syrup has cooled completely.

Prepare the Apricot Filling: This filling is simply 100% apricot fruit spread that you buy at the store—easy as spooning out of the jar. I use 100% apricot fruit spread as it has less sugar and more flavor than jam.

Make the Leaf Doily, if Using: Pick all the camellia leaves off of the stems and place them in a bowl. Have your glue gun hot and many glue sticks available. Place your fabric on a work surface; you will be working from the edge inward. Place a dot of glue on the underside of a leaf, near the stem end, and affix it to the edge of the fabric with the majority of the leaf hanging over the edge. Repeat with another leaf, placing it right next to the first one, and slightly overlapping the long edges. Continue all the way around the edge of the fabric.

Don't strive for perfection. In fact, it looks best if the edges of the leaves are somewhat jagged. When the first row is done, begin your second row. You want all subsequent rows to overlap the one made before. The edges of the leaves you are affixing should hang down halfway over the leaves from the former row. Just like in a theater, where the seats are staggered, similarly stagger the placement of the leaves. Continue until enough of the fabric is covered so that the cake itself fully covers any unadorned part. The finished doily is pretty sturdy and can be gently folded or rolled up and refrigerated until time to display the cake.

Assemble the Cake: Before assembling, have all the components made and ready to use. Have all your tools and equipment on hand, and make sure there is space for the tiers in the refrigerator.

1 Level and torte the cake layers (see pages 27–29).
2 Moisten the cake layers, fill, and assemble each tier (see pages 29–32) as follows: Cardboard, first cake layer, syrup, Hazelnut Praline Buttercream, corresponding second cake layer, syrup, Apricot Spread, third cake layer, syrup, Hazelnut Praline Buttercream, corresponding fourth layer, syrup.
3 Apply the crumb coat with Vanilla Buttercream (see page 32). Chill until firm. Meanwhile, prepare your cake base (see page 37).
4 Apply the final smooth coat of Vanilla Buttercream (see page 35). While the buttercream is still soft, press the roughly crushed praline to the bottom third of each tier (see page 46 for instructions). Place the 12-inch tier on the center of your cake base. Affix the 8-inch tier to the separator plate (see page 41). Chill overnight.

↪ For the "leaf doily," you need a 40-inch round of dark green fabric—a twill weight works well. You need a hot glue gun and many glue sticks, too. (The number depends on their size. Explain to the craft store clerk what you are trying to accomplish and they should be able to guide you.) If you don't have a glue gun, you can pick one up for less than $10 at a fabric/craft store, or borrow one.

↪ For the doily leaves, order camellia leaves from the florist. You will probably need 4 large bunches, but as bunch and leaf sizes vary, bring the fabric with you to the florist, explain what you want to accomplish, and have them assess what you need.

I typically use medium size leaves and discard very small or large ones. The center 12 inches of the fabric does not need to be covered; that is where you will place the cake. The rest of the fabric should be covered with leaves.

You should order the leaves a week ahead, in case they need to special-order them; they are a pretty common item, though, so it shouldn't be a problem. Preparing this table cover takes time so plan ahead.

Wedding Day

Place the Tiers on Pillars, Decorate, and Present! At the site of the wedding, place the leaf doily in the center of a tablecloth-covered display table, if using. Place the cake base containing the 12-inch tier on the center of the doily or tablecloth. Trim the pillars so that there will be a 2-inch separation between the layers. Attach the separator plate to the pillars (see page 40 for information on working with pillars and separator plates).

Arrange bunches of grapes and lilacs in between the tiers and on top (see photo for inspiration). If you have extra camellia leaves, you may tuck them here and there. Serve at room temperature.

CHOCOLATE-COVERED CARAMEL CAKE

If you love chocolate-covered caramel candies, you will flip over this funky and decadent cake. The caramel flavor appears on the inside in the form of Caramel Buttercream Filling and a rich Caramel Moistening Syrup for the layers of Chocolate Cake. Then comes a Milk Chocolate Buttercream frosting on the outside, and finally the cake is "covered" with bittersweet chocolate tiles. With its stylized, hip look, this cake would be as appropriate at a chic urban wedding (think slinky sleeveless white wedding dress) as at a casual reception. A contemporary cake topper, like a silver or glass sculpture of a bride and groom (3 to 6 inches tall), would fit perfectly if you can find one.

Serves 100

RECIPE COMPONENTS

- Chocolate Cake
- Caramel Moistening Syrup
- Caramel Buttercream Filling
- Milk Chocolate Buttercream Frosting

DECORATION

- Bittersweet chocolate tiles

SPECIAL EQUIPMENT

- Two 6 × 2-inch, two 10 × 2-inch, and two 14 × 2-inch square pans with corresponding cardboard squares
- 1/4-inch-thick wooden dowels (1 yard)
- 16-inch square cake base (can be covered with dark chocolate–colored foil)
- A white striped tablecloth will accent the contemporary feel; a deep burgundy will give it elegance
- 6 Sheets of acetate (see Equipment Tips)
- Medical-grade rubber gloves
- Sharp Xacto knife (optional)
- Flat, smooth baking sheets (see Equipment Tips)

TIMELINE

- **Up to 1 Month Ahead:** Make the Milk Chocolate Buttercream Frosting and the Caramel Buttercream Filling
- **Up to 1 Week Ahead:** Make the Bittersweet Chocolate Tiles
- **2 Days Ahead:** Make the Chocolate Cake
- **1 Day Ahead:** Make the Caramel Moistening Syrup, Assemble and Decorate the Cake
- **Wedding Day:** Present!

Up to 1 Month Ahead

Make the Milk Chocolate Buttercream Frosting: Make the Essential Buttercream (page 69) 4 times with the following changes: add 14 ounces melted and cooled milk chocolate to each finished batch. Then beat the batches together to ensure a perfectly uniform color for all the buttercream.

Make the Caramel Buttercream Filling: Make the Caramel Buttercream, following the instructions on page 144, but prepare it using only 2 batches of caramelized Essential Buttercream, with 1 cup of Caramel Sauce added to each batch (you will only need to make the Caramel Sauce once).

Up to 1 Week Ahead

Make the Bittersweet Chocolate Tiles: These are made of tempered bittersweet chocolate that is spread onto sheets of acetate (which make it very shiny), cooled, and then broken into odd-sized pieces. The "tiles" are then easily pressed into the soft buttercream. You are making enough tiles to fill 6 baking sheets, but you can make them in batches with the number of sheets you have.

BITTERSWEET CHOCOLATE TILES

6 pounds bittersweet couverture chocolate

1 Cut the acetate sheets to fit baking sheets.
2 Temper the chocolate according to the instructions on page 13. (If you are making the tiles in batches, then temper smaller batches of chocolate as you go.) Pour the tempered chocolate onto the acetate-lined sheets and spread with an offset spatula to a 1/8-inch thickness. (You won't use all the chocolate at once—if you're doing this in batches.) Refrigerate the sheets until the chocolate has hardened, usually about 30 minutes. The timing is not as important as the texture of the chocolate; it should be completely chilled through and therefore firm enough to handle.

Equipment Tips:

- Use a stainless steel lined pan when making caramel so that you can see the color of the caramel as it darkens. A dark pot makes this assessment very difficult.
- Acetate sheets are shiny, flexible clear plastic, and will give the tempered chocolate a nice, high shine. You can purchase them from art supply stores.
- Make sure the pans that support the acetate sheets are perfectly flat and smooth, as the chocolate will pick up the texture of any dents or bumps. Having 6 sheet pans would let you make all the tiles at once, but you can make them in batches.

3 Now, don the rubber gloves, as you will be handling the chocolate. You can either break up the chocolate by hand, or you can cut it into shapes. Either way, you want pieces that range from about 1 inch to 2¹/₂ inches long and slightly less wide. Take a look at the photo and you will get the idea of the shapes and proportions.

4 To break it up by hand, place the sheet of chocolate top-side down onto a large clean piece of parchment, with the acetate now on top. Peel the acetate off and begin breaking off suitably sized pieces. They can be placed in single layers, separated by parchment paper, in airtight containers, and refrigerated until ready to be used.

5 Cutting pieces with the Xacto knife gives a different effect: it is more precise and you can control the shapes of the pieces. Peel off the acetate as described above, then cut the chocolate into desired shapes. If the chocolate is too cold, it will shatter, so let the chocolate set for a few minutes to warm slightly before cutting. Store as mentioned above.

2 Days Ahead

Make the Chocolate Cake: Make the Essential Chocolate Cake (see page 66) in 6-inch, 10-inch, and 14-inch square sizes, in the following way: For the 6-inch square make the 8-inch round recipe; for the 10-inch square, make the 12-inch round recipe, for the 14-inch square, make the 6-inch round recipe once and the 10-inch round recipe twice. Baking times might be a bit longer than for round cakes of similar size.

1 Day Ahead

Make the Caramel Moistening Syrup: This is simply regular moistening syrup boiled until it becomes a deep, golden amber. Make this caramelized version of Essential Moistening Syrup (see page 68) 2 times.

CARAMEL MOISTENING SYRUP

2 cups sugar
2 cups water, divided

Three stages of caramel: too light; just right; too dark

1 Place the sugar and 1 cup of the water in a deep saucepan and stir to wet the sugar. Bring to a boil over medium-high heat. Boil until it turns a deep, golden amber; this might take as long as 10 minutes (see photo). Temperature is not as important as color.

2 Remove from the heat and slowly pour in an additional 1/2 cup water. Be careful as the caramel will sputter and boil up towards the top of the pot. Swirl the pot gently to combine the mixture after the bubbling has subsided.

3 Place the pot over medium heat to combine the sugar syrup and water and to dissolve any hard caramel bits that might have formed. Add an additional 1/2 cup water, if necessary, to create a thick caramel syrup. Cool to room temperature. Store in an airtight container at room temperature until needed.

Assemble and Decorate the Cake: Before assembling, have all components made and ready to use. Have all your tools and equipment on hand, and make sure there is space for the tiers in the refrigerator.

1 Level and torte the cake layers (see pages 27–29).

2 Moisten the cake layers, fill, and assemble each tier (see pages 29–32) as follows: Cardboard, first cake layer, syrup, Caramel Buttercream, corresponding second layer, syrup, Caramel Buttercream, third cake layer, syrup, Caramel Buttercream, corresponding fourth layer, syrup.

3 Apply the crumb coat with Milk Chocolate Buttercream (see page 32). Chill until firm. Meanwhile, prepare your cake base (see page 37).

4 Apply the final smooth coat of Milk Chocolate Buttercream (see page 35). Place the 14-inch tier on the center of the cake base.

5 Using dowels for support (see pages 38–39), center and stack the remaining tiers at 90-degree angles so that their corners bisect the sides of the tier below (see photo). Make sure to place dowels beneath where subsequent tiers will rest. (If using a heavy cake topper, support it with additional dowels in the top tier—see page 38.)

6 While the buttercream is still soft, press the chocolate "tiles" into the buttercream (while wearing gloves) all over the sides and tops of the tiers. Chill overnight.

Wedding Day

Present! At the site of the wedding, place the cake in the center of the tablecloth-covered display table. Serve at room temperature.

VALENTINE'S DAY CAKE

his cake erupts with symbols of love and romance! Red roses, chocolate truffles, and chocolate-dipped strawberries burst from between the tiers, turning this chocolate cake into a giant valentine. On the inside, crème de cacao gives an added flavor note to the classic combination of Chocolate Cake and Chocolate Buttercream. The cake is intensely chocolate throughout! The tiers themselves are simply decorated and separated with pillars—all to better show off the decor in between! With so much love in the air—and on the plate—who knows what will happen?

Serves 100

RECIPE COMPONENTS

- Chocolate Cake
- Crème de Cacao Moistening Syrup
- Crème de Cacao Buttercream Filling
- Chocolate Buttercream Frosting

DECORATIONS

- Cocoa-dusted dark chocolate truffles (90; each about 1 inch wide)
- Large red roses (24)
- Chocolate-Dipped Strawberries
- Chocolate Curls
- Chocolate Shavings

SPECIAL EQUIPMENT

- Two 6 × 2-inch, two 10 × 2-inch, and two 14 × 2-inch round pans with corresponding cardboard rounds
- One 7-inch and one 11-inch separator plate
- 8 trimmable pillars
- 18-inch base (can be covered with gold foil)
- A deep red tablecloth looks exceptional
- Nontoxic chocolate brown or gold spray-paint

TIMELINE

- **Up to 1 Month Ahead:**
  Prepare the Separator Plates and the Pillars, and Make the Crème de Cacao Buttercream Filling, the Chocolate Buttercream Frosting, and the Moistening Syrup Base
- **2 Days Ahead:**
  Make the Chocolate Cake and the Chocolate Curls and Shavings
- **1 Day Ahead:**
  Finish the Crème de Cacao Moistening Syrup, Make the Chocolate-Dipped Strawberries and Assemble the Cake
- **Wedding Day:**
  Place the Tiers on Pillars, Decorate, Present!

Up to 1 Month Ahead

Prepare the Separator Plates and the Pillars: Always spray paint in a well ventilated area; if you can do this outside, so much the better. Spread newspaper on your work surface and place all the pillars and separator plates on the paper. Start with the plates, and spray-paint one side and the edges thoroughly, covering every surface.

Allow them to dry (about 10 minutes for spray paint), then flip them over and paint the other side. To paint the pillars, I find it easiest to hold them while spray-painting them. Since the plates and pillars may be painted whenever you like, why not paint them 1 month ahead? Store them carefully so as not to chip the paint.

Make the Crème de Cacao Buttercream Filling: Make the Essential Buttercream (see page 69) 2 times with the following changes: beat 1/4 cup crème de cacao (or more or less, to taste) into each batch.

Make the Chocolate Buttercream Frosting: Make the Essential Buttercream (see page 69) 3 times with the following changes: beat in 12 ounces of melted and cooled semisweet or bittersweet chocolate per batch. Then beat the batches together to ensure a perfectly uniform color for all the buttercream.

Make the Moistening Syrup Base: The moistening syrup can be made ahead but should not be flavored with crème de cacao until right before using. Make the Essential Moistening Syrup (see page 68) 2 times but do not use the vanilla bean or vanilla extract.

2 Days Ahead

Make the Chocolate Cake: Make the Essential Chocolate Cake (see page 66) in the 6-inch, 10-inch, and 14-inch sizes.

Make the Chocolate Curls and Shavings: Make the chocolate curls according to the instructions on page 112, using 5 pounds semisweet or bittersweet couverture chocolate. While making the curls, there will probably be some small shavings that are generated as a by-product of making the larger curls and you can use them to embellish the sides of the cake. Alternately, you can make the small shavings deliberately. Take a block of semisweet or bittersweet chocolate (such as a 1-pound piece) and use a sharp chef's knife to shave bits off of various corners of the chocolate. By shaving off the corners you will make smallish shavings, which is what you want. Look at photograph to see the sizes of shavings I used.

1 Day Ahead

Finish making the Crème de Cacao Moistening Syrup: Stir in about 1 1/4 cups crème de cacao (or more or less, to taste) to the entire batch. If you are making the syrup now, do not add the liqueur until the syrup has cooled completely.

Ingredient Tip:

↬ Use a high quality bittersweet couverture chocolate for the curls and chocolate-dipped strawberries, such as Valrhona Equatoriale or Scharffen Berger Bittersweet.

Decoration Tips:

↬ The pillars and separator plates are painted with a nontoxic paint to help them blend with the cake's decor. A dark gold will add an elegant touch of color, while a chocolate brown will blend in to the background. I prefer spray-paints, but you can use a brush-on type.

↬ I suggest buying and not making the truffles. There are many high quality varieties available, and making them, while not difficult, is time-consuming. If you would like to make your own, there are many books to guide you, and you can make them way ahead and freeze them.

The chocolate-dipped strawberries should be made as close to serving time as possible, preferably the same day, although they can be held overnight. If you're pressed for time, use plain strawberries, undipped. After all, no one is going to feel shortchanged of chocolate with this cake.

Buy the roses a few days ahead so that they can open and relax a bit. If they are at least partially open, they will give a more lush look.

Make the Chocolate-Dipped Strawberries: If you have time, it's even better to make these the day of the wedding, but they will be OK refrigerated for 1 night.

Use 24 large or long-stemmed strawberries and 2 pounds semisweet or bittersweet chocolate. Gently wash and dry the strawberries. Make sure they are completely dry. Line 2 baking sheets with parchment or aluminum foil. Temper the chocolate according to the instructions on page 13. Hold a strawberry by the stem and dip it three-quarters of the way into the chocolate. Gently shake it to encourage any excess chocolate to drip back into the pot. Place the berry on the prepared sheet pan; repeat with the remaining berries.

Let the berries cool to room temperature, then place the sheets in the refrigerator until the chocolate completely hardens, about 20 minutes. Keep refrigerated until needed, at a maximum, overnight.

Assemble the Cake: Before assembling, have all the components made and ready to use. Have all your tools and equipment on hand, and make sure there is space for the tiers in the refrigerator.

1 Level and torte the cake layers (see pages 27–29).

2 Moisten the cake layers, fill, and assemble each tier (see pages 29–32) as follows: Cardboard, first cake layer, syrup, Crème de Cacao Buttercream, corresponding second layer, syrup, Crème de Cacao Buttercream, third cake layer, syrup, Crème de Cacao Buttercream, corresponding fourth layer, syrup.

3 Apply the crumb coat with Chocolate Buttercream (see page 32). Chill until firm. Meanwhile, prepare your cake base (see page 37).

4 Apply the final smooth coat of Chocolate Buttercream (see page 35). Sprinkle shavings here and there on the top quarter of the tiers' sides as well as on the first outer inch or so of the tiers' tops. A random look is fine (see photo for inspiration). Place the 14-inch tier on the center of the covered base.

5 Affix the 6-inch and 10-inch tiers to the separator plates. Nestle the truffles side by side around the base of each tier, pressing them gently into the soft buttercream (when the buttercream chills, it will hold them in place). Chill overnight.

Wedding Day

Place the Tiers on Pillars, Decorate, Present! At the site of the wedding, place the cake in the center of a tablecloth-covered display table. Trim the pillars so that there will be a 3-inch separation between layers. (You may make the separation any height you like, but make sure to leave space for the curls, roses, and berries.) Attach the separator plates to the pillars, which have been sunk into the tiers (see page 42).

Creatively arrange the chocolate curls, strawberries, roses, and any leftover chocolate truffles between the tiers and on the top tier, using the photograph as a guide. They should look gently mounded on the top tier. Serve at room temperature.

ITALIAN RUM CREAM AND FRUIT CAKE

This cake is delicate and quite flavorful at the same time, and wonderfully vivid in color. It starts with our White Cake, generously brushed with a rum-laden moistening syrup. The Vanilla Bean Pastry Cream Filling makes for ultra-moist cake tiers. Vanilla Buttercream Frosting, piped in ridged columns, surrounds the outside, while a mosaic of fresh fruit completely covers the tops of the tiers. This panoply of color and texture is highlighted by a glistening apricot glaze, which is brushed over the fruit. This cake is best served indoors where you can control the ambient temperature. The entire cake should be served at a cool room temperature, where the pastry cream on the inside stays cool and the buttercream outside remains soft. At the very least, if you serve it outside, avoid the mid-summer heat!

Serves 100

RECIPE COMPONENTS

- White Cake
- Rum Moistening Syrup
- Vanilla Bean Pastry Cream Filling
- Vanilla Buttercream

DECORATION

- Fresh fruit under Apricot Glaze

SPECIAL EQUIPMENT

- Two 6 × 2-inch, two 10 × 2-inch, and two 14 × 2-inch round pans with corresponding cardboard rounds
- Ateco #802 tip and Ateco #844 tip
- Pastry brush (see Equipment Tip)
- 16-inch round base (can be covered with dark green foil)
- 7-inch and 11-inch separator plates
- 8 trimmable pillars
- Dark green tablecloth for dramatic effect, a simpler patterned white for subtlety
- Nontoxic orange spray-paint

TIMELINE

- **Up to 1 Month Ahead:**
  Prepare the Separator Plates and the Pillars, Make the Moistening Syrup Base and the Vanilla Buttercream Frosting
- **Up to 1 Week Ahead:**
  Make the Apricot Glaze for the Fruit
- **Up to 3 Days Ahead:**
  Make the Vanilla Bean Pastry Cream Filling
- **2 Days Ahead:**
  Make the White Cake
- **1 Day Ahead:**
  Finish Making the Rum Moistening Syrup, Prepare the Fruit for Decoration, and Assemble and Decorate the Tiers
- **Wedding Day:**
  Place the Tiers on the Pillars, Present!

Up to 1 Month Ahead

Prepare the Separator Plates and the Pillars: Always spray paint in a well ventilated area; if you can do this outside, so much the better. Paint the plates and pillars orange according to the instructions on pages 38–42.

Make the Moistening Syrup Base: The moistening syrup can be made ahead but should not be flavored with rum until right before using. Make the Essential Moistening Syrup (see page 68) 2 times but do not use the vanilla bean or vanilla extract.

Make the Vanilla Buttercream Frosting: Make the Essential Buttercream (see page 69) 4 times with the following changes: beat in 1 tablespoon vanilla extract to each batch.

Up to 1 Week Ahead:

Make the Apricot Glaze for the Fruit: The yield is less than the original amount of preserves because some solids are strained out and discarded.

APRICOT GLAZE

Makes about 2¹/₄ cups

2¹/₂ cups apricot preserves
¹/₃ to ¹/₂ cup water

Stir together the apricot preserves and ¹/₃ cup water in a small saucepan. Bring to a boil over medium heat. Immediately strain into a small bowl—press firmly through the strainer, leaving bits of apricot chunks in the strainer. Allow the strained jam to cool to a warm temperature; it should still be fluid. If it is not, add the additional water. It should flow and be liquidy. Refrigerate the glaze in an airtight container until needed. It may be reheated on top of the stove or in the microwave.

Equipment Tip:

➷ Make sure your pastry brush is soft and clean (not one you have used for basting chicken with barbecue sauce). A 1¹/₂-inch size is perfect. It is worth buying a new one for your cake. There are new ones on the market made from silicone that are wonderful; search them out. (They can be thrown in the dishwasher, do not retain flavors between uses, do not shed any bristles, and are very pliable.)

Ingredient Tips:

➷ The rum syrup is an important part of this cake. The cake is meant to be very "rummy." (Consequently, this is not a good cake to make for non-drinkers.) I think gold or dark rum is best; I made it once with Bacardi 151 and it was amazing.

➷ The pastry cream is enhanced with vanilla bean, not just extract, which should not be substituted in this particular recipe. Look for very plump, moist vanilla beans. Also, this pastry cream is deliberately made a bit thick with a large amount of flour so that it stays put when you spread it between the layers.

The fruit for decoration should be vivid, ripe, but firm, and blemish-free. The recipe suggests buying quite a bit of each type of fruit because for every half-pint of raspberries, for instance, you might only pick out a dozen perfect ones to use. Use any leftover fruit for a fruit salad or smoothies.

Decoration Tip:

The decoration and color on this cake are provided by the fruit, so you should take extra care in choosing and preparing it. For berries (strawberries, raspberries, blackberries, and blueberries) make sure they are ripe, yet very firm and dry.

If the stone fruits (plums, apricots, and pluots—a fruit that's half plum, half apricot) are not in season, go with what is fresh, vivid in color, and flavorful. I have used clementine segments to great effect. All of the fruit should be prepped the morning of decorating the cake tiers, which will be the day before your event.

Up to 3 Days Ahead

Make the Vanilla Bean Pastry Cream Filling: Make this pastry cream 2 times. This thick, smooth, and creamy pastry cream is used as the filling of this cake.

VANILLA BEAN PASTRY CREAM

Makes 5 cups

4 cups whole milk
2 vanilla beans, split lengthwise
14 large egg yolks
1 cup sugar
Pinch salt
2/3 cup all-purpose flour

1 Bring the milk and the vanilla beans to a boil in a large nonreactive pot. Remove from the heat, but keep warm. Let the beans steep for 30 minutes.

2 Meanwhile, in a nonreactive bowl, whisk together the yolks and sugar until creamy. (Refrigerate or freeze the egg whites for the Essential Buttercream!) Whisk in the salt and flour until smooth.

3 Remove the vanilla beans from the milk and scrape all the seeds into the milk using a blunt butter knife or a spoon. Whisk to break up the sticky clumps of vanilla beans. Reheat the milk. Pour about 1/4 of the warm milk over the egg yolk mixture, whisking gently. Add the remaining milk and stir to combine. Immediately pour the mixture back into the pot and cook over a low-medium heat. Stir continuously, but do not let it boil. The mixture will eventually thicken. If you pull your spoon across the bottom of the pot, you should be able to see the bottom of the pot for a moment. The pastry cream will cook in about 10 minutes.

4 Allow the pastry cream to cool; stir it frequently to release heat. When almost at room temperature, scrape the pastry cream into a storage container, press plastic wrap directly onto the surface to prevent a skin from forming, then snap on an airtight lid. Refrigerate at least 4 hours or until thoroughly chilled. It will become quite thick upon cooling, which is what you want.

2 Days Ahead

Make the White Cake: Make the Essential White Cake (see page 64) in the 6-inch, 10-inch, and 14-inch sizes.

1 Day Ahead

Finish making the Rum Moistening Syrup: stir in about 2 cups (or more or less, to taste) of gold or dark rum to the entire batch. If you are making the syrup now, do not add the liqueur until the syrup has cooled completely.

Prepare the Fruit for Decoration: Your fruit should be prepped the day you assemble the cake. For your fruit decoration, make sure the berries are as ripe, yet firm, as possible. Grapes should be very firm.

FRUIT FOR DECORATION

3 pints raspberries
3 pints blackberries
2 pints blueberries
2 pints strawberries
6 kiwis (green, gold, or both)
5 pluots, apricots, plums or clementines
2 pounds red seedless grapes
2 pounds green seedless grapes

1 The raspberries, blackberries, and blueberries should be uniform in size and firm. (I rinse and dry the blueberries, but leave the others as is.) Any soft or wet berries should be avoided. Pick through them and choose the medium-sized, dry, firm, unblemished ones. These will be used whole.

2 The strawberries should be rinsed and dried thoroughly. Choose berries that are all the same size, be it small or medium. Forgo very large berries for this endeavor. Use a strawberry huller to remove the stems or cut carefully, so that the heart shape of the berry is preserved, then cut the berries in half, right down the center lengthwise.

3 The kiwis should be carefully peeled so that they retain their round shape. Slice off the two ends and discard. Cut them into 1/4-inch slices and then in half crosswise.

Piping ridged, vertical columns of buttercream

Removing peaks of buttercream from ridged vertical columns

4 Pluots or other stone fruit should be halved or quartered, depending on size, and pits removed. For clementines, peel and separate them into individual sections. Remove all of the white fibrous strings.

5 The grapes should be rinsed and dried. Sort out and choose ones of medium size and slice them in half lengthwise.

Assemble and Decorate the Tiers: Before assembling, have all the components made and ready to use. Have all your tools and equipment on hand, and make sure there is space for the tiers in the refrigerator.

1 Level and torte the cake layers (see pages 27–29).

2 There is a particular technique that I use with this cake to help the layer of pastry cream remain in between the cake layers and not seep out. The pastry cream is thick, but this is a safety measure to make sure your wedding cake is as great as it can be. Using a pastry bag fitted with an Ateco #802 tip (which gives you a 1/4-inch round opening) pipe a continuous circle of the Vanilla Buttercream Frosting around the outer edge of each cake layer. This will act as a barrier for the pastry cream that you will spread within the circle.

3 Now, moisten the cake layers, fill, and assemble each tier (see pages 29–32) as follows: Cardboard, first cake layer, generous amount of syrup, pastry cream, corresponding second layer, syrup, pastry cream, third cake layer, syrup, pastry cream, corresponding fourth layer, syrup. A small offset spatula is best for spreading the pastry cream.

4 Apply the crumb coat with Vanilla Buttercream (see page 32). Chill until firm. Meanwhile, prepare your cake base (see page 37).

5 Use an Ateco #844 tip to pipe vertical ridged columns of buttercream. Piping from the bottom of each tier to the top for each column gives the best results. Make the columns right next to one another so that the crumb coat is completely covered, but do not allow the columns to overlap (see photo). Each column should be perfectly vertical. End the columns so that they are just slightly higher than the tops of the tiers. Don't worry about the tops being neat, as they will be covered by rosettes.

Use a small offset spatula to even out the tops of the columns as follows: take the spatula and swipe it over the tops of each column, from the outside of the cake towards the inside, so that the columns are even with the top of the cake. You are just trying to remove the peaks of the columns to bring them level with the top of the cake (see photo). Chill, if time permits.

6   Place the 14-inch tier on the center of the cake base. Affix the 6-inch and 10-inch tiers to the separator plates. Using the same Ateco #844 tip, pipe rosettes along the tops of each tier, covering the tops of the piped, ridged columns. Make sure the rosettes along the top outer edge make a continuous ring, as it will help keep the apricot glaze in place on top of the tiers. If the bottoms of your vertical columns do not cover the cardboards underneath each tier, then pipe rosettes along the bottom edges as well. Chill, if time permits.

7   Now is the time to arrange the fruit and you can make some creative and aesthetic decisions. You can make concentric rings of the same type of fruit (a ring of strawberries, a ring of grapes, etc.) or you can make clusters of fruit of the same sort, which is what I did for this cake. The key is to cover the entire surface of the cake with fruit; you shouldn't be able to see any buttercream beneath. Also, since the centers of the lower tiers will be shadowed by the ones above, take care to make the edges, which will peak out, as visually appealing as possible.

There is no one way to do this, but here are some suggestions: first of all, whether you are making rings or clusters, think color. Don't put two dark fruits, like blueberries and blackberries next to one another. For raspberries and blackberries, place them side-by-side, top side up. For blueberries, they can be slightly leaning on their sides, one against one another. Strawberries can be placed, cut side down, overlapped, if they are small. Grapes are also placed cut side down, and, depending on their size, they can be overlapped. Kiwis should be set cut side down and overlapped. Plums, apricots, and pluots can be placed cut side down if halved, or gently overlapped if quartered. Clementines can be arranged broad side down and nestled against one another, slightly overlapping. I like to make odd-shaped groupings of fruit, so that there is a free-flowing nature to the design. (Refer to photo for inspiration.)

8   Have the glaze in a warmed liquid state. Dip the pastry brush in the glaze to get a generous amount and gently dab it on top of the fruit, allowing the glaze to drip down and around the fruit. Do this gently so as not to upset the arrangement of fruit. You want to completely cover the fruit and make a layer of shiny glaze over all. Repeat for all the tiers. Chill overnight.

Wedding Day

Place the Tiers on the Pillars, Present! At the site of the wedding, place the cake base containing the 14-inch cake in the center of a tablecloth-covered display table. Trim the pillars so that there will be a 3-inch separation between the layers. (You may make the separation any height you like, but make sure you can see a good bit of the fruit.) Sink the pillars into the tiers and attach the separator plates to the pillars (see pages 38–43 for information on pillars and separator plates); you might have to move some fruit aside in order to insert the pillars. Serve at room temperature.

BROWN SUGAR, PECAN, AND PEACHES CAKE

T his cake is best in summer when fresh peaches are at their peak. While the no-frills decoration creates a casual air, the cake's basket-weave pattern is like a simple stage that lets the flowers become the star—voluptuous roses and ranunculus that sprout from each tier in complementary colors of orange and burgundy. This is the cake for showing off a truly sophisticated palette of flowers at their peak. The color range of the flowers is important, because it harmonizes with the colors of the cake: delicate beige Brown Sugar Pecan Cake (yellow cake made with brown sugar and bits of toasted pecans) moistened with Peach Liqueur Moistening Syrup, and richly flavored and colored Caramel Buttercream.

Cutting through the richness is a layer of fresh sliced peaches nestled within the filling. On the outside, the caramel color of the buttercream further echoes the color of a real basket. (The basket weave might look complicated, but it is not, and the photographs will help you. In fact, it is easier than making ultra-smooth sides with buttercream and an icing spatula!) You may, of course, use whatever color or type of flowers that you like. Colorful gerbera daisies would look nice, too.

Serves 100

RECIPE COMPONENTS

- ᠕ Brown Sugar Pecan Cake
- ᠕ Peach Liqueur Moistening Syrup
- ᠕ Fresh Sliced Peaches
- ᠕ Caramel Buttercream

DECORATION

- ᠕ Flowers in full bloom, half burgundy-colored roses and half orange- and yellow-toned ranunculus (3 dozen total)

SPECIAL EQUIPMENT

- ᠕ Two 6 × 2-inch, two 10 × 2-inch, and two 14 × 2-inch round pans with corresponding cardboard rounds
- ᠕ Ateco #10 tip
- ᠕ 16-inch round base (can be covered in bronze-colored foil)
- ᠕ 1/4-inch-thick wooden dowels (1 yard)
- ᠕ Patterned cream-colored tablecloth to complement the basketweave, or a russet tablecloth with beige lace overlay

TIMELINE

- ᠕ **Up to 1 Month Ahead:**
  Make the Moistening Syrup Base and the Caramel Buttercream
- ᠕ **2 Days Ahead:**
  Make the Brown Sugar Pecan Cake
- ᠕ **1 Day Ahead:**
  Finish Making the Peach Liqueur Moistening Syrup, Prepare the Peaches for the Filling, and Assemble the Cake
- ᠕ **Wedding Day:**
  Decorate, Present!

Up to 1 Month Ahead

Make the Moistening Syrup Base: The moistening syrup can be made ahead but should not be flavored with peach liqueur until right before using. Make the Essential Moistening Syrup (see page 68) 2¹/₂ times but do not use the vanilla bean or vanilla extract.

Make the Caramel Buttercream: Caramel Buttercream is made by combining a caramelized version of the Essential Buttercream and a thick caramel sauce, which should be made first. Make the Caramel Sauce 2 times.

CARAMEL SAUCE

Makes 2²/₃ cups

2 cups heavy cream
2 cups sugar
1 cup water
2 teaspoons vanilla extract

1 Bring the cream to a boil over medium heat in a medium-sized saucepan; set aside, keeping warm. Place the sugar and water in a large heavy-bottomed pot. Stir to moisten the sugar and cook over a low-medium heat, without stirring, until the syrup begins to color. Wash down the sides of the pot once or twice with a damp pastry brush.

2 When the syrup is a golden amber color (see the photo on page 128 for proper color), remove from the heat and carefully pour in the warm cream. The mixture may bubble up furiously. Allow the mixture to calm down, then gently whisk until smooth. (If the cream is too cool, it will cause the caramel to seize. If this happens, place the pot back over a low heat and stir until the sauce liquefies.) Stir in the vanilla off the heat. Store refrigerated in an airtight container. It should be room temperature and fluid when added to the buttercream. Reheat in a double boiler or microwave before using, if necessary.

After you have made the Caramel Sauce, make the Essential Buttercream (see page 69) 5 times with the following changes:

You will cook the sugar syrup for the Essential Buttercream until it caramelizes. As it boils, watch it carefully and cook it until it turns a deep golden amber (see photo on page 128). Do not let it turn dark brown, or it will taste burned. The temperature will be about 325°.

↪ For the peach liqueur, you can use peach schnapps, which is inexpensive, but rather sweet. I prefer the more expensive peach eau de vie. Its taste is far more subtle.

↪ The peaches should be ripe, but not too soft or they will exude too much juice. Taste before you buy; they should taste exceptionally peachy. If they do not, nectarines would make a fine substitute. If you can't find either, it's OK to omit them.

Equipment Tip:

↪ To boil the sugar syrup for the Caramel Buttercream, use a pot with a stainless steel interior, so you can see the color of the syrup as it changes color. A dark pan makes this very difficult.

ᔎ The roses and ranunculus really make a statement on this cake. They are fresh and elegant and unusually colored. Because you want to have as much choice as you can with the color palette, you will most likely have to be preorder them. Better yet, maybe you can work with a local flower purveyor from a green market.

The look I wanted to accomplish was one of warm colors in gradations ranging from orange through the terra cotta tones, and into the deep burgundy color range. Discuss this with your florist; they should be able to help you get what you need.

Order them so that they arrive 2 days before the event. If they are very tightly closed, freshly cut the stems and place in warm water in a warm room. You want them to be somewhat open and lush looking. When they open sufficiently, they can be put in cold water in the refrigerator (if you have space) or a cool room.

Remove syrup from the heat and allow to cool to about 260°. Then, use it in place of the regular sugar syrup and proceed with the Essential Buttercream recipe.

When the buttercream is finished and all of the butter has been added and the mixture is smooth, beat 1 cup of the Caramel Sauce into each batch of buttercream. The Buttercream is now ready to use and may be stored and reconstituted as for regular Essential Buttercream. While this buttercream can be made 1 month ahead and frozen, it tastes best when fresh.

2 Days Ahead

Make the Brown Sugar Pecan Cake: Make the Essential Yellow Cake (see page 61) in the 6-inch, 10-inch, and 14-inch sizes with the following changes: use packed light brown sugar instead of white sugar. Additionally, for the 6-inch recipe, add 1/3 cup chopped toasted pecans along with the flour mixture. Add 3/4 cup pecans to each 10-inch recipe (you make the 10-inch recipe twice for the 14-inch layer). (To toast pecans: Spread in an even layer on a baking sheet, and bake in a 350° oven until just light golden brown and beginning to turn fragrant, about 8 minutes.)

1 Day Ahead

Finish making the Peach Liqueur Moistening Syrup: stir about 1 1/2 cups peach liqueur (or more or less, to taste) into the entire batch. If you are making the syrup now, do not add the liqueur until the syrup has cooled completely.

Prepare the Peaches for the Filling: The center layer of filling is comprised of Caramel Buttercream with fresh, sliced peaches nestled into it. The peaches should be prepared within an hour of assembling the cake, preferably right before you need them. Use 5 medium ripe, but firm, peaches.

Fill a deep saucepan with water and bring to a boil over high heat. Drop in 2 or 3 peaches at a time, bring back to a boil, and boil for 1 minute. Check the skin on 1 of the peaches. As soon as it has loosened, remove the peaches to a colander and rinse with cold water to stop cooking. Repeat with the remaining peaches.

Slip the peels off of the peaches and discard. Slice the peaches very thinly, about 1/8 inch thick, and lay in a single layer on clean paper towels to absorb excess moisture. The peach slices are now ready to use.

Assemble the Cake: Before assembling, have all the components made and ready to use. Have all your tools and equipment on hand, and make sure there is space for the tiers in the refrigerator.

1 Level and torte the cake layers (see pages 27–29).

2 Moisten the cake layers, fill, and assemble each tier (see pages 29–32) as follows: Cardboard, first cake layer, syrup, buttercream, corresponding second cake layer, syrup, buttercream. Now pause and nestle fresh peaches in this center layer of buttercream by placing slices over the entire layer. They should be touching and placed as close together as possible without overlapping. Finish with third cake layer, syrup, buttercream, corresponding fourth layer, and syrup.

3 Apply the crumb coat with the buttercream (see page 32). Chill until firm. Meanwhile, prepare your cake base (see page 37).

4 Apply the final coat of buttercream in a basket weave pattern to each tier as follows: To make basket weave, fit the Ateco #10 tip on your pastry bag with a coupler. You will use this tip for both vertical and horizontal lines forming the weave pattern.

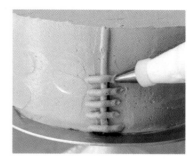

Piping horizontal lines across initial vertical line

To begin, pipe a vertical line going from bottom of the tier to the top. Then pipe horizontal lines, each approximately 1 inch long, across the vertical line (see photo). The number will depend on the height of the tier. Space them so that additional lines will just fit in between and all of them will cover the side of the tier. Make the first horizontal line along the bottom edge of the cake. The next line will be one line's width up from it, and so on, until you reach the top of the tier.

Pipe a second vertical line to the right of the horizontal lines, slightly overlapping the edges of the horizontal ones (see photo). Then pipe more horizontal lines across this vertical line, filling in the spaces formed by the previous horizontal lines. This set of horizontal lines will be started just to the left of the second vertical line and go for 1 inch toward the right.

Piping second vertical line so that it covers ends of horizontal lines

Repeat this pattern, working all around the cake. (If you are a lefty, you can work toward the left.) As you approach the end, space it so that the last set of horizontal lines complements the first set. They should dovetail and fit together neatly. When finished, chill the tier and repeat with the other tiers. I like to start with the largest tier, which gives me a sense of accomplishment when it's done. Chill all the tiers well.

> **Technique Note:** Making a basket weave does take a while and your hands can overly warm up the buttercream in the pastry bag, so fill it only partially at any given time. If the buttercream becomes too warm, the nice round shape of the lines will soften and become less distinct. Chill the tier and buttercream at any time, if necessary, then resume.

Making a rope border

5 Place the 14-inch tier on the center of your cake base. Center and stack the remaining tiers using dowels for internal support (see page 38). Use Ateco #10 tip to pipe a small rope border along the outer top and bottom edges (see photo). Chill overnight.

Wedding Day

Decorate, Present! At the site of the wedding, place the cake in the center of a table-cloth-covered display table. Trim flower stems to about $^1/_2$ to 1 inch. Arrange the flowers on the tops of the tiers and on top of the cake (see photo for inspiration) or anywhere you would like. Peel off individual rose petals from any extra flowers, if desired, and scatter around the cake on the table. Serve at room temperature.

Gilded Mocha Cake

꧅꧅

This is a very elegant cake, perfect for a second wedding, or for use as a groom's cake—
or if you love mocha! Here we take our yellow cake, fold bittersweet chocolate shavings into the batter and brush Kahlua-flavored syrup on each layer. A deep dark bittersweet chocolate ganache, along with Espresso Buttercream, fill the tiers, while smooth
Espresso Buttercream decorates the outside. The top of each oval tier is gently flooded with
an additional layer of rich bittersweet chocolate ganache and embellished with flecks of real,
edible 24-karat gold and crunchy, rich chocolate-covered espresso beans. If you want to add
a floral element, deep-red roses look smashing on this cake.

Serves 80

RECIPE COMPONENTS

- Yellow Cake with Bittersweet Chocolate Shavings
- Kahlua Moistening Syrup
- Bittersweet Chocolate Ganache
- Espresso Buttercream

DECORATION

- Chocolate-covered espresso beans (48 or more)
- Gold leaf (5 sheets)
- Ganache glaze

SPECIAL EQUIPMENT

- Two $5^5/_8 \times 7^3/_4 \times$ 2-inch, two $7^5/_8 \times 10^3/_4 \times$ 2-inch, and two $9^7/_8 \times 13 \times$ 2-inch oval pans with corresponding cardboard ovals
- Ateco #10 tip
- 16-inch oval or round base (can be covered with gold foil)
- $1/_4$-inch-thick wooden dowels (1 yard)
- Tablecloth can echo the gold and brown colors from cake, or go with burgundy velvet tablecloth (especially if you use red roses)
- Tweezers for applying gold leaf

TIMELINE

- **Up to 1 Month Ahead:**
  Make the Espresso Buttercream and the Moistening Syrup Base
- **Up to 1 Week Ahead:**
  Make the Bittersweet Chocolate Ganache
- **2 Days Ahead:**
  Make the Yellow Cake with Bittersweet Chocolate Shavings
- **1 Day Ahead:**
  Finish the Kahlua Moistening Syrup, Assemble and Decorate the Cake
- **Wedding Day:**
  Present!

Up to 1 Month Ahead

Make the Espresso Buttercream: Make the Essential Buttercream (see page 69) 4 times with the following changes: add 1/4 cup instant espresso powder that has been dissolved in a scant 3 tablespoons of warm Kahlua (or warm water) to each batch. Just beat it in after the Essential Buttercream is done. Make sure that the color of each batch is as similar as possible. To ensure even color, beat all the batches together bit by bit so that there is even color throughout.

Make the Moistening Syrup Base: The moistening syrup can be made ahead but should not be flavored with Kahlua until right before using. Make the Essential Moistening Syrup (see page 68) 2 times but do not use the vanilla bean or vanilla extract.

Up to 1 Week Ahead

Make the Bittersweet Chocolate Ganache: This ganache recipe makes quite a bit, as it will be used to glaze the tops of the tiers as well as to fill the central layer in each tier. Make the ganache recipe 2 times; this is enough for the filling and the glaze. Refrigerate until ready to use.

Ingredient Tip:

↬ I use Scharffen Berger bitter-sweet chocolate for the shavings and ganache in this cake and Medaglia D'Oro instant espresso powder for the coffee elements (in addition to the Kahlua). It gives a better flavor to this cake than regular instant coffee would.

Decoration Tips:

↬ Make sure the espresso beans are real beans covered with dark chocolate. Some candies are just shaped like espresso beans, but are really just chocolate through-and-through.

↬ Buy gold leaf that is at least 22 karats. Any lesser karat will have too many impurities. People ask me all the time whether it is safe to "eat" gold. In these small amounts, it is just fine. In fact, you can find liqueurs on the market that have gold leaf floating in the bottles.

BITTERSWEET CHOCOLATE GANACHE

Makes 5 cups

24 ounces bittersweet chocolate, finely chopped
2$\frac{1}{2}$ cups heavy cream

1 Place the chocolate in a very large mixing bowl.

2 Heat the cream in a saucepan until it comes to a simmer. Immediately, but slowly, pour the hot cream into the bowl of chocolate in a circular motion, covering all of the chocolate. Allow it to sit for about 3 minutes; the heat from the cream will melt the chocolate.

3 Gently stir the ganache to blend the cream and chocolate. The ganache should be dense and smooth, with few air bubbles, so stir with a spoon when you make it, as opposed to whisking, which would add air. The mixture should become smooth and pourable. Allow it to cool slightly until the mixture has thickened but is still pourable.

4 You may use the ganache right away, or, if chilled, it can be melted in the top of a double boiler until the desirable texture is achieved. (If you are handy with your microwave, try melting it on 30% power.) The ganache used for filling should be a spreadable consistency; the ganache used for glaze should be pourable.

> **Technique Note:** Occasionally ganache will separate, but you can save it. You will know if it is separated as it will not look smooth—it might appear grainy or an oily film might form. There are two solutions. If you have an immersion blender, use it to blend the mixture. This usually does the trick and it turns silky smooth. Alternatively, add a little bit of cold cream (a tablespoon at a time) and stir gently; the mixture should smooth out and blend.

2 Days Ahead

Make the Yellow Cake with Bittersweet Chocolate Shavings: See page 112 for instructions on making chocolate shavings. Make the Essential Yellow Cake (see page 61) in oval sizes in the following way: for the 5⅝ × 7¾-inch oval, make the 8-inch round recipe. Fold 1½ ounces bittersweet chocolate shavings into the completed batter. For the 7⅝ × 10¾-inch oval, make the 10-inch round recipe. Add 2½ ounces of bittersweet chocolate shavings. For the 9⅞ × 13-inch oval, make the 12-inch round recipe. Add 4 ounces of bittersweet chocolate shavings.

1 Day Ahead

Finish Making the Kahlua Moistening Syrup: stir in about 1¼ cup (or more or less, to taste) of Kahlua to the entire batch. If you are making the syrup now, do not add the liqueur until the syrup has cooled completely.

Assemble and Decorate the Cake: Before assembling, have all the components made and ready to use. Have all your tools and equipment on hand, and make sure there is space for the tiers in the refrigerator.

1 Level and torte the cake layers (see pages 27–29).
2 Moisten the cake layers, fill, and assemble each tier (see pages 29–32) as follows: Cardboard, first cake layer, syrup, Espresso Buttercream, corresponding second layer, syrup, ganache, third cake layer, syrup, Espresso Buttercream, corresponding fourth layer, syrup.
3 Apply the crumb coat with Espresso Buttercream (see page 32). Chill until firm. Meanwhile, prepare your cake base (see page 37).
4 Apply the final smooth coat of buttercream (see page 35). Place the 14-inch tier on the center of your cake base.

Ganache beginning to flood top tier

5 Center and stack the remaining tiers using dowels for internal support (see page 38). Fit a pastry bag and coupler with Ateco #10 tip. Pipe a bead border along the outer top and bottom edges. Make sure that the border along the top outer edges is pronounced and continuous. Its function is not just to add decoration but also to form a barrier to hold the poured ganache in place.

6 Press the chocolate-covered espresso beans into the bead border at approximately 2-inch intervals, or however you think looks best. Keep them nestled in the bead border and not too far down—don't let them touch the cake itself—as this is where the ganache will be poured. They can be pressed into the bottoms of the tiers, too, as we did for the bottom tier (see photo). Chill well.

7 Have the remaining ganache pourable (but not hot, which would melt the buttercream) and ready to go. Slowly pour ganache on top of all of the tiers. The ganache should cover the surfaces, but not overflow the borders (see photo). Chill overnight.

> **Technique Note:** To pour the ganache on the tier tops, there are a couple of techniques to try. Pouring it from a spouted measuring cup works well. Then, if there are any small or hard to reach parts, drip it from a teaspoon or demitasse spoon.

8 Use tweezers to pull off pieces of gold leaf and apply here and there to the ganache (see photo for suggestions). You may use as little or as much as you like.

> **Technique Note:** The easiest way to work with gold leaf for this cake is to pick off pieces with a tweezer. Allow one edge of the gold to touch the still soft ganache, then drop the other part. If it doesn't flatten out well enough, blow gently over it, straight down; it will stick as soon as it hits the ganache. It's okay if the gold is somewhat bunched up and three-dimensional.

Wedding Day

Present! At the site of the wedding, place the cake in the center of a tablecloth-covered display table. Serve at room temperature.

CHOCOLATE-COVERED CHERRY CAKE

O n the outside, this cake is a study of white-on-white, with delicate vines, leaves, and white chocolate roses molded by hand adding visual and textural dimension. Inside, there are delicious surprises in store. Bittersweet chocolate shavings are folded into the white cake batter along with kirsch-soaked dried cherries. Kirsch is also added to the syrup for brushing on the layers. Real chocolate-covered cherries are chopped and added to vanilla buttercream for the filling, while a vanilla buttercream covers the exterior.

The decorations for this cake are the most complex in the book. The white chocolate plastic roses, leaves, and tendrils are made by hand and do take some time. I have provided you with step-by-step photos to make the process as clear as possible. The cake base in the photograph is an elegant, formal, silver-plated cake stand and can be purchased from Beryl's (see Sources). Your local rental store might have similar ones as well. (If you choose to use one, make sure that you have enough refrigerator space because the base will add height to the final cake.)

Serves 100

RECIPE COMPONENTS

- White Cake with Bittersweet Chocolate Shavings and Kirsch-Soaked Dried Cherries
- Kirsch Moistening Syrup
- Chocolate-Covered Cherry Buttercream Filling
- Vanilla Buttercream

DECORATION

- White Chocolate Plastic Roses, Leaves, and Tendrils
- Confectioners' sugar for dusting (optional)

SPECIAL EQUIPMENT

- Two 6 × 2-inch, two 10 × 2-inch, and two 14 × 2-inch round pans with corresponding cardboard rounds
- Ateco #10 tip
- 16-inch round cake base (can be covered with silver foil, or use silver cake base as in photo)
- 1/4-inch-thick wooden dowels (1 yard)
- White-on-white, textured tablecloth
- Small gum paste rolling pin and board for rolling out chocolate plastic
- Three sizes of rose petal cutters
- Three sizes of leaf shape cutters
- Veining mat

TIMELINE

- **Up to 1 Month Ahead:**
  Make the White Chocolate Plastic Roses, the Moistening Syrup Base, the Vanilla Buttercream, and the Chocolate-Covered Cherry Buttercream Filling
- **2 Days Ahead:**
  Make the White Cake with Bittersweet Chocolate Shavings and Kirsch-Soaked Dried Cherries
- **1 Day Ahead:**
  Finish Making the Kirsch Moistening Syrup, Make the White Chocolate Plastic Leaves and Tendrils, and Assemble and Decorate the Cake
- **Wedding Day:**
  Present!

Up to 1 Month Ahead

Make the White Chocolate Plastic Roses: Since the white chocolate plastic roses are made far ahead of the leaves and tendrils, you may end up making the white chocolate plastic recipe twice. Leftover white chocolate plastic may be stored, well wrapped in plastic, then slipped into a ziplock bag, for up to a few weeks, if necessary.

While chocolate plastic can be made with either real chocolate or chocolate coating. I suggest using chocolate coating, which makes the plastic easier to work with as it has a higher melting point. If you have never worked with chocolate plastic before, I suggest using a coating such as Wilton's Candy Melts in white. Otherwise, use a high quality brand of white chocolate such Valrhona or Callebaut. The other thing that makes a difference is the warmth of your hands. Some folks have much hotter hands than others, and this prematurely softens the chocolate plastic and makes it very difficult to mold the roses.

Refer to photos on page 158 that accompany instructions for making roses.

WHITE CHOCOLATE PLASTIC ROSES

28 ounces white chocolate coating, finely chopped
2/3 cup light corn syrup

1 Melt the chocolate coating in the top of a double boiler or microwave. Stir the corn syrup into the melted chocolate until the mixture comes together. It might look grainy, but that is typical at this stage. It will smooth out upon kneading later on. Scrape it out onto a large piece of plastic wrap and wrap it up well. It will look like a large thick puddle. Let it sit for at least 4 hours at a cool room temperature, or until it is firm enough to roll.

2 Cut off one 4-inch-square piece at a time and knead it until it is soft. If it is very hard, hold it in your palms for a minute or two to warm it up, then knead it until it is absolutely smooth.

3 Dust your small board with cornstarch or confectioners' sugar. Roll out the plastic with the small rolling pin as thinly as possible without being able to see the board underneath—this will be about 1/8 inch. Another option to consider is to use a pasta maker to roll out the chocolate plastic. I have a pasta machine that I have reserved for the purpose. If yours has been used for a lot for pasta, it might be coated with excess flour, in which case do not use it.

4 Cut out 4 petals from the rolled-out plastic with the same sized rose petal cutter for every small, tight rose. Cut out 7 to 10 petals to make larger roses. Use the rolling pin to thin out the tops of the petals (the broader, rounded edge). Alternatively, you can hold the base of the petals and pinch the petal edges between your thumb and index finger to thin them out. The edges should be as thin and delicate as possible for a realistic look.

Ingredient Tips:

ॐ Use high quality bittersweet chocolate for the shavings in the batter; I like Scharffen Berger Bittersweet for this cake.

ॐ Not all chocolate-covered cherries are created equal. Try the hand-crafted ones from Kee's Chocolates in New York City. They will ship them to you (see Sources). They use delicious dark chocolate on the outside and moist flavorful cherries.

Equipment Tips:

ॐ I particularly like the 6-inch acrylic rolling pins and the green boards available through Beryl's (see Sources). The green color shows off whatever you are working with (such as any color chocolate plastic, marzipan, etc.).

ॐ Ask for rose leaf cutters in a few different sizes and a veining mat that is suitable for rose leaves and the size cutters you have purchased.

ॐ A veining mat has raised or etched veins that make natural-looking indentations and patterns on your plastic leaves when you press your leaves onto the mat.

ॐ Having a small offset spatula on hand is very important! You will need it to loosen pieces of rolled and cut white chocolate plastic up off of the rolling surface.

Decoration Tips:

↝ The roses can be made up to 1 month ahead, which is a true convenience. They need to be stored very carefully in a single layer in an airtight container to preserve their shape.

↝ The leaves should be made the day before the event as they must be soft and pliable; you want to be able to bend and shape them as you place them on the cake, and if they are made way ahead of time they will be dry and may crack. The tendrils can be rolled and placed on the cake as you go and can be made from the scraps of fresh white chocolate plastic leftover from making the leaves.

5 Now, form the center of the rose. Take 1 petal and hold the center top of the petal between your index finger and thumb. If you have a thumbnail of any length, use it to gently pinch an indentation to mark the center spot. Now take your right hand and gently but tightly roll the upper right hand part of the petal diagonally toward the middle. The top (where you made the indentation) will be the tip and should be tighter and narrower. When you get to the middle, remove your thumb and finger and continue folding. (Reverse directions if you are a lefty.) When you are done, you should have a cone-shaped "center."

6 At this point, you have a choice as to the way to proceed, and your decision will depend on what feels easier to you. You can either affix the base of the rose's center to your rolling board, or you can work up in the air with your two hands. You will have to see which works better for you as you begin to add subsequent petals.

7 Take 1 of the petals and gently pinch the bottom, making the petal more of a curved, cup shape. If the top is not thinned out and delicate, you can gently flatten it by squeezing it flat between your thumb and index finger at this point. Then, gently bend the top toward the back, forming a tight outward furl. Some asymmetry is allowed and even desired. All real roses have imperfections. Repeat with the remaining petals.

8 Place 1 petal against the cone base with the pinched end down. Flatten one side against the cone, leaving the other side open and not contacting the cone. You will tuck the last petal beneath it so that they all overlap.

9 Place one edge of the second petal in the middle of the first petal and flatten this second petal against the center. Your third petal will be started in the center of the second petal and then be tucked under the first. It will be pressed against the center cone, and the first petal's open edge will be pressed against it. These 3 petals formed over the center create a tight rosebud. You may add additional petals, each beginning in the middle of the one underneath. The more you add the larger the rose will become in diameter. This rosebud may be left as is, but most likely will need a little tweaking. Use your fingers to reshape the tips of the petals as you see fit to make an aesthetically pleasing shape. Unfurl them toward the outside, or press them further toward the center to make the rose tighter. I suggest making many different variations.

10 To form a large bud, keep the petals somewhat tight against the center. For a full-blown rose, make the outer layers more and more open and less tightly furled. At this point, the base of the rose might be thick and wide. That's OK because it provides a base for the rose to sit upon during storage. If you are using the roses right away, or you are ready to place them on the cake, the rose bases may be trimmed. If your rose is

Rolling out chocolate plastic

Cutting out rose petals from chocolate plastic

Forming the rose's center

Finishing forming the rose's center

Forming a rose petal

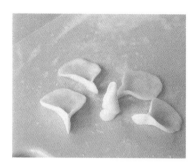

Rose center with four petals ready to use

Placing first petal around center

Placing second petal on rose

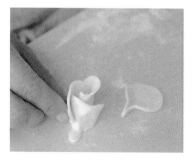

Wrapping first petal around third petal

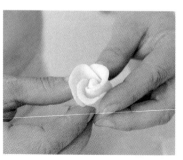

Shaping a small rose with three petals

Adding petals to make chocolate rose

attached to your board release it from your work surface with a small offset spatula. (Carefully slide it beneath the flower loosening its grip.) Trim any excess chocolate plastic from the base with a sharp paring knife. You want to coax the base into a reverse cone shape. This end will be nestled into buttercream and under chocolate plastic leaves, so it doesn't have to be perfect. You can also roll the bottom back and forth between your fingers to create a narrow shape. When you are done, use a fluffy, soft brush to dust off any extra confectioners' sugar or cornstarch.

11 The rose is now basically done. You may bend the petals inward or outward and mold it into the shape that you want. Make at least 20 roses of various sizes. Make sure at least 7 of them are large. Store them in a cool dry place. Place a Blue Magic insert in the container to help stave off moisture.

Make the Moistening Syrup Base: The moistening syrup can be made ahead but should not be flavored with kirsch until right before using. Make the Essential Moistening Syrup (see page 68) 2 times but do not use the vanilla bean or vanilla extract.

Make the Vanilla Buttercream: Make the Essential Buttercream (see page 69) 5 times with the following changes: to each batch beat in 1 tablespoon vanilla extract. Some of the Vanilla Buttercream will be used to make the Chocolate-Covered Cherry Buttercream Filling. Reserve 12 cups of the Vanilla Buttercream for the filling (see below).

Make the Chocolate-Covered Cherry Buttercream Filling: The filling for this cake is scrumptious. It starts innocently enough with Vanilla Buttercream (see above). Then, chopped chocolate-covered cherries are folded in for a unique, luscious filling with a lot of textural interest. Use 6 cups chocolate-covered cherries. (The number depends on size but there should be about 20 cherries per cupful if using the source I suggest.)

Have the 12 cups of Vanilla Buttercream soft and ready to go in the bowl of a mixer (you can do this in two batches if you like). Quarter the cherries, then add them to the buttercream and beat them in on low speed just until combined. Don't overblend. You want some texture from the chopped cherries to remain. And make sure to include all the liquid from the centers of the chocolate-covered cherries!

> **Technique Note:** If your chocolate-covered cherries have stems, simply remove them and discard. To chop the chocolate-covered cherries for the filling, I suggest chopping them individually. They are all about the same size and quartering them should do the trick. When you beat them into the buttercream, they will break down further, giving you just the amount of textural interest that you want to have.

2 Days Ahead

Make the White Cake with Bittersweet Chocolate Shavings and Kirsch-Soaked Dried Cherries: Make the Essential White Cake (see page 64) in the 6-inch, 10-inch, and 14-inch sizes, with the following changes: for the 6-inch cake recipe, chop $^1/_3$ cup of tart dried cherries and toss them with 2 teaspoons kirsch; microwave on high power for 30 seconds until the liquid is absorbed or, alternatively, heat in a small saucepan. Allow to cool. If there is any unabsorbed liquid, drain and discard. Meanwhile, shave 1 ounce of bittersweet chocolate (see page 112 for instructions on shaving chocolate). Fold both cherries and chocolate shavings into the finished batter. Bake for about 30 minutes.

For each 10-inch recipe, use $^3/_4$ cup dried cherries, $1^1/_2$ tablespoons kirsch, and $2^1/_2$ ounces chocolate. The 14-inch cake is made from two 10-inch recipes. Bake the 10-inch cake for about 45 minutes and the 14-inch cake for about 55 minutes.

1 Day Ahead

Finish Making the Kirsch Moistening Syrup: stir in about $1^1/_4$ cups (or more or less, to taste) of kirsch to the entire batch. If you are making the syrup now, do not add the liqueur until the syrup has cooled completely.

Make the White Chocolate Plastic Leaves and Tendrils: Make a second batch of white chocolate plastic. For the leaves, knead the chocolate plastic until pliable. Roll out to about 1/8-inch thickness and cut out leaf shapes with cutters. Remove excess plastic from around the leaf shape, just like when making cookies. Loosen the leaf shapes from the board with a small offset spatula. Align and press the leaves against the veining mat to transfer the vein pattern onto the chocolate leaves.

To make tendrils, simply take a small portion of chocolate plastic (you can use the scraps from between the leaves) and roll into long, thin rope shapes that taper at the ends (6 to 10 inches long). Make the leaves and tendrils right before you are going to use them.

Assemble and Decorate the Cake: Before assembling, have all the components made and ready to use, including the white chocolate plastic roses and leaves (you will make the tendrils as needed). Have all your tools and equipment on hand, and make sure there is space for the tiers in the refrigerator.

1 Level and torte the cake layers (see pages 27–29).

2 Moisten the cake layers, fill, and assemble each tier (see pages 29–32) as follows: Cardboard, first cake layer, syrup, Chocolate-Covered Cherry Buttercream Filling, corresponding second layer, syrup, filling, third cake layer, syrup, filling, corresponding fourth layer, syrup. (When filling, be sure to leave a $1/4$-inch empty border around the edge of the layers, so no filling will peek through the pure whiteness of the finished cake; the space can then be filled in with Vanilla Buttercream.)

3 Apply the crumb coat (see page 32) with Vanilla Buttercream. Chill until firm. Meanwhile, prepare your cake base or silver cake stand (see page 37).

4 Apply the final smooth coat of Vanilla Buttercream. Chill again, if time allows. Place the 14-inch tier on the center of your cake base.

5 Center and stack the remaining tiers using dowels for internal support (see page 38). Fit a pastry bag and coupler with Ateco #10 tip. Pipe a bead border of Vanilla Buttercream along the base of the tiers (see photo, page 45).

6 Now apply the roses, leaves, and make and apply the tendrils. Begin by placing 3 of the prettiest large roses on the top of the cake (see photo for inspiration). Arrange some leaves over the bottoms of the roses and around them and add tendrils radiating out. Tuck small roses here and there. The goal is to create a rounded cake topper selecting from your varied chocolate plastic shapes. Place roses, leaves, and tendrils here and there along the tops of the tiers and along the bottom of the cake. Some of the leaves and tendrils can be flat against the tops and sides of the cake. Others can be draped and shaped for a more realistic look (again, using photo for ideas). Chill overnight.

Wedding Day

Present! At the site of the wedding, place the cake in the center of a tablecloth-covered display table. Dust the cake with confectioners' sugar sprinkled through a sieve, if desired. Serve at room temperature.

SOURCES

August Thomsen Corp. (Ateco)
36 Sea Cliff Avenue
Glen Cove, NY 11542
(516) 676-7100
(800) 645-7170
FAX (516) 676-7108
www.atecousa.com

This company distributes all of the Ateco products, including cake turntables, icing spatulas, and a large variety of decorating tips.

༈༈༈༈༈༈༈༈༈༈༈༈

Beryl's Cake Decorating and Pastry Supplies
P.O. Box 1584
North Springfield, VA 22151
(703) 256-6951
(800) 488-2749
FAX (703) 750-3779
www.beryls.com

This is one of my first stops for wedding cake supplies. Beryl will often answer the phone herself—she provides highly personal and professional customer service and her company supplies pans of all shapes and sizes, food colors, pastry bags and decorating tips, gum paste cutters, gum paste tools, cardboard rounds, cake drums, masonite boards, books, and more. A print catalog is available on CD-ROM.

Blue Magic
The Luce Corporation
336 Putnam Avenue
P.O. Box 4124
Hamden, CT 06514
(203) 787-0281

Blue Magic moisture absorbers are small devices a little larger than a walnut that have a clear glass bottom and metal perforated top. Inside is a dry chemical that absorbs moisture. It's called "blue" magic because the chemical changes from blue to pinkish-white as it absorbs moisture. When it has completely turned pinkish-white, you just dry it out in the oven or toaster oven and when it's blue again, it's ready to use once more. I place one in any container that's storing crystallized flowers to keep them crisp and dry.

༈༈༈༈༈༈༈༈༈༈༈༈

The Chef's Catalog
3631 West Davis Street
Suite D
Dallas, TX 75211
(800) 338-3232
FAX (972) 401-6306
www.chefscatalog.com

This is a great mail-order catalog with very competitive prices. You'll find KitchenAid mixers, large professional-sized rubber spatulas, extra-long hot mitts, parchment paper, and more. Catalog available.

Chocoshpere
(877) 99CHOCO
FAX (877) 912-4626
www.chocosphere.com

If you are looking for high quality chocolate, make this your first stop. This company specializes in all my favorite chocolates that are great to eat and to use in your baked goods. Owners Joanne and Jerry Kryszek offer excellent personal service, and they ship nationwide.

༈༈༈༈༈༈༈༈༈༈༈༈

Crate and Barrel
Customer Service Dept.
1860 West Jefferson Avenue
Naperville, IL 60540
(630) 369-4449
(800) 967-6696
FAX (630) 527-1404
www.crateandbarrel.com

This company has retail locations as well as a mail-order catalog. They are a great source for platters and tiered cake stands, such as the ones we used for the cupcake tower.

Da Vinci Gourmet
7224 First Avenue South
Seattle, WA 98108
(206) 768-7401
(800) 640-6779
FAX (206) 764-3989
www.davincigourmet.com

If you would like to add flavors to your Essential Moistening Syrup, but not add any alcohol, then flavored syrups are for you. This company makes dozens of flavors including amaretto, cherry, raspberry, blackberry, hazelnut, orange, coffee, rum, chocolate, and even white chocolate. You can order them online, or they will refer you to a nearby retail outlet.

❧❧❧❧❧❧❧❧❧❧❧❧❧❧

Fauchon
442 Park Avenue (at 56th Street)
New York, NY 10022
(212) 308-5919
(866) 784-7001
www.fauchon.com

This French company, which is now on our shores, has many, many high quality ingredients, including chocolate, jams and jellies, and the most perfect glacéed fruit you have ever seen. They call them "comfit," so for glacéed orange wedges and whole clementines, that's what you should ask for. They are pricey, but nothing else will give you the same beautiful effect. It's a wedding: Splurge!

Fresh Petal
P.O. Box 638
Watsonville, CA 95076
(831) 728-5970
info@freshpetal.com

This company offers fresh rose petals, roses, and other flowers specifically for weddings.

❧❧❧❧❧❧❧❧❧❧❧❧❧❧

Garden Valley Ranch
498 Pepper Road
Petaluma, CA 94952
(707) 795-0919
www.gardenvalley.com

Dozens and dozens of varieties of roses are available through this company. Many are the old-fashioned English style roses, but they also have some gorgeous hybrids. Go to the website and look under the Fresh Cut Roses section for photos of every available rose. You can search by color, which makes it very easy to find what you want. They try to use "low spray" methods wherever possible. The minimum order is 2 bunches, 10 stems each of one variety.

❧❧❧❧❧❧❧❧❧❧❧❧❧❧

Green Valley Growers
10450 Cherry Ridge Road
Sebastopol, CA 95472
(707) 823-5583
www.greenvalleygrower.com

This company specializes in hydrangeas, flowering herbs, fruit on the branch,

and more. You can obtain many unsprayed greens from them too. Jerry Bolduan will be happy to quote a market price. You'll find kumquats, lemons, persimmons, wild rose hips, and more. They will also search for things that they do not grow, to purchase for you. They can provide blackberries on the vine for the Lemon Blackberry Cake.

❧❧❧❧❧❧❧❧❧❧❧❧❧❧

Kee's Chocolates
80 Thompson Street
New York, NY 10012
(212) 334-3284

Kee Ling Tong makes the most exquisite chocolate-covered cherries, which I use in my recipes. Consider calling her for your chocolate candy needs.

❧❧❧❧❧❧❧❧❧❧❧❧❧❧

King Arthur Flour, The Baker's Catalogue
P.O. Box 876
Norwich, VT 05055
(800) 827-6836
(802) 649-3881
FAX (802) 649-5359
www.kingarthurflour.com

This catalog, which is updated often, offers high-quality flours, extracts, chocolates, candied fruit and citrus rinds, scales, measuring cups (including ones in odd sizes), and more. They carry the wonderful American Almond brand of almond paste. Catalog available.

KitchenAid
P.O. Box 218
St. Joseph, MI 49085
(800) 541-6390 (small appliance
information)
(800) 422-1230 (major appliance
information)
www.kitchenaid.com

Go directly to this website for a complete listing of their great products. All
of my cakes were tested in a KitchenAid
oven and made with a KitchenAid mixer.
I bought my mixer almost 20 years ago
and it is still going strong—this is a worthwhile investment for any avid baker.

ᨆᨆᨆᨆᨆᨆᨆᨆᨆᨆᨆᨆ

La Cuisine
323 Cameron Street
Alexandria, VA 22314
(800) 521-1176
(703) 836-4435
FAX (703) 836-8925
www.lacuisineus.com

This company has an amazingly comprehensive array of equipment as well
as ingredients. Shop here for top quality chocolates, gold leaf, French black
steel baking sheets and other baking
equipment, vanilla beans, and more.
They carry peeled (or "skinned") whole
hazelnuts. Their catalog may be down-
loaded online.

Meadowsweets
173 Kramer Road
Middleburgh, NY 12122
(888) 827-6477
meadows@midtel.com
www.candiedflowers.com

This company makes the most perfect
crystallized flowers. Toni Elling takes
care with each and every bloom to
make sure you get the most exquisite
crystallized flowers available. If you do
not want to make your own, this is the
source to use. Her website features
photographs of many different cakes
decorated in a variety of ways. Check it
out for inspiration!

ᨆᨆᨆᨆᨆᨆᨆᨆᨆᨆᨆᨆ

Melissa's
P.O. Box 21127
Los Angeles, CA 90021
(800) 588-0151
www.melissas.com

This company is a specialty food pro-
ducer. When I need kumquats or other
unusual or exotic items to use with
cakes I check my supermarket for their
produce. You can often find a section of
interesting fruits and vegetables in and
amongst the regular produce and it will
often bear their label. Or, call the number above to find out where you can
buy their products.

New York Cake and Baking Distributors
56 West 22nd Street
New York, NY 10010
(212) 675-2253
(800) 942-2539
FAX (212) 675-7099
www.nycake.com

This New York institution offers a variety of high quality chocolates, food colors, gold and silver powders, pastry
bags and decorating tips, gum paste
cutters and tools, cake pans, Magi-Cake
Strips, parchment paper, cardboard
rounds, colored foils, microplane zesters,
and basically anything you need to con-
struct a sturdy wedding cake. Just call
and ask for what you want.

ᨆᨆᨆᨆᨆᨆᨆᨆᨆᨆᨆᨆ

Parrish's Cake Decorating Supplies, Inc.
225 West 146th Street
Gardena, CA 90248
(310) 324-2253
(800) 736-8443
FAX (310) 324-8277

This company carries my favorite cake
pans called Magic Line. They are made
of heavy-duty aluminum, conduct heat
evenly, and the square versions have
perfectly squared-off edges. They also
have general cake decorating equipment, such as cake decorating turntables, masonite boards, and beautiful
clear acrylic columns, and separator
plates. Call for a catalog.

Penzey's Spices
P.O. Box 993
W19362 Apollo Drive
Muskego, WI 53150
(800) 741-7787
FAX (262) 785-7678
www.penzeys.com

Check out this company for top-quality vanilla extract, vanilla beans, and spices, among other ingredients. Catalog available.

✎✎✎✎✎✎✎✎✎✎✎✎✎✎✎

Pfiel & Holing
58-15 Northern Boulevard
Woodside, NY 11377
(718) 545-4600
(800) 247-7955
FAX (718) 932-7513
Info@cakedeco.com
www.cakedeco.com

This company offers everything from colors to cake pans, gold leaf to cake turntables, cake drums to most any wedding cake related item you might need. The catalog costs $15, which is refundable with your first order.

Sur La Table
Pike Place Farmer's Market
84 Pine St.
Seattle, WA 98101
(206) 448-2244
(800) 243-0852
www.surlatable.com

This company has everything from mixers to spatulas, cake pans to books, thermometers to microplane zesters. They are a great one-stop-shopping resource for equipment. Catalog available.

✎✎✎✎✎✎✎✎✎✎✎✎✎✎✎

Sweet Celebrations/Maid of Scandinavia
7009 Washington Avenue South
Edina, MN 55439
(952) 943-1661
(952) 943-1508
(800) 328-6722
FAX (952) 943-1688
www.sweetc.com
www.maidofscandinavia.com

This company used to be called Maid of Scandinavia, but is now called Sweet Celebrations. They offer a huge array of equipment, including pastry bags and decorating tips, decorator's combs, microplane zesters, chocolates, and many wedding cake related items, such as cardboard rounds, colored foils, pillars, etc. Catalog available.

Williams-Sonoma
P.O. Box 7456
San Francisco, CA 94120
(415) 421-4242
(800) 541-2233
FAX (415) 421-5253
www.williams-sonoma.com

Famous for their mail-order catalog, they also have stores nationwide. You will find well-made, accurate measuring tools, KitchenAid mixers, vanilla extract, some chocolate and cocoa, and other baking equipment, including pans and spatulas of all sorts.

✎✎✎✎✎✎✎✎✎✎✎✎✎✎✎

Wilton Industries, Inc.
2240 West 75th Street
Woodbridge, IL 60517
(630) 963-7100, ext. 4811
(800) 794-5866
FAX (888) 824-9520
www.wilton.com

They have a great catalog with heavy-duty pans, pastry bags and decorating tips, food colors, cookie cutters, decorator's combs, parchment paper, chocolates, cocoa, and much more.

INDEX

Acetate sheets, 126
Almond(s)
  extract, 14
  gold-dusted whole, 108
  paste, 108
  sliced, decorating sides, 109
Apricot
  Filling, 122
  Glaze, 137
  and Hazelnut Praline Cake,
    118–123
Assembly
  of layers, 32
  pillar separated tiers, 41–43, 55
August Thomsen Corp., 162

Baking basics
  batter preparation, 21–22, 60
  cooling, 25–26
  doneness, testing, 25
  even layers, 17, 23
  filling pans, 23
  measuring/weighing, 22
  pan preparation, 18, 21
  sample cake, 20
Baking core, 17, 23–24
Baking powder, 12
Baking schedule, 49, 50
Baking soda, 12
Baking times, 25, 66
Basketweave pattern, 36, 46, 146
Batter preparation, 21–22, 60
Beaded border, 44
Beryl's Cake Decorating and Pastry
  Supplies, 162
Bittersweet chocolate, 13
Blackberry
  Jam Filling, 81
  Lemon Cake, 79–83
Blue Magic moisture
  absorbers, 19, 162
Brainstorming ideas, 2–3
Brown Sugar, 10
  Pecan, and Peaches Cake,
    142–147
Budget, and cake design, 4–5
Butter
  creaming, 21
  storing, 11
Buttercream. See also Frosting;
Piped buttercream decorations
  amounts per layer, 31, 33
  applying, 33–37

Caramel, 144
chilling/rewarming, 72
Chocolate, 132
Chocolate, Light, 112
Chocolate, Milk, 126
crumb coat, 32–33
emergency repairs, 51, 53, 55
Espresso, 33, 150
Essential, 68, 69–72
Lemon Curd, 82
Orange, 116
temperature, 37
Vanilla, 76, 90, 102, 108, 136, 159
Buttercream Filling
  Caramel, 126
  Chocolate-Covered Cherry, 159
  Crème de Cacao, 132
  Hazelnut Praline, 121
  Orange Marmalade, 108
  Raspberry, 92

Cake(s). See also Cake layers;
  Cupcake(s); Cake tiers
  Brown Sugar, Pecan, and
    Peaches, 142–147
  Chocolate-Covered Caramel,
    124–129
  Chocolate-Covered Cherry,
    154–161
  Hazelnut Praline and Apricot,
    118–123
  Lemon Blackberry, 79–83
  Marble, Swirled, with Sour
    Cream Fudge Frosting,
    84–87
  Marzipan and Orange Essensia,
    106–109
  Mocha, Gilded, 148–153
  moisture content, 63
  Nutella, 110–113
  Orange Mocha, 114–117
  Raspberries and Cream, 88–93
  Rum Cream and Fruit, Italian,
    134–141
  Strawberry Shortcake and
    Meringue, 100–105
  Valentine's Day, 130–133
  Vanilla Wedding, The Essential,
    75–77
Cake bases, 18–19, 37–38, 98, 155
Cake drums, 18, 37, 38
Cake flour, 10
Cake layers. See also Baking basics;
  Cake tiers
  Chocolate Cake, Essential, 66–67
  even, 17, 23, 28

leveling, 27–28
moistening, 29–31
storing, 26
torting, 28–29
White Cake, Essential, 64–65
Yellow Cake, Essential, 61–63
Cake mixes, 63
Cake pans. See Pans
Cake servers, 56
Cake tiers. See also Buttercream;
    Buttercream Filling; Filling;
    Frosting; Moistening Syrup
  assembly of layers, 32
  assembly with pillars, 41–43
  cutting and serving, 56–57
  extra, for serving, 8
  freezing, 27
  front, 39
  largest, baking, 23–24
  vs. layers, 8
  pillar separated, 37, 40–42, 55,
    56–57, 105
  size/number of servings, 9, 11
  stacked, 37, 38–40, 51, 52
  storage of, 33
  transporting, 39–40, 42–43
Caramel
  Buttercream, 144
  Buttercream Filling, 126
  Chocolate-Covered Cake,
    124–129
  Moistening Syrup, 128
  Sauce, 144
Cardboard rounds, 18
Chef's Catalog, The, 162
Cherry(ies)
  Chocolate-Covered,
    Buttercream Filling, 159
  Chocolate-Covered, Cake,
    154–161
  dried, kirsch-soaked, 160
Chocolate
  Buttercream, 132
  Buttercream, Light, 112
  Buttercream, Milk, 126
  Cake, Essential, 66–67
  Caramel Cake, -Covered,
    124–129
  Cherry, -Covered, Buttercream
    Filling, 159
  Cherry, -Covered, Cake,
    154–161
  Frosting, Sour Cream Fudge, 86
  Ganache, Bittersweet, 150–151
  Ganache Espresso Filling, 116
  Hazelnuts, -Dipped, 112

melting, 14
Shavings, 132, 152
sources, 162–163
storing, 12
Strawberries, -Dipped, 133
tempering, 13
thermometer, 18
Tiles, Bittersweet, 126–127
types of, 12–14
weighing, 22
White. See White Chocolate
Yellow Cake, Marbled, 86
Chocolate chips, 13
Chocolate Curls, 132
  Gianduja, 112
  White, 90–91
Chocosphere, 162
Cocoa, 14
Coconut
  Cupcakes, White, 98
  Lemon Cupcake Tower,
    94–99
  long-shred, decorating with, 99
  sweetened and unsweetened, 96
  toasting, 99
Colors, food, 14–15
Confectionary coating, 14
Confectioners' sugar, 10–11
Cookie cutters, 19, 91
Cooling racks, 17, 25
Cooling techniques, 25–26
Cost by slice, 4
Couverture chocolate, 14
Crate and Barrel, 98, 162
Cream of tartar, 12
Crème de Cacao Buttercream
    Filling, 132
  Moistening Syrup, 132, 138
Crumb coat, 32–33
Crystallized flowers, 77, 91, 96, 99
  homemade, 96
Cupcake(s)
  Coconut White, 98
  liners, 98
  Tower, Lemon Coconut,
    94–99
Curls. See Chocolate Curls
Cutting cake, 56–57

Da Vinci Gourmet, 163
Day of week, cake design and, 4
Decorating turntable, 18, 28, 29,
  32, 34
Decorations. See also Chocolate
    Curls; Flowers, fresh; Piped
    Buttercream decorations

Almonds, Gold-Dusted Whole, 108
candied peel, 117
chocolate for, 14
Chocolate Shavings, 132, 152
Chocolate Tiles, Bittersweet, 126–127
coconut, long-shred, 99
crystallized flowers, 77, 91, 96, 98, 99
display table, 55
espresso beans, chocolate-covered, 150, 153
fruit for, 137, 138–139
fruit, glacéed, 109, 117
gold leaf, 150, 153
grape clusters, 120–121
Hazelnuts, Chocolate-Dipped, 112
leaf doily, 122
Monogram, White Chocolate, 102
overview, 43
on pillars/separator plates, 40, 43, 132
plastic leaves and tendrils, white chocolate, 160, 161
plastic roses, white chocolate, 156–159, 161
at reception site, 43, 47, 55
on serving plate, 57
sides, 46–47, 86, 87, 109
Strawberries, Chocolate-Dipped, 133
Decorator's comb, 46–47
Display, 54–55, 98
Doily, leaf, 122
Doneness, testing, 25
Dowels, in stacked tiers, 39–40, 52
Dry ingredients, measuring, 18, 22

Eggs, separating, 11–12
Egg whites, whipping, 71
Emergency kit, 51, 55
Equipment. See also Icing Spatula; Ovens; Pans
baking core, 17, 23–24
Blue Magic moisture absorbers, 19, 162
cake bases, 18–19, 37–38, 98, 155
cake drums, 18, 37, 38
cardboard rounds, 18
chocolate thermometer, 18
cookie cutters, 19, 91
cooling racks, 17, 25
decorating turntable, 18, 28, 29, 32, 34

decorator's comb, 46–47
food processor, 16
gum paste cutters, 19
leaf veiners, 19
Magi-Cake strips, 16, 23, 24
measuring cups/spoons, 18
mixers, 15
oven thermometer, 15, 18
pastry bag and decorating tips, 19, 36, 43–46
pastry brush, 29, 136
scales, 16, 22
slicing knife, 17, 28
sources for, 162–165
Espresso
beans, chocolate-covered, 150, 153
Buttercream, 33, 150
Ganache Filling, 116
Essensia Cake, Marzipan and Orange, 106–109
Extracts and oils, 14

Fauchon, 163
Filling. See also Buttercream Filling
amounts per layer, 31
Apricot Jam, 121, 122
Blackberry Jam, 81
Espresso Ganache, 116
Lemon Curd, 97
Nutella, 113
Peach, 145
spreading, 32
thickness, 32
Flavor choices, 5, 6–7
Flour, 10, 22
Flouring pans, 21
Flowers, crystallized, 77, 91, 96, 99
homemade, 96
Flowers, fresh
color palette, 116, 119, 120, 145
edible, 48
frilly, 105
petals, 77, 86, 87
placement of, 47
Flower spikes, 47
Fondant, 47, 68
Food colors, 14
Food processor, 16
Formality level, and cake design, 4
Freezing
layers, 26
tiers, 27
Fresh Petal, 163
Frosting. See also Buttercream
with pastry bag and tip, 19, 36
patterns in, 46–47

pillars, separator, 14
softening, 87
Sour Cream Fudge, 86
with spatula, 33–35, 36
square cakes, 34, 108
swirls in, 47, 86, 87
varieties, 68
Fruit
glacéed, 109, 117
glazed, for decoration, 137, 138–139
and Rum Cream Cake, Italian, 134–139
Fudge Frosting, Sour Cream, 86
Ganache
Bittersweet Chocolate, 150–151
Espresso Filling, 116
pouring, 153
separated, saving, 151
Garden Valley Ranch, 163
Gianduja Chocolate Curls, 112
Gilded Mocha Cake, 148–15
Glaze, Apricot, 137
Gold leaf, 150, 153
Granulated sugar, 10
Grape cluster decorations, 120–121
Green Valley Growers, 163
Guests, number of, 4
Gum paste cutters, 19

Hand mixers, 15
Hazelnut(s)
Chocolate-Dipped, 112
Moistening Syrup, 112, 121
paste, 120
Praline and Apricot Cake, 118–123
Yellow Cake, 121

Icing. See Buttercream; Frosting
Icing spatula, 17, 33–35, 108
offset, 17, 32, 34–35, 108
triangular-shaped, 36
Ingredients. See also Measuring ingredients
basic, 10–15
sources for, 162–165
substitutions, 15
Italian Meringue Buttercream, 68, 69–71
Italian Rum Cream and Fruit Cake, 134–141

Kee's Chocolates, 162
King Arthur Flour, The Baker's Catalogue, 163
Kirsch Moistening Syrup, 160

KitchenAid, 164
Knife, slicing, 17, 28

La Cuisine, 164
Leaf border, 45–46, 83
Leaf doily, 121, 122
Leaf veiners, 19, 156
Leaves, white chocolate plastic, 156, 157
Lemon
Blackberry Cake, 79–83
Coconut Cupcake Tower, 94–99
Curd Buttercream, 82
Curd Filling, 97
Moistening Syrup, 82, 97
zesting, 82
Liqueurs, in moistening syrup, 29
Liquid ingredients, measuring, 18, 22

Magi-cake strips, 16, 23
homemade, 24
Magic Line pans, 21
Marble Cake, Swirled, with Sour Cream Fudge Frosting, 84–87
Marmalade, Orange, Buttercream Filling, 108
Marzipan and Orange Essensia Cake, 106–109
Masonite cake bases, 19, 38
Meadowsweets, 164
Measuring ingredients
dip and sweep method, 10
dry/liquid, 18, 22
tools, 16, 18, 22
weighing, 16, 22
Melissa's, 164
Meringue
Buttercream, Essential, 68, 69–71
Cake, Strawberry Shortcake and, 100–105
Discs, 103
Microwave oven, 16
Milk, 12
Milk chocolate, 14
Mixers, 1
Mocha
Gilded Cake, 148–153
Orange Cake, 114–117
Moistening Syrup
amounts per layer, 30–31
applying, 29
Caramel, 128
Crème de Cacao, 132, 138
Essensia, 109

Essential, 68
Hazelnut, 112, 121
Kirsch, 160
Lemon, 82, 97
liqueur-enhanced, 29
Orange, 117
Peach Liqueur, 145
Raspberry Eau de Vie, 90, 91
Rum, 136, 138
Vanilla Bean, 76, 86, 102
Monogram, White Chocolate, 102
Monogram template, 105

New York Cake and Baking
    Distributors, 164
Nonstick spray, 21
Nutella Cake, 110–113

Offset icing spatula, 17, 32, 34–35,
    108
Orange
    Buttercream, 116
    Marmalade Buttercream Filling,
        108
    and Marzipan Essensia Cake,
        106–109
    Mocha Cake, 114–117
    Moistening Syrup, 117
    Zest, 116
Oval tier, number of servings, 9
Ovens
    level, 15
    microwave, 16
    size, 16–17
Oven thermometer, 15, 18

Pans
    dent-free, 16
    filling, 23
    lining with parchment, 18, 21
    preparation, 21
    selecting, 21
    steel, 90
Pan size
    larger, oven fit, 16–17
    number of servings, 8–9
    volume and, 8, 10
Parchment cones, 18, 105
Parchment paper, lining pans, 18, 21
Parrish's Cake Decorating Supplies,
    164
Pastry bag and decorating tips, 19,
    36, 43–46
Pastry brush, 29, 136

Pastry Cream, Vanilla Bean, 136,
    137
Peach(es)
    Brown Sugar, and Pecan Cake,
        142–147
    Filling, 145
    Liqueur Moistening Syrup, 145
Pecan, Brown Sugar, and Peaches
    Cake, 142–147
Pedestal cake plate, 98
Penzey's Spices, 165
Pfiel & Holing, 165
Pillar separated tiers, 37, 40–43,
    56–57, 105
Piped buttercream decorations
    basketweave pattern, 36, 46, 146
    beaded border, 44–45
    leaf border, 45–46, 83
    with pastry bag and tip, 19,
        43–46
    ribbon border, 44–45
    rope border, 44, 146
    shell border, 44
    vertical ridged columns,
        104–105, 139–140
Planning and organization, 2–19
    brainstorming ideas, 2–3
    flavor choices, 5, 6–7
    questionnaire for, 3–5
Plate decoration, 57
Praline, Hazelnut, and Apricot
    Cake, 118–123

Raspberry(ies)
    Buttercream Filling, 92
    and Cream Cake, 88–93
    Moistening Syrup, Eau de Vie,
        91
Reception site
    cutting and serving, 56–57
    emergency kit, 51, 55
    final decorations, 43, 47, 55
    presentation of cake, 54–55
    timing arrival, 54
Rectangular cake, number of
    servings, 9
Ribbon border, 44–45
Rope border, 44, 146
Roses
    fresh, 116, 145
    petals, fresh, 77, 86, 87
    plastic, white chocolate,
        156–159, 161
Round tier, number of servings, 9

Rum
    Cream and Fruit Cake, Italian,
        134–139
    Moistening Syrup, 136, 138

Sample cake, 20
Sauce, Caramel, 144
Scales, 16, 22
Schedule, baking/organizing, 49–50
Seasonality, and cake design, 4
Semisweet chocolate, 13
Separator plates, 41, 42
Servers, cake, 56
Serving plates, decorating, 57
Servings
    number of, 8–9, 11
    size of, 4, 9
Shell border, 44
Sour Cream, 12
    Fudge Frosting, 86
Spatula, icing, 17, 33–35, 108
    offset, 17, 32, 34–35, 108
    triangular-shaped, 36
Spiked pillars, 41
Square cakes, frosting, 34, 108
Square tier, number of servings, 9
Stacked tiers, 37, 38–40, 51, 52, 57
Steel pans, 90
Storage
    butter, 11
    cake, freezing, 26, 27
    cake, refrigeration, 33, 51
    chocolate, 12
    cupcakes, 98
Strawberry(ies)
    Chocolate-Dipped, 133
    Shortcake and Meringue Cake,
        100–105
Sturdiness, of stacked tiers, 38–40
Style/mood, and cake design, 5
Substitutions, 15
Sugar, 10–11, 96
Sweet Celebrations, 165
Swirled Marble Cake with Sour
    Cream Fudge Frosting,
        84–87
Swirls, frosting, 47, 86, 87
Syrup. See Moistening Syrup

Tablecloths, 55
Tables, display, 54, 98
Tempered chocolate, 13
Thermometer
    chocolate, 18

oven, 15, 18
Tiers. See Cake tiers
Tiles, Bittersweet Chocolate,
    126–127
Tips, decorating, 19, 36, 43–46
Torting cake layers, 28–29
Transportation
    driving safety, 52–53
    emergencies, 53–54
    separated tiers, 42–43
    stacked tiers, 39–40, 52
Trimmable pillars, 41
Turntable, decorating, 18, 28, 29,
    32, 34

UHU Tac, 98
Unmolding cakes, 25
Unsweetened chocolate, 12–13

Valentine's Day Cake, 130–133
Vanilla
    Buttercream, 76, 90, 96, 102,
        108, 136, 159
    extract, selecting, 14
    Meringue Discs, 103
    Wedding Cake, The Essential,
        75–77
Vanilla Bean Moistening Syrup, 76,
    86, 102
    Pastry Cream, 136, 137
Volumes, for cake pans, 10

Weighing ingredients, 16, 22
White Cake, Essential, 64–65
White Chocolate
    about, 14
    Cake, 91
    Curls, 90–91
    Monogram, 102
    plastic leaves and tendrils, 160,
        161
    plastic roses, 156–159, 161
Williams-Sonoma, 165
Wilton Industries, 165
Work surface, level, 28

Yellow Cake, Essential, 61–63
Yield, determining, 11

Zest
    lemon, 80, 82
    orange, 116

Get Ready to Make the Cake

■ **Set Your Budget**—Even if you have $2 per person, you can have a custom-made cake. If you have more, the sky's the limit!

■ **Numbers Count!**—A small wedding will require a small cake. A large party gives you more flexibility; all of the cake can be on display, or, if you're on a budget, showcase a small decorated cake and keep an extra undecorated cake in the kitchen to slice and serve.

■ **Note the Date**—A midsummer wedding suggests a different cake from what would be desirable at a winter holiday reception. A winter-white color scheme, anyone?

■ **Pick Your Flavor**—Your wedding cake should feature flavors that you love. If you love puckery lemon, then include it. Are both of you chocoholics? Don't leave out chocolate!

■ **Determine Your Style**—Is your wedding formal or on-the-beach casual? Your cake should fit your level of formality.

■ **Logistics Lowdown**—Assess your ability and situation. Do you have the time to make the cake? Will you need to borrow or buy any equipment? Do you have refrigerator space?

■ **Make Lists**—Lists are helpful for organizing ingredient and equipment needs as well as your week-to-week and day-to-day approach.

■ **Practice!**—From piping buttercream decorations to get them even to making a sample miniature version of your cake, familiarize yourself with techniques and try out the flavors you've chosen before making the final commitment.